10.02.12
Ward A6   To W.T.G
                 From B.J.F. & J.M.F.

LEST WE
FORGET

LEST WE FORGET

FORGOTTEN VOICES
FROM 1914-1945

In association with
the Imperial War Museum

Max Arthur

EBURY
PRESS

5 7 9 10 8 6

Published in 2007 by Ebury Press,
an imprint of Ebury Publishing

A Random House Group Company

Text © Max Arthur 2007
Illustrations © Imperial War Museum 2007

Max Arthur has asserted his right to be identified
as the author of this Work in accordance with the
Copyright, Designs and Patents Act 1988

The Random House Group Limited Reg. No. 954009

Addresses for companies within the Random House Group
can be found at www.randomhouse.co.uk

A CIP catalogue record for this book
is available from the British Library

The Random House Group Limited supports The Forest Stewardship
Council (FSC®), the leading international forest certification organisation.
Our books carrying the FSC label are printed on FSC® certified paper. FSC
is the only forest certification scheme endorsed by the leading environmental
organisations, including Greenpeace. Our paper procurement policy can be
found at www.randomhouse.co.uk/environment

MIX
Paper from
responsible sources
FSC® C016897

To buy books by your favourite authors and register for offers visit
www.randomhouse.co.uk

Printed and bound by CPI Group (UK) Ltd, Croydon, CR0 4YY

ISBN 9780091922948

CONTENTS

PREFACE

In *Lest We Forget* I have combined personal testimonies from *Forgotten Voices of the Great War* with *Forgotten Voices of the Second World War*.

I have sought to show how both wars affected people in the front line and at home. Sometimes these stories are quite short, while others are several pages long. I have put the accounts under chapter headings such as 'The Coming Storm and the Call to Arms', 'The Fighting Spirit', 'Grim Reality', 'Fears, Tears and Laughter' and 'The Human Cost'.

As the 90th anniversary of the end of the Great War in 2008 draws near, so likewise does the 70th anniversary of the outbreak of the Second World War in 2009. I hope that this book will show what previous generations endured in order to bring peace to this country. Let us never forget that those two wars cost Britain a million lives to ensure that peace.

Max Arthur
London
August 2007

1

THE COMING STORM
AND THE CALL TO ARMS

You are blind like us. Your hurt no man designed,
And no man claimed the conquest of your land.
But gropers both through fields of thought confined
We stumble and we do not understand.
You only saw your future bigly planned,
And we, the tapering paths of our own mind,
And in each other's dearest ways we stand,
And hiss and hate. And the blind fight the blind.

When it is peace, then we may view again
With new-won eyes each other's truer form
And wonder. Grown more loving-kind and warm
We'll grasp firm hands and laugh at the old pain,
When it is peace. But until peace, the storm
The darkness and the thunder and the rain.

'To Germany'
CHARLES HAMILTON SORLEY

William Ewen

English student in Germany, 1914

One sensed a tremendous expectancy of war in the near future. A favourite bestseller in all the bookshops was *Weltmacht oder Untergang* – World Dominion or Decline. I bought a copy of it and read it myself. Oh! They had the plan for the conquest of the whole of Europe laid out bare. One could feel tremendous resentment in the British attitude towards Germany. We were the band of fellows, we had brought about this *Einkreisung* – this encirclement of poor unfortunate Germany that seemed to worry them all so much. We had a music hall song – *'Tis the Navy, the Fighting Navy, We will keep them in their place, For they know they will have to face, The gallant little lads, in Navy blue.'* Oh, they resented that one!

Robert Poustis

French student, 1914

When I was a boy, in school and within the family, we often spoke about the lost provinces – Alsace-Lorraine, which had been stolen from France after the war of 1870. We wanted to get them back. In the schools the lost provinces were marked in a special colour on all the maps, as if we were in mourning for them. When I became a student and went to the university, there was always the same ardent feeling. Speaking together we would say maybe war is coming. Sooner or later, we'd say, we don't know when, but we, the young people in those times, we very much wanted to get back the provinces.

[5]

In the first days of mobilisation there was of course a lot of enthusiasm. Everybody was shouting and wanted to go to the Front. The cars, the railway wagons loaded with soldiers were full of tricolour flags and inscriptions: 'A Berlin, à Berlin.' We wanted to go to Berlin immediately, with bayonets, swords and lances, running after the Germans. The war, we thought, was to last two months, maybe three months.

DORIS BEAGHAN

ENGLISH SCHOOLGIRL, 1914

We had been on holiday in France for ten days. Although there had been rumours of war, my father didn't believe them. But then war broke out, so we made our way to Le Havre by boat. We went to a hotel, had a clean-up and then went out in the town and then the excitement began. It was absolutely incredible. The British Expeditionary Force was coming in. The soldiers were marching in, all singing. French people, all excited, madly waving, dashing about and rushing up to the soldiers, pulling off their buttons as keepsakes, kissing them and oh! terrific excitement! It was marvellous that here they were. So we stayed there during the day and then we got the boat to Southampton at night. We arrived in the early hours of the morning and went up to London and there the contrast was incredible. From the excitement in France to the gloom of London. Everybody there with long faces and an 'Oh, isn't it terrible' sort of attitude. You could hardly believe it was possible, that there was such a change from the two sides of the Channel.

Germaine Soltau

Belgian schoolgirl, 1914

I was in Brussels, and at an age when all events seem to leave a permanent impression on you. Of course we were not expecting the Germans to invade Belgium, we were hoping they would respect our neutrality, so the invasion came as a very great shock to us all. We had heard in Brussels what was happening at the frontier – the killing, the shooting, the atrocities and of course it was awful, but the fortresses of Liège were holding and that gave us some hope. Brussels then was very silent, and the Grande Place had never been so beautiful, with all the big flags flying on the old historical buildings. But there was much sadness and emotion.

Then on the 18th of August the government in Brussels left the capital to go to Antwerp. Soon Liège fell and the Germans were on their way to Brussels. They were preceded by streams of refugees, telling us more stories of atrocities in the villages and small towns of the Ardennes. We heard about friends from a little village – the young woman who was shot dead in front of her child just after her husband had been taken away to be shot. That happened hundreds and thousands of times, always the same story.

Then on Thursday the 20th of August, a date I will never forget, the Germans entered Brussels. It was a glorious day of sunshine but in my mind I still keep a vision of grey, these grey-clad hordes marching in the streets. It was a sinister, greenish grey, even their helmets were covered in grey. They had with them all their heavy guns, field kitchens and officers on horseback, and it all went in long, long, endless streams of grey. And the dust that was raised by all these thousands of feet and all those weapons of war – one had the feeling that the dust was hiding the sun. And their music, the music that we were going to hear for four years and three months – the sound of drum and fife and always the same tune. It made us cry when we heard that and thought about our soldiers and of the Allies on the front line. And then in the evening, on our beautiful Grande Place, they put up their field kitchen and started making their soup.

Men Marching at Night
PAUL NASH

KITTY ECKERSLEY

MILL WORKER, 1914

I worked in the mill, I was a ring-spinner, and we worked six days a week, from six o'clock in the morning until half-past five at night, and I got the large sum of fifteen and six a week. Anyway, I had a nice friend and we used to go out at night – and we met these two young men, and I liked mine very much and he liked me. So eventually we started courting, and I learned that he was only in lodgings, that he had no father and no mother, and that he was a very steady young man, very big and fair, and he was all that a young woman would wish to see. He was a lovely man, really good, and he was a member of St Cross's Church at Clayton. We eventually made our minds up that we would get married, but we wanted a house, so we saved our money up, and eventually got a house in Clayton for three and sixpence a week which we furnished. He would go to his work and I would go to the mill. We were very happily married. Very, very happy because we were very much in love, he thought the world of me and I thought the world of him. And at times, at nights when he used to be at home, I had lovely hair in those days, and he used to do my hair up for me, in all kinds of styles.

And then it came to be that the war started. Well, we had a friend in Canada who had enlisted over there, and when he came back, he visited one night and asked us, 'Would we go to the Palace?' He had booked seats for the Palace and would we like to go? We didn't know what was on, of course, but it was a great treat for us. So we went. And when we got there everything was lovely. Vesta Tilley was on stage. She was beautifully dressed in a lovely gown of either silver or gold. But what we didn't know until we got there was that also on stage were army officers with tables all set out for recruiting. She introduced those songs, 'We Don't Want To Lose You, But We Think You Ought To Go' and 'Rule Britannia', and all those kind of things. Then she came off the stage and walked all round the audience – up and down, either sides, down the middle – and the young men were getting up and following her. When she got to our row she hesitated a bit. I don't quite know what happened but she put her hand on my husband's shoulder – he was on the end seat – and as the men were all following her, he got up and followed her too.

When we got home that night I was terribly upset. I told him I didn't want him to go and be a soldier – I didn't want to lose him. I didn't want him to go at all. But he said, 'We have to go. There has to be men to go.'

PRIVATE GODFREY BUXTON

ROYAL ARMY MEDICAL CORPS, 1914

I'd had one year up at Cambridge and then volunteered for the Army. We were quite clear that Germany would be defeated by the 7th of October when we would go back to Cambridge.

PRIVATE F. B. VAUGHAN

12TH BATTALION, YORKS AND LANCS, 1914

I said to the boss, 'I want to join the Army, I want to be released from my job.' So he said to me, 'Here in the steelworks you are doing just as much for your country, just as much for the nation, as though you were in the Army.' Well, I couldn't see myself catching the 8.40 to Brightside every morning and leaving for home in the afternoon, doing little jobs in the evening, and all the time my pals were suffering – probably dying somewhere – they were serving their country. I couldn't see myself carrying on in that particular way, so I said, 'I'm awfully sorry but I have made up my mind, I must go.'

And he saw that I was determined and he said, 'Well then, go to the wages office and they will pay you whatever is due to you. But we shall not save your job for you when you come back and we shall not pay you anything while you are away.' I said, 'All right, I accept those conditions.' My mind was made up, the die was cast, and when I finally joined the Sheffield Battalion, as 256, Private F. B. Vaughan, Sheffield Battalion York and Lancasters – all at a bob a day – you know I was a very happy man.

It was not just a sudden decision that I made to join the Army. My pals were going, chaps I had kicked about with in the street, kicking tin cans or a football, and chaps I knew very well in the city. And then if you looked in the newspapers we saw that Canadians were coming, Australians were coming, South Africans were coming – they were catching the first available boat to England to get there before the war was over.

Then when you went to the pictures you'd be shown crowds of young men drilling in Hyde Park or crowding round the recruiting office, or it might be a band playing 'Tipperary'. The whole thing was exciting, and even in the pulpits – although it started rather shakily at first – they eventually decided to come down on the side of the angels and blessed our little mission.

I don't know whether patriotism entered into it or not, possibly so. We were stirred, I know, by the atrocities, or the alleged atrocities, when the Germans invaded Belgium and France. The other great factor was that the womenfolk, fifty per cent of the population, were very keen on the war. Before long they were wearing regimental badges, regimental buttons, little favours in their hats or coats, and they were offering to do the jobs men had done in civil life, so that men could be released. Some of them would stop us in the street and say, 'Well, why aren't you in khaki?' In other words the whole effect was cumulative, but we were not pressed, we made our own decisions.

Heinrich Beutow

German schoolboy, 1914

My memories are those of a child of course. I was in a small German garrison town in 1914 and I remember very well the tremendous enthusiasm. Of course, we schoolboys were all indoctrinated with great patriotism when war broke out. My father was an active infantry officer and I shall never forget the day when they marched out to the trains. All the soldiers were decorated with flowers, there was no gun which did not show a flower. Even the horses I think were decorated. And of course all the people followed them. Bands playing, flags flying, a terrific sort of overwhelming conviction that Germany now would go into war and win it very quickly.

Private Thomas McIndoe

12th Battalion, Middlesex Regiment, 1914

It was seeing the picture of Kitchener and his finger pointing at you – any position that you took up, the finger was always pointing to you – it was a wonderful poster really.

I was always a tall and fairly fit lad. When I confronted the recruiting officer he said that I was too young, although I had said that I was eighteen years of age. He said, 'Well, I think you are too young son. Come back in another year or so.' I returned home and never said anything to my parents. I picked up my bowler hat, which my mother had bought me and which was only to wear on Sundays, and I donned that thinking it would make me look older. I presented myself to the recruiting officer again, and this time there was no queries, I was accepted. Birth certificates were not asked for, although I had one, not with me but I had one. My mother was very hurt when I arrived home that night and told her that I had to report to Mill Hill next morning. I was sixteen in the June.

Rifleman Norman Demuth

London Rifle Brigade, 1914

As well as being given white feathers, there was another method of approach. You would see a girl come towards you with a delightful smile all over her face and you would think to yourself, 'My word this is somebody who knows me.' When she got to about five or six paces from you she would suddenly freeze up and walk past you with a look of utter contempt and scorn as if she could have spat. That was far more hurtful than a white feather – it made you curl up completely and there was no replying because she had walked on.

However, I was given a white feather when I was sixteen, just after I had left school. I was looking in a shop window and I suddenly felt somebody press something into my hand and I found it was a woman giving me a white feather. I was so astonished I did not know what to do about it. But I had been trying to persuade the doctors and recruiting officers that I was nineteen and I thought, well, this must give me some added bounce because I must look the part, and so I went round to the recruiting offices with renewed zeal.

RIFLEMAN HENRY WILLIAMSON

LONDON RIFLE BRIGADE, 1914

During our training in Crowborough in Sussex it was a month of great heat, we sweated tremendously. We carried about 60 lb of ammunition, kit and our rifle. We got blisters, but we did about fifteen or sixteen miles a day, with ten minutes' halt every hour. We lay on our backs gasping, water bottles were drunk dry, people in cottages, women in sun bonnets come up with apples and jugs of water and we passed some of the battalions who had been in front of us whose headquarters were in some of the poorer quarters of London, and I remember so well the dead white faces, many with boils, lying completely exhausted, sun-stricken in the hedges, hundreds of them.

FUSILIER WILLIAM HOLBROOK

4TH BATTALION, ROYAL FUSILIERS, 1914

There was a periodical going at that time called *John Bull*. It was published by a man named Bottomley. Well, when we got to Cowes and were waiting on the beach I saw on the side of a house, covering the whole wall, a placard advertising *John Bull*. The words were 'The Dawn of Britain's Greatest Glory'. That was all it said. I was lying there, and I thought to myself, I wonder whether it will be or not.

LIEUTENANT CHARLES CARRINGTON

1/5TH BATTALION, ROYAL WARWICKSHIRE REGIMENT, 1916

When they came to us they were weedy, sallow, skinny, frightened children − the refuse of our industrial system − and they were in very poor condition because of wartime food shortages. But after six months of good food, fresh air and physical exercise they changed so much their mothers wouldn't have recognised them. We weighed and measured them and they put on an average of one stone in weight and one inch in height. But far more than that, at the end of six months they were handsome, ruddy, upstanding, square-shouldered young men who were afraid of nobody − not even the sergeant-major. When we'd pushed them through this crash programme of military training, out they went to France in batches.

American Troops at Southampton Embarking for France
THOMAS DERRICK

SERGEANT MELVIN KRULEWITCH

UNITED STATES MARINE CORPS, 1918

We left New York and sailed in a convoy of seven or eight
ships, including some very important warships. We were, of
course, under twenty-four-hour alert; we had submarine
warnings about halfway across, and several submarine attacks
during the trip. As we neared the French coast and the coast
of Ireland – in that general line from Ireland to France –
we were met by a group of camouflaged destroyers. It was
a most welcome sight, because we were in a danger zone,
and they would flit in and out between the ships, giving us
an assurance of safety.

We came through all right, with no losses, and landed at Brest. On the trip across we'd had to impose many restrictions: sleeping quarters were tight and we all slept in hammocks; and we had an allowance of just a small amount of water each. That water was used for brushing the teeth, then washing the face, then for washing your hands and finally for washing your clothes – all in the same bucket.

We had submarine attack exercises every day, when some men went to the gun crews and others to the boats in order to prepare us for an emergency, should it come about. Some of the men hadn't had any experience of sailing abroad and they were a little – shall we say – queasy at times. But by and large the crossing was a tremendous success, and all the men in my platoon were well trained and active, and ready and eager to get into the battle itself.

When we got to France there was intensive training from French and British instructors, who had already had three years' experience of the war and could give us the benefit of that right at the start. We learned trench practice and how to handle ourselves in night raids and night marches. We learned how to handle a knife, which we hadn't learned before, although all of us carried a dirk. We also learned the raider attack, which was common in trench warfare, because both sides would occasionally make a night raid to a part of the enemy line to get a prisoner, or some information or documents.

So we were trained right down to the bone. These men were like eagles newly washed, which I think is what Churchill called the British soldiers landing at the Dardanelles. And our boys were ready for war; we awaited the call; we were no jingoes, we were no screamers around for this or that, but we were regular marines and we were trained for war – that was our profession. We didn't like the waiting behind the lines. We heard in March or April that one of our brother outfits – the 1st Division – had had a raiding operation up north, and we waited for our opportunity. And then the day finally came, and we loaded into the famous forty-and-eight box cars. And there we were, shouting and gay, the finest type of young American.

FREDERICK WINTERBOTHAM

SECRET INTELLIGENCE SERVICE, 1939

We had an agreement with our man in Warsaw that he would let us know the moment hostilities started. And I think it was when the first bomb dropped on Warsaw that he got through to us at once – and I had the signal brought in to me and I was sleeping in the office, of course, at the time. I had the pleasure of ringing up the Secretary to the Cabinet, who was sleeping at that time, and happened to be a friend of mine. I said, 'I've got a job for you. War has broken out and I think you'd better advise the Cabinet.' I won't repeat his language at the other end, because he didn't get another wink of sleep that night. But we were now at war. Chamberlain talked about the subject on the radio a few days later.

EVELYN WHITE

CIVILIAN IN BIRMINGHAM, 1939

I remember vividly 'peace in our time' – Neville Chamberlain coming back from Munich. We thought, 'Thank God, it's going to be peace. It's not going to be war.' But, of course, events proved wrong. I began thinking, 'Is it going to be like the First World War?' when thousands of men were killed. In a way, they were human fodder. I thought, 'Is it going to be a repeat? What's going to happen to my brothers?'

JUTTA BUDER

JEWISH GIRL LIVING IN GERMANY, 1939

We were on vacation in September 1939 and we were playing on the beach – and our parents came running down to the beach and told us war had broken out, and that we had to go home immediately. I thought it was very exciting, even though I didn't want to leave the beach – and we all pushed into trains and everybody had to go home.

Mysterious things were beginning to happen. We lived in a duplex, and the radio used to be on the wall facing us – and my parents moved the radio to an inside wall of the house and away from our neighbours, and they would keep it very low, because they were listening to foreign stations – which was, of course, forbidden. Sometimes my mother listened from under a blanket so that nobody could hear outside – and we were told not to talk about that outside our home.

EDWARD DOE

FORMER SOLDIER WHO HAD FOUGHT IN THE SPANISH CIVIL WAR, 1939

Looking round, I could see that we were quite unprepared to enter a war of any magnitude – we just weren't ready. We never had the kit and we never had the men. We never had anything – we had so far lagged behind.

Us chaps who had been in the service were under no illusion as to what the word 'war' itself meant. We had no illusions on that score. However, I answered the call the same as many thousands of others and reported myself at Winchester, and we were there a total of two days. Everything was in chaos because the barracks not only housed the King's Royal Rifle Corps, it also housed the Rifle Brigade and also the Hampshire Regiment. You can imagine the chaos as literally hundreds and hundreds were pouring through the gates those first three days – all reserves answering the call.

LIEUTENANT DICK CALDWELL

LIEUTENANT-SURGEON, ROYAL NAVY, 1939

As war approached, I think the thought of going to war was exciting. The day war was declared, the admiral called us together in the wardroom and gave us champagne and gave us a toast – 'Damnation to Hitler'.

PILOT OFFICER DOUGLAS GRICE

32 SQUADRON, RAF, 1939

On September 3rd 1939, I seem to remember listening to the wireless, as it was called – hearing the announcement that we were at war with Germany. And there was, I mean a suppressed cheer – the thought that at long last we would earn our keep was really quite exhilarating. We didn't know quite what was going to follow. But at the time, we were all fully trained – well, as trained as we could have been for fighting. I mean we didn't know then that our tactics were all wrong – but anyway, we could fly our aeroplanes rather well.

Our tactics had never been tested in warfare – unlike the Germans, who had the Spanish Civil War to practise in. We had a set series of attacks – they were number one, two, three, four, five and six. And there were various manoeuvres you had to go through, like going from flying in Vic formation to flying in line astern. Attacking bombers from above, behind – the side – none of which was the slightest bit of use when you came to the point of actually finding the enemy and wanting to fire your gun.

GUNTHER RALL

LUFTWAFFE FIGHTER PILOT, 1939

There was a big, depressed mood throughout the country, 'What is going on?' But as a fighter pilot I also felt, if there is a war, then I want to be successful and be a fighter pilot and do my duty. But the population as such was very much shocked by the war, there's no doubt.

LADY ISABEL NAPIER

CIVILIAN LIVING IN LONDON, 1939

We had a butler – four staff, I think. But the moment, of course, the war broke out, everything dissolved around me.

The butler went off to join up. The cook left – she was frightened she might be bombed. The nursery governess left to help evacuate the LCC [London County Council] children – the London children. All the kids were evacuated as quickly as possible, and anyone living in the country with a spare room was liable to have these evacuees sent to them. And some of them, of course, had never seen the country – never seen the sea or farm animals and all the rest of it. I don't think, really, it was a great success.

The Evacuation of Children from Southend, Sunday 2nd June 1940
ETHEL LEONTINE GABAIN

Ronald McGill

Evacuee from Vauxhall, South London, 1939

We waved goodbye. The parents stayed on one side of the road and they all cried their eyes out – it was terrible, but we were all happy and joking by then. We'd had our apple, bagged our gasmask and we'd said our goodbyes.

We got into Vauxhall Station, and it was like entering a tomb – all tiled and dark. We had to wait down there until the train came in. It was a Southern Railway train that went round the loop line to Reading.

It really was packed! What I remember is the noise – ten carriages of children, and half of them were hanging out the windows. A lot of police there. It was just bedlam. I felt the teachers were very, very harassed, and in retrospect, they did a marvellous job. They shepherded us all there, looked after us – and they were worried themselves – some of their own children were with us.

Mum said that after we left it was like a cathedral, it was so quiet, the whole area. In the evenings, she said, it was unbelievable. They didn't realise 'til then the noise of children playing. The streets had been our playgrounds.

On the train we were all happy – thrilled, adventurous. We whizzed under funny old archways at Clapham Junction and Wandsworth Town; we could see people lined up above it all, waving to us, and that cheered us up no end. We were joyful for them. We went through Richmond, across the Thames, and you knew we were in the countryside. It wasn't long before we saw cows – we were thrilled. It was a tremendous adventure for us.

Henry Metelmann

German youth railway apprentice, 1939

Germany had invaded Poland, and to us it was something great. With shame I express this feeling now, because I had no idea what it really meant to the people there, to be invaded by a foreign army – and anyway, to be honest, I didn't care. I thought of the German greatness and I thought, 'Well, anyway, the Poles are second-rate and they have treated our German people living there very badly. It serves them right.' And also, to think that Germany now could occupy Poland, then surely we would be a powerful state in central Europe – that appealed to me.

People in general did not like it, because many of the neighbours, they remembered the First World War. My father had been a soldier. He said, 'I remember at first it was all great, the colours and all this and fighting for the Kaiser and the Empire. But then later on, things turned and changed, and it could well happen again, because it could be a long war.'

The Blitzkrieg was a great idea. With our superior technology in warfare, we would smash that little lot – yet within a few days France and England came in. We made a point of it, that it was not Germany who had declared war on England or France – but it was the ultimatum they sent to us, saying, 'If you are not out of Poland by so and so, we consider ourselves to be at war with you.' That was a strong propaganda line. 'We have not declared war on the western democracies – they have declared war on us!' and they should have kept out of our arrangement we had with the Poles – that was our business.

I thought a war was a great thing. We were being told it cleanses the nation, and a war is necessary in order to get the rubbishy element out of our blood – and I believed it.

ORDINARY SEAMAN DOUGLAS STEVENS

SIGNALLER ABOARD HMS *SAON*, 1939

I was called up by the RNVR – people seemed to cheer you on your way and wish you all the best. People at the bus-stop, when I caught the bus to the Embankment with my kitbag. People seemed to want to pat you on the back as you went.

CHARLES 'BERTIE' NASH

CIVILIAN LIVING IN LONDON, 1939

On my wedding day, which was 12th October 1939, at four o'clock in the afternoon I received a little buff envelope asking me, in reference to my volunteering, I should report to the Acton Town Recruiting Office and get myself sworn in and attested. I must admit I was rather shattered at receiving this on my wedding day.

FLIGHT LIEUTENANT PETER BROTHERS

32 SQUADRON, RAF, 1939

The first hint of war came into my life with the Munich crisis, when I began to think, yes, this is deadly serious.

I was sent to Uxbridge first, for ground training, getting kitted out and so on. At Uxbridge there was this splendid First World War pilot, Ira Taffy Jones, who stuttered terribly. One day he stood up and said, 'There is going to be a b-b-bloody wa-wa-war and you ch-chaps are going to be in it. I'll give you one piece of advice – wh-wh-when you fir-first get into a co-combat, you will be fu-fu-fucking fr-frightened. Ne-never forget the ch-chap in the other cock-cockpit is tw-twice as fu-fucking fr-frightened as you are.' I reckon he saved my life with that piece of advice. In my first combat over France, I suddenly thought, 'My God, the chap in that other cockpit must be having hysterics,' and shot him down. But I give all credit to Taffy.

GWENDOLINE SAUNDERS

CIVILIAN IN WEYMOUTH, 1939

On Monday I went back to the library. There was a fair stir about, and by the end of that week, this other girl had already been scouting round, apparently, to find what she could do. She'd been up to this air force station. She said, 'It's rather exciting. I think I shall like this. I've signed for a plotter.' So I said, 'What is that?' 'Well,' she said, 'I think we shall plot the operations, but I'll have to go for training. I had to sign a form. It was either for the duration or for four years.' So I said, 'What did you do?' She said, 'I signed for the duration. It can't go on longer than four years, can it?'

2

INTO BATTLE

*The naked earth is warm with Spring,
And with green grass and bursting trees
Leans to the sun's gaze glorying,
And quivers in the sunny breeze;
And Life is Colour and Warmth and Light,
And a striving evermore for these;
And he is dead who will not fight;
And who dies fighting has increase.*

*The fighting man shall from the sun
Take warmth, and life from the glowing earth;
Speed with the light-foot winds to run,
And with the trees to newer birth;
And find, when fighting shall be done,
Great rest, and fullness after dearth.*

From 'Into Battle',
Julian Grenfell

2

INTO BATTLE

The naked earth is warm with spring,
And with green grass and bursting trees
Leans to the sun's gaze glorying,
And quivers in the sunny breeze;
And Life is colour and warmth and light,
And a striving evermore for these;
And he is dead who will not fight;
And who dies fighting has increase.

The fighting man shall from the sun
Take warmth, and life from glaring earth;
Speed with light-foot winds to run,
And with the trees to never birth;
And find, when fighting shall be done,
Great rest, and fullness after dearth.

FROM 'INTO BATTLE'
JULIAN GRENFELL

Sergeant Stefan Westmann

29th Division, German Army, 1914

During our advance through Belgium we marched on and on. We never dared take off our boots, because our feet were so swollen that we didn't think it would be possible to put them on again. In one small village the mayor came and asked our company commanders not to allow us to cut off the hands of children. These were atrocity stories which he had heard about the German Army. At first we laughed about it, but when we heard of other propaganda things said against the German Army, we became angry.

Private Clifford Lane

1st Battalion, Hertfordshire Regiment, 1914

We moved to the Front in thirty or forty London omnibuses. When we boarded these omnibuses everybody wanted to get on the top because it was quite a nice day, fairly bright for November. But we had not been going very long before it started to rain, so we got thoroughly soaked. We must have travelled for quite a few hours, for it was dark when we eventually reached our destination, Vlamertinge.

We were lined up and given a very generous issue of rum. I didn't even drink beer. So in no time we were quite euphoric really. We were quite happy. We did not know where we were going, but the moon broke through the clouds and it was a lovely night. And I can remember, as we marched along, we passed a Roman Catholic priest who removed his hat and murmured his blessings.

We spent a cold night in a field. In the morning we were told to go up a wooded hillside where we found dugouts. We could rest there much more comfortably – in a dugout you could lay down. We stayed that day, but did not go to sleep. When it was light we simply came out to survey our surroundings.

We could see a road running towards Ypres from our hillside, and on it we saw a group of French soldiers. While we were watching there was the sound of heavy gunfire and, after a few seconds, three violent explosions. When the smoke had cleared we saw this group picking up one of their number and immediately start to dig a grave for him, so the shell had killed him. That was the first time we realised what the war was about – what the Germans could do.

Nightfall: Zillebeke District
PAUL NASH

Rifleman Henry Williamson

London Rifle Brigade, 1914

It is true to say that we enjoyed our first visit to the trenches. The weather was dry, we went through a wood under Messines Hill. We were brigaded with regulars who wore balaclava helmets. The whole feeling was one of tremendous comradeship, and these old sweats who were survivors of Mons and Aisne, they had no fear at all, and any apprehension we had of going in under fire was soon got rid of in the trenches.

We could also go in estaminets and have omelettes, and café rum for about a halfpenny, it was great fun. We had to go on working parties at night in the woods, and then after four more nights we were in the trenches again, back slithering into the trenches and doing it all over again.

One night in the second week of November there was a tremendous storm blowing, lightning was flashing and flares were still going up. Rain splashed up about nine or ten inches in no man's land, and it went on and on and on. That stopped the first battle of Ypres which was raging up north. Our sector north of Armentières ceased. The condition of the latrines can be imagined and we could not sleep, every minute was like an hour. The dead were lying out in front. The rains kept on, we were in yellow clay, and the water table was 2 ft below. Our trenches were 7 ft deep. We walked about or moved very slowly in marl or pug of yellow watery clay. When the evening came and we could get out of it, it took about an hour to climb out. Some of our chaps slipped in and were drowned. They couldn't even be seen, but were trodden on later.

We were relieved after the fourth night and some of us

had to be carried out. I noticed that many of the tough ones were carried out, while the skinny little whippersnappers like myself could somehow manage, we got out somehow as we had not the weight to carry. We marched back – slouched back – and eventually got to our billet at Plug Street (Ploegsteert), a mile and a half away. We fell on the floor and slept, equipment on and everything. Everything was mud-slabbed – overcoats, boots and everything. We were dead beat.

Sergeant Stefan Westmann

29th Division, German Army, 1915

We got orders to storm the French position. We got in and I saw my comrades start falling to the right and left of me. But then I was confronted by a French corporal with his bayonet to the ready, just as I had mine. I felt the fear of death in that fraction of a second when I realised that he was after my life, exactly as I was after his. But I was quicker than he was, I pushed his rifle away and ran my bayonet through his chest. He fell, putting his hand on the place where I had hit him, and then I thrust again. Blood came out of his mouth and he died.

I nearly vomited. My knees were shaking and they asked me, 'What's the matter with you?' I remembered then that we had been told that a good soldier kills without thinking of his adversary as a human being – the very moment he sees him as fellow man, he's no longer a good soldier. My comrades were absolutely undisturbed by what had happened. One of them boasted that he had killed a poilu with the butt of his rifle. Another one had strangled a French captain. A third had hit somebody over the head with his spade. They were ordinary men like me. One was a tram conductor, another a commercial traveller, two were students, the rest farm workers – ordinary people who never would have thought to harm anybody.

But I had the dead French soldier in front of me, and how I would have liked him to have raised his hand! I would have shaken it and we would have been the best of friends because he was nothing but a poor boy – like me. A boy who had to fight with the cruellest weapons against a man who had nothing against him personally, who wore the uniform of another nation and spoke another language, but a man who had a father and mother and a family. So I woke up at night sometimes, drenched in sweat, because I saw the eyes of my fallen adversary. I tried to convince myself of what would've happened to me if I hadn't been quicker than him, if I hadn't thrust my bayonet into his belly first.

Why was it that we soldiers stabbed each other, strangled each other, went for each other like mad dogs? Why was it that we who had nothing against each other personally fought to the very death? We were civilised people after all, but I felt that the thin lacquer of civilisation, of which both sides had so much, chipped off immediately. To fire at each other from a distance, to drop bombs, is something impersonal, but to see the whites of a man's eyes and then to run a bayonet into him – that was against my comprehension.

Corporal Sidney Amatt

7th Battalion, Essex Regiment, 1916

They never asked for volunteers, they'd say, 'You, you, you and you,' and you suddenly found yourself in a raiding party.

They went over at night, in silence, and the parties were always arranged in the same way. Number one was the rifleman, who carried a rifle, a bayonet, fifty rounds of ammunition and nothing else. The next man was a grenade thrower and he carried a haversack full of Mills hand bombs. The next man was also a bomb-thrower, he helped the first man replace his stock when it was exhausted. And the last man was a rifle and bayonet man, and all he carried was a rifle and fifty rounds of ammunition in a bandolier slung over his shoulder.

The idea was to crawl underneath the German wire and jump into their front-line trench. Then you'd dispose of whoever was holding it, by bayonet if possible, without making any noise, or by clubbing over the head with the butt. Once you'd established yourself in the trench you'd wend your way round each bay. A rifleman would go first, and he'd stop at the next bay, which was normally unoccupied. The bomb-thrower would then throw a grenade towards the next bay, and when that exploded the rifleman who was leading would dash into the trench and dispose of any occupants that were still left. And so we'd go on until we'd cleared the whole trench.

Two or three other parties would be doing the same thing until we'd cleared about a hundred yards of trench between us and brought back some prisoners. Anybody that had survived any grenades would be more or less stupefied, so we'd disarm them and get them back so they could identify which regiment they were with. They'd be taken, first of all, to the unit's headquarters to be interviewed by one of the officers. Then they'd be taken right back to brigade and divisional headquarters to be questioned by interrogating officers hoping to glean whatever information they could about who was holding the line in front of us.

Signallers
WILLIAM ROBERTS

It was usually the biggest man in the raiding party who was chosen to lead, because he had the best chance of fighting the Germans, who were nearly all much bigger than us. All the other smaller chaps were used to throw grenades. But the raiding parties were rarely successful because by the time we got halfway across no man's land and come up against the Jerry wire, the Germans had usually realised something was going on and opened up their machine-guns on that area. So we'd have to scuttle back to our own lines before we all got killed.

I got in several German trenches but only one that was manned. The Germans nearly always held the higher ground and so had constructed dugouts, which they retired to after any strafing by our artillery, leaving the trenches more or less vacant. But if one of them was occupied, once you'd got in the trench amongst them the Germans nearly always put their hands up and shouted 'Kamerad!' without any opposition at all.

FATHER CHARLES-ROUX JEAN

OFFICER, FRENCH CAVALRY, 1940

When the German attack came on the 10th May 1940, I was in bed at three in the morning, and there was a frightful noise, and I didn't know what it meant. It sounded like a storm and an earthquake all at the same time. Then I realised that it was an artillery bombardment.

GUNTHER RALL

LUFTWAFFE PILOT, 1940

There was another quiet period of time until our attack into the Netherlands, Belgium and France. This was my first confrontation with the French air force – it was 12th May 1940. My squadron had a mission to locate a German reconnaissance plane which had been deep in France, and escort it back to Germany. We took off with ten aircraft and we saw the plane we were looking for. But behind we saw ten dots chasing our plane. These were twelve P46s. Our reconnaissance plane escaped, but we were engaged in this dogfight. This was a tremendous excitement, especially as it was the first time I had come that close to the enemy – I could see his head and his eyes in the cockpit.

I chased one who turned and turned, and he got right in front of me, so I shot him down. But I also took a lot of bullets into my aeroplane, because there was a plane on my tail. When I got back to base, I realised that he had hit my aeroplane seriously, but I was conscious and confident. This was my first victory, which had a very important psychological effect. You have proved that you can do the job.

EVELYN JAULMES

DAUGHTER OF FORMER BRITISH INTELLIGENCE OFFICER, LIVING IN PARIS, 1940

We saw the Belgians and the Dutch fleeing with anything they could bring. We knew this was a dangerous period and so we left on the 11th June and three days later the Germans entered Paris. There were thousands and thousands of us with all the cherished things we could bring, mattresses on the tops of cars. Miles and miles of us and we hindered the French army a lot because all the roads were completely blocked by refugees and the army couldn't get their tanks and troops through to the front to fight the Germans. There was such a panic – we all knew the Germans were coming and we had to go.

SERGEANT LEONARD HOWARD

210 FIELD COMPANY, ROYAL ENGINEERS, 1940

We got into Dunkirk around five o'clock in the evening – we hadn't eaten and it was really chaos. The sand was littered with bodies and crowds of chaps all hoping to get off.

I was exhausted, and I went to sleep. I lay in the sand in

the dunes, and I slept, because I was really completely exhausted. The next morning, my mate Bill Baldry was still around, and he and I went into the water, hoping to get picked up. But there was no hope. They tried to organise queues, but it was very difficult. People were not only being Stuka-ed, but there was also panic on the beaches themselves.

I saw British men shoot British troops. On one occasion, a small boat came in – and they piled aboard it to such a degree that it was in danger of capsizing. The chap in charge of this boat decided he must take some action. He ordered one man who was hanging on the side to get away – but he didn't, so he shot him through the head. From the people around there was no reaction at all. There was such chaos on the beach that that didn't seem to be out of keeping. There were chaps who were going round the bend. I saw chaps run into the water screaming, because mentally it had got too much for them.

I was wearing a battledress blouse and slacks, and it was bitterly cold at night. I came out of the water and I removed a corporal's overcoat from a corpse on the beach.

They landed some beachmasters, who were in service dress, and they had red bands on their arms – trying to organise the evacuation. They'd come over from the UK to try and organise the queues on the beach. Well, frankly, the chaps who'd made it to Dunkirk didn't want chaps with service dress and Sam Brownes and red bands round their arm trying to organise them into queues.

There was a very flimsy canoe, and two chaps paddled out in this canoe. A Stuka had come down and machine-gunned them, and they both leaned the same way and they were both drowned. The canoe was upside-down, and it was floating some way off the beach. Bill swam out to this canoe and pulled it ashore, and we emptied it of water, got a couple of spades off an abandoned lorry, and we paddled out. HMS *Whitehall* came past us with its gun blazing away at these Stukas, threw us a line and we were pulled aboard.

Ordinary Seaman Stanley Allen

HMS *Windsor*, Dunkirk evacuation, 1940

A megaphone asked if there was anyone who would volunteer to crew up a fishing boat, where some of the crew had been machine-gunned. This boy of seventeen – who'd been sunk twice that day – volunteered immediately. He got cheered by the sailors and the soldiers who were on board.

One old, three-badge able seaman – which meant he'd had thirteen years of undetected crime – said to me, 'With youngsters like that, how can we effing-well lose?' And really it was something. It did us the world of good. It was a real tonic that this boy who had gone down twice in that morning, instead of coming back to England to his family, volunteered again.

What I couldn't help marvelling about as well, was how the soldiers, who were very tired and very hungry – were squatting down sending rapid fire up at the aircraft. I took my hat off to them – everybody did.

Some Spitfires appeared, and a couple of Stukas got shot down. They were cheered into the sea. But our first-lieutenant – after the incident was over, he appealed to the soldiers, 'Please don't fire, because you are putting our machine-gunners on the bridge in jeopardy in your enthusiasm.' He said it so calmly and nicely that all the soldiers laughed.

As we were going out with these boats, it came to me –

and came to a lot of us – that we'd had a heck of a pasting the day before and today we must be untouchable. Nothing could hit us. It was rather a strange feeling – that we'd got through, and we were going to get through it again.

When we got alongside at Dunkirk and secured, a file of Scottish soldiers who were wearing khaki aprons over their kilts, came along led by an officer who'd got his arm in a sling. He called out to the bridge, 'What part of France are you taking us to?' One of our officers called back, 'We're taking you back to Dover,' so he said, 'Well, we're not bloody well coming.' They turned round and went back to continue their war with the Germans on their own. It was something remarkable.

The *Crested Eagle* – the old London pleasure ship which used to go between Tower Bridge down to Clacton – was a hospital ship, painted up with red crosses. She'd been bombed and settled in the water. But the German aircraft were still machine-gunning her. That wasn't cricket. There was no real hatred about the Germans, really, except they just weren't playing the game. That wasn't the right way to win a war – to have a go at wounded people.

There was a little dog, a terrier-type mongrel, who came on board with some of the soldiers. He had a harness on him with pouches. He only understood French. When I spoke to him he wouldn't leave me. That little dog came back with us on the other two trips that we made. He didn't understand any English, which rather tickled some of the soldiers. One of our sub-lieutenants felt that Kirk, as we called him, should not be destroyed to keep to the necessary anti-rabies laws, so after Dunkirk was all over, Kirk was collected by a PDSA [People's Dispensary for Sick Animals] van to go into quarantine for six months before, as the sub-lieutenant put it, 'being taken on the staff of the parish where his father was vicar'. All of us cheered the old dog off. It was a very nice human touch amongst all that carnage of Dunkirk – as though people, in spite of all, were still caring.

The other thing was seeing all the soldiers coming back without their equipment. We began to think it was sort of the end of our way of life. We didn't know how long we'd be able to hold Jerry off in England. We knew we had the Navy, and that we would fight – but we didn't know what the soldiers would be able to do if Jerry had landed – because they had nothing.

The Withdrawal from Dunkirk, June 1940
CHARLES ERNEST CUNDALL

BERNT ENGELMAN

LUFTWAFFE PILOT, 1940

On the beaches and in the dunes north of Dunkirk, thousands of light and heavy weapons lay in the sands, along with munitions crates, field kitchens, scattered cans of rations and innumerable wrecks of British Army trucks.

'Damn!' I exclaimed to Erwin. 'The entire British Army went under here!' Erwin shook his head vigorously. 'On the contrary! A miracle took place here! If the German tanks and Stukas and navy had managed to surround the British here, shooting most of them, and taking the rest prisoner, then England wouldn't have any trained soldiers left. Instead, the British seem to have rescued them all – and a lot of Frenchmen too. Adolf can say goodbye to his Blitzkrieg against England.'

FREDERICK WINTERBOTHAM

SECRET INTELLIGENCE SERVICE, 1940

I think the most important signal we had decrypted through ULTRA right at the beginning of the Battle of Britain, was Goering establishing his strategy with his commanders. He told them that they were to fly over Britain and bring the whole of the Royal Air Force up to battle, because only in that way could it be destroyed in the time they had.

That was the key for Dowding – to fight the battle with very small units every time they came over, gradually wearing them down and always having aeroplanes to send up. It became evident that Hitler and his generals wouldn't contemplate invasion unless they had absolute control of the air over the Channel.

FLYING OFFICER ALEC INGLE

605 SQUADRON, RAF, 1940

On the 8th September we met all these Heinkel IIIs, and literally we took them head-on. We were spread out – we were coming straight in, with Walter Churchill leading us. Unfortunately, his eyesight wasn't very good, and he didn't see these things as soon as most people did, so he was directing us to where they were, and we all went in that direction. We met them – and it was a fairly shattering experience. You were closing very quickly, and before you knew what was happening you had a huge aircraft just in front of you, and you were coming straight at it. We advanced on those IIIs and shot, and broke away underneath them. There was a fellow pilot, Jack Fleming – a New Zealander – he got a hit directly and was just a sheet of flame. I think he was hit in the header tank, and the next thing we knew of Jack, he was in a maternity hospital some-where in Kent – he'd arrived near here, very badly burned.

It was fairly shattering to see an aircraft just go whoof alongside you. But it all happened so quickly, when you are closing at those speeds. You are not talking about minutes – you are talking about seconds. You are there, you fight, you break out of that particular attack and on a number of occa-sions, by the time you've come back again, you can't see another aircraft in the sky. The whole thing has passed you by.

This friend of mine, Passey, who was flying with me – he was rather an extrovert sort of character with a large dog called Havoc. They were a rather curious pair – but anyhow, poor old Passey – he was flying around one day, and he was shot down. He arrived on the ground in something of a hurry, and when he was found, with his aircraft, he was sitting in a seat and the aircraft – bits of the aircraft – were scattered for hundreds of yards around the place. But he was perfectly all right, sitting strapped in his seat on the ground. He had the luck of the devil, I think.

FREDERICK DELVE

LONDON FIREMAN, 1940

The first daylight raid occurred on Croydon Airport. Before the war, Croydon Airport was known throughout the world. They used to run these huge Hannibal aircraft to and from Paris. The German raiders came over in the middle of the day – no sirens had been sounded at all, and they literally destroyed the whole of Croydon Airport. I was on the scene at the time and people at the airport were able to identify the pilots, because apparently these were former Lufthansa pilots who had used the airport almost daily. 'One man – we could tell him like our fingerprint – the way he always came into the airport – and he picked out every building that there was to be damaged.' Near Croydon Airport was this very large building where they were manufacturing textiles – that had a direct hit and a very large number of women were killed. The senior police officer was with me when we passed by this building, you could see arms and limbs among the debris.

When they came at dusk it was blackout conditions, and fortunately for us, the total area of the London region is 700 square miles, so it wasn't in the same streets every night that the bombs fell. They were obviously picking out area by area, which was most helpful to the fire service because we were able, generally, to extinguish most fires before the following night – otherwise they would have formed a beacon for the raiders that were coming later.

I learned after the war that the Germans chose their raid time when the water in the Thames was at its lowest. It was only possible for fire boats to be right in the centre of the river, and for firemen to take hoses ashore it would mean them standing up to their shoulders in mud to struggle ashore with lines of hose. The volume of water that could be delivered in that way was quite infinitesimal compared to what was required to deal with the fire situation that had followed, because there were more than 2,500 fires burning surrounding St Paul's. Our problem was that if you have one jet of water with just a three-quarter-inch diameter nozzle, you require 70 gallons per minute to make that jet effective.

Able Seaman Bob Tilburn

Aboard HMS *Hood*, 1941

On the 22nd May 1941, the *Hood* set sail with the *Prince of Wales* in pursuit of the *Bismarck* and the *Prinz Eugen*, which were on their way to attack Atlantic convoys supplying Britain. The *Prince of Wales* had only just come out of the maker's yard, and still had some civilian employees on board, working on her gun turrets. We went over to Iceland and refuelled there. All the time we were wondering which way the *Bismarck* was going to come. There were three possible ways she could break out – via the Denmark Strait between Iceland and Greenland, or either north or south of the Faroe Islands. The *Norfolk* and

Suffolk, 8-inch-gunned cruisers, were keeping a look-out in the Denmark Strait. The next morning, 23rd May, *Suffolk* spotted the *Bismarck*, and *Norfolk* and *Suffolk* shadowed her from then on.

The *Bismarck* was approximately 300 miles away. We set off after her and at 2000 hours, went into action stations because we expected to pick her up at midnight. Then the weather deteriorated and at midnight there was a blizzard, so we couldn't see anything. But we still had reports from the *Suffolk*, saying in which direction they had last seen her. We switched off our radar in case the *Bismarck* could pick up our transmissions and know there was somebody shadowing her. We were travelling at full speed – about 29.5 knots. Then, between 0500 and 0600 on the morning of the 24th May, we sighted the *Bismarck* in the distance, turned in towards her and opened fire at about 25,000 yards. I was manning one of the 4-inch AA guns on the port side. The *Bismarck* answered immediately with three shells, each getting closer and closer and closer.

Then the fourth, fifth and sixth shells hit us. Everyone, even the gun crews, was ordered to go into the shelter deck. There were three of us from our gun who didn't take cover. Then a shell hit the upper deck and started a fire. The ammunition in our ready-use locker was on fire and started exploding. The gunner's mate told us to put out the fire, but we said, 'When it stops exploding, we will.' He went back inside to report to the gunnery officer, and at that moment, a shell flew into the shelter and killed the lot – 200 blokes. We three were still alive, lying flat on our faces on the deck with everything going off around us.

The next shell came aft, and the ship shook like mad. I was next to the gun-shield, so I was protected from the blast, but one of my mates was killed and the other had his side cut open by a splinter. It opened him up like a butcher, and all his innards were coming out. Bits of bodies were falling over the deck, and one hit me on the legs. I thought, 'I'm going to be sick,' so I got up and went to the ship's side to throw up. Then I looked up and saw the bows coming out of the water, and started to strip off – tin hat, gas mask, duffel coat and all the rest. By then the water had reached me and I was swimming.

I had my sea boots on and a very tight belt. I paddled around in the water and took my knife and cut my belt so I could breathe properly. Then I looked around and saw the *Hood* was rolling over on top of me. It wasn't a shadow – it was a big mast coming over on top of me. It caught me across the back of the legs and the radio aerial wrapped around the back of my legs and started pulling me down. I still had my knife in my hands, so I cut my sea-boots off and shot to the surface. I looked up to see the *Hood* with her bows stuck in the air – then she slid under.

It was 0600 in the morning. It was dark and cloudy, but there was good visibility. A heavy swell, about fifteen or twenty foot. There wasn't anybody in sight.

Further away I could see a lot of clobber in the water, so I swam over. I thought I would get myself one of those little rafts, made of wood and about a metre square. But they were in a fuel oil slick, and I didn't want to go in. So I paddled around, and I was getting really cold by then. I spotted two other survivors on rafts – Ted Briggs and Midshipman Dundas. But there was nobody else . . . nobody else. No bodies . . . nobody else alive or dead out of 1,400 men. Just we three.

Eventually, I was getting tired and cold, so I got one of these rafts, laid my chest on it and paddled over to Briggs. You know, someone to talk to. He wasn't feeling very well, because he had swallowed some of the oil fuel, but Dundas was sitting on his raft. He'd been on the bridge, forty feet up in the air. Tell me how he did it – he must have flown.

I tried to sit on my raft, but every time I pulled it down, the other side came up and so I packed it in, because it was falling on my face all the time. We were on three separate little rafts – Dundas, Briggs and me. Where could we go? I mean, the nearest land was one mile straight down. You can't swim, you've just got to hope for the best. An aeroplane came over once, but obviously didn't see us.

I'd read one or two of Jack London's books, where in the very cold conditions of Canada, you go to sleep and you die. So I thought I might as well go to sleep. So I actually tried to go to sleep on this thing that was tossing up and down. I thought, 'If I'm going to die, I might as well die in my sleep.' Then Dundas shouted, 'What's that?' And I woke up a bit and looked behind me – and there was this destroyer coming – the *Electra*. What a beautiful sight. Then it went straight past us – but I could see the signalman on the bridge, who was looking aft – and he suddenly sighted us and gave the flash, and told the skipper and he turned to pick us up. It was a marvellous sight.

BOMBARDIER RAY ELLIS

ROYAL ARTILLERY, WESTERN DESERT, 1941

By the middle of the morning, as the heat of the day became more intense, you could walk about without compunction. They could see you – but only in a distorted way. They did the same thing, and we would see them walking about – but you'd see a man walking upside down fifteen foot in the air – distorted visions – you couldn't aim at it, because you

didn't know where he was really. Sometimes by a trick of
the light, or by fate, it would all revert back to normal again
in a second and they had a complete view of the front again,
maybe for quarter of an hour, and then it would go again.
You'd be looking out and everything would be distorted;
then it would clear and everyone dived for cover as the war
started again.

A man could walk up, one shot could be fired and he would
be killed. We thought about this a lot, actually. You looked for
all sorts of omens – I can remember looking for omens in the
sky – shapes of clouds which would suggest good things. Your
mind was involved in this sort of thing. What were the omens
or the chances? But I never thought of being killed – it was
always the other man who was going to die. You had this
feeling that, yes, you would survive – but at the back of your
mind you realised you were kidding yourself.

Digging Slit Trenches: El Dab'a, Western Desert
Ivor W G Beddoes

Sergeant George Cook

No. 4 Commando, Dieppe Raid, 1942

Mountbatten gave us a lecture – said he wished he was coming with us. Once we realised where we were going, I think 200 blokes thought, 'I wish he were going instead of us.' But yes, very nice talk. We cheered him – off he went. Then we started priming grenades, drawing ammunition. Our troop were doing the demolitions, so we drew explosives and we'd a fair amount of stuff which we packed up – ammunition, spare Bren pouches, spare mortar shells, grenades – which we'd all primed. Then we had a meal and we sailed – a beautiful evening, as we went down the Solent and past the Isle of Wight.

Suddenly an officer said, 'Oh – they've got all the harbour lights lit.' I looked over the prow of the boat and you could see lights on the shore. The lighthouse at Varengeville was flashing, so I thought, Cor blimey – everybody awake. We're going to have a pretty bad welcome here.

When we landed, there was some barbed wire. We'd a roll of wire netting which we threw over the barbed wire so we could run over it. The Germans were firing tracers from their pill-boxes, and Lord Lovat said, quite casually, 'They're firing too high.' He was about six foot – I'm five foot four – so I thought, 'If they're firing over his head, there's no danger they're going to hit me' – but they did fire their mortars, and four or five blokes were killed on the beach.

We kept firing as we moved, but we were getting a lot back. Somebody shot a bloke out of the ack-ack tower. He did a lovely swallow-dive off the top. We arrived in an orchard, and Sergeant Horne and I had to cut some barbed wire. He started cutting, and then I heard an 'Ugh' – and when I looked, there was Sergeant Horne, blood spurting out of his chest. He looked as though he was dead – which was a bit of a shock to me, because he was about the toughest fellow I ever knew, was Geordie Horne. Then I got hit in the face and the shoulder. That was me out of it.

LIEUTENANT DONALD DAY

1ST BATTALION, 4TH GURKHA RIFLES
FAR EAST, 1942

The Gurkhas were a bit bewildered. We keep lambasting the Jap and then had to retire. They did not understand this constant retreat. Every time they met the Jap they beat them, and then had to retire.

Gurkhas prefer the kukri to the bayonet, they can cut a man in half with it. A standard blow is cross-cut to the shoulder. They cut off heads. It is a terrifying weapon and, used in the hand of the Gurkha, is lethal. I have used the kukri in anger only once. I was using it to sharpen a pencil by a haystack, when a Jap suddenly appeared round the corner, and I had to hit him with my kukri as I had nothing else to attack him with. My orderly was so convulsed with laughter at my ineptness, he failed to dispatch the chap quickly. The Gurkhas have a strange sense of humour. I made a mess of him and my orderly finished him off.

Sapper Stanley Fennell

23rd Field Company, Royal Engineers
Italy, 1944

The Americans were astonished at the Grenadier Guards. They were used in all the bad places where the enemy were probing. We went with them and gave them support, in that we laid minefields for them, or did demolitions for them. These brave Guardsmen whom I watched go into action – I cringed at the sight, because I was sitting in an enormous armoured car, and they were completely soft-skinned, as it were. The shells burst amongst them, and they marched steadily forward in the attack.

The Irish Guards, the Scots Guards – to see them go forward in attacks was awe-inspiring. I suppose it's esprit de corps, and that's a kind of morale-booster. We thought we were better off than the infantry, but the infantry said they wouldn't like to do our job.

The Yankees went rolling past in their Shermans, which brewed up very easily. They used to wave to us, and throw us tins of food. If they were going into action, they wanted to get rid of it anyway. We used to look at them and say 'You poor devils!' – and they used to look down at us, clearing mines, and say, 'Wouldn't do that for a fortune.'

When I was captured, the Germans treated us very reasonably – they kept saying, 'We are the front swine. You are the front swine.' And we laughed. They seemed to have a very simple kind of humour – very straightforward. As the daylight came and the shellfire slackened, they marched us back along the road that we had been attacking. It was strewn with the debris of our original advance. Our vehicles and tanks, still smouldering, and the bodies of our people were strewn everywhere. It sobered us to see the shambles of it all. We'd been pushed back miles.

Yvonne Cormeau

Agent, F Section, SOE [Special Operations Executive]. Working with the French Resistance, 1944

We listened to the radio for messages all the time. The men could not, of course. It fell to the people who were in the home – whether it was grandma or children – everyone contributed to try and listen in. The main times were the six and nine o'clock broadcasts from the BBC. One day we had a message, which said, 'Listen in to the broadcasts twenty-four hours a day,' so the boss and I installed a little set in the hay up in a loft outside the farm, and we listened. We were told it might happen any time, 'You must listen in, you might hear your message. Get yourselves ready, put on the clothes you will wear for work when you go away and make all arrangements for those who stay at home looking after the animals, that they have food.' Then finally the message came through that the armada had sailed, and there was terrific rejoicing, and a little crowd came up to our village during the night. We had been up all the time, cleaning what weapons we had. They had been hidden in the beehives. Then by morning, the others had turned up, and we allocated them to various people in the village we knew we could trust. They went out, despite the fact that they'd only had about five hours' sleep – they went out as soon as possible to blow up the railways and bridges, get trees knocked down so as to block the roads – the bigger the tree the better.

LIEUTENANT-COMMANDER CROMWELL LLOYD-DAVIES

HMS *GLASGOW*, D-DAY, 1944

The scene in the Channel was quite amazing. It was almost like Piccadilly Circus – there were so many ships there, and it was incredible to us that all this could be going on without the Germans knowing anything about it. But we never saw a German aircraft the whole time. Our air force had kept them completely out of the air. We arrived off the approaches to Normandy, and Glasgow was then told to take the head of the line of the force going into the Omaha Beach. As we steamed down the line, the padre said to me, 'Shouldn't we say a prayer?' And so I said, 'Why not say Nelson's Prayer?' because it was exactly right for this day. So he started to read Nelson's Prayer, and as we passed the *Texas*, all their ship's company took off their helmets as they heard us reading the prayer going in.

MAJOR PETER MARTIN

2ND BATTALION, CHESHIRE REGIMENT, 1944

As the mist began to clear on the morning of the 9th September, the enemy tanks started to take a toll of our tanks and transport. Our anti-tank guns were having no effect on the well-concealed German armour although a German commander who stood up in the hatch of his tank, shouting in English, 'I want to die for Hitler!' had his wish fulfilled by one of my platoons. As the mist continued to lift, Du Pré, one of my platoon commanders, spotted a Tiger 100 yards away, facing in the opposite direction. He crawled to a nearby Sherman and directed its fire into the Tiger, brewing it up. This seemed to mark the turn of the battle.

The enemy may have sensed that they were in a very sticky position and began to withdraw. As soon as their tanks came out of hiding, they were good targets for our anti-tank guns and Vickers. By about 1400 hours, the enemy were all accounted for – hardly a man, gun or tank escaped. I found a young German hiding in a barn. I was very angry as one of my best soldiers, Private Price, had been killed during the night, just outside this barn, and I felt this young man was partly responsible. Price had been with me right through the war. I was hopping mad, pointing my finger at this chap, shouting at him in fury. He was wounded. He said he was only seventeen and had been in the army just three months. His friends had stripped him of everything of value, his watch and money.

Sergeant Doug Woodcraft

9th Parachute Battalion, 1944

On about the 14th June, I was told to go into Escoville and see if it was still held by the Germans, So off we went, followed a track to the edge of the wood and there, six or seven hundred yards away, was the village. At the edge of the wood was a slit trench occupied by Jocks from the 51st Highland Division. I asked them if the Germans were in Escoville. The answer I got was in broad Scots and had more fucks than a Sergeant-Major's blessing. They didn't know – they didn't want to know. They were up to here with Normandy – give them the Western Desert any day.

It took the best part of an hour to make our way along a hedge through the thick undergrowth until we were almost to the village. I saw two Frenchmen digging a hole beside a very dead cow. After a bit, I managed to attract their attention. They dropped their shovels and to my horror, came running over, shouting 'Tommy! Tommy!' at the tops of their voices, with me shushing away like mad.

We followed them to the village centre, where there was a small café with eight or nine Frenchmen seated around, each with a glass in front of him and there was a war going on outside! I shook hands with everyone, then the owner of the café came from behind the bar, moved a small carpet and pulled up a loose floorboard, and came up with a bottle of clear liquid. I didn't know it at the time but I was about to be introduced to Calvados – the real stuff – you could run buses on it.

We all toasted De Gaulle, Roosevelt, Churchill and Stalin, each swallow causing a minor explosion at the back of my throat. All the time, I was pointing in all directions and saying, 'Boche? Boche?' whilst everyone replied in a torrent of French. I was getting nowhere when I suddenly remembered that we had been issued with a leaflet that contained a number of English–French phrases and it was in my wallet. Also in my wallet, which I had forgotten about, were five contraceptives, loose, no packaging. As I opened the wallet, they fell on to the floor. One Frenchman, with a yell of delight that could be heard in Caen, grabbed them, held them above his head and punched the air with his fist, screaming, 'British Tommy jig-a-jig!' At this the small crowd started cheering and clapping. It was obvious there were no Germans in the vicinity with all this noise going on and I decided to get away as soon as possible.

Before we could leave, the Frenchman went into a house opposite and returned with a dozen big brown eggs. My pouches were full with Sten magazines and my pockets had grenades in them, so I placed the eggs carefully inside my smock, said, 'Au revoir,' and left.

On the way back, we heard the now-familiar sound of German mortars firing. As one man, the three of us dived headlong into a ditch and as the bombs burst around us, I became aware of a wetness spreading over my chest and stomach. I thought, 'God! I've been hit!' Then it dawned on me. I'd landed on the eggs.

Major Tod Sweeney

2nd Battalion, Oxfordshire and Buckinghamshire Light Infantry, Rhine crossing, 1945

Quartermaster Bill Allsop shouldn't have been flying into action – he was quite old, about forty, but the commanding officer wanted him there. As his glider was coming in to land, he saw first the left-hand pilot slump over his joystick and then the right-hand pilot do the same. They had both been shot, and the glider was hurtling down to the ground. So he pushed one of them aside, and had a guess at what he should do. He sat down and as the glider plunged towards earth, he pulled the joystick back. He had no idea how to apply the brake or the rudder or anything else, but at least he straightened the glider out and it landed and ran on before coming safely to rest.

He spent the rest of the day sat in our headquarters without saying a single word. He was in shock – absolutely devastated by what had happened. The commanding officer had a sense of humour and put him in for a Distinguished Flying Cross. He didn't get it.

3

FOG OF WAR

I am the man who looked for peace and found
My own eyes barbed.
I am the man who groped for words and found
An arrow in my hand.
I am the builder whose firm walls surround
A slipping land.
When I grow sick or mad
Mock me not nor chain me:
When I reach for the wind
Cast me not down:
Though my face is a burnt book
And a wasted town.

'WAR POET'
SIDNEY KEYES

BOMBADIER J. W. PALMER

ROYAL ARTILLERY, 1915

Our lads weren't moved for some days – the dead weren't moved, the wounded were – and for days after when I was laying the wire out I had to pass over those bodies, whose faces were turning more and more blue and green. As a matter of fact it was a terrible sight and we had one or two frosts those evenings which made matters worse. Well, on the left of us, there was the Hohenzollern Redoubt, one of the strongest points of the war at that time, I know our Guards had two or three attempts to do it without any luck at all. I was told to lay a wire up to the Hulluch Crossroads. Well, I went over the first and second line of trenches and I got right up to where some German trenches had been captured when an officer came down and he said, 'Where are you going?' I said, 'I've got to lay a wire to the Hulluch Crossroads.' He said, 'You'd better bugger off. We haven't captured it yet.'

CAPTAIN MABERLY ESLER

ROYAL ARMY MEDICAL CORPS, 1915

In our front-line dugout we had first-aid dressings and morphia and that was all. We'd never attempt any major surgery or anything like that in the trenches – one couldn't do it. The only thing you could do was to cover a wound to keep it from getting infected, or stop a haemorrhage by compression on the main vessel if they were bleeding to death.

If a limb had been virtually shot off and they were bleeding profusely you could stop the whole thing by putting a tourniquet on, but you couldn't keep it on longer than an hour without them losing the leg altogether. So it was necessary to get the field ambulance as soon as possible so they could ligature the vessels, and the quicker that was done the better. But even so, several people got tetanus afterwards from an infection in the ground which was carried in shelled areas – very much like it was carried in farmland in the Fens. The ground had been shelled for such a long time it was in a rather septic sort of condition.

But it was all first-aid work. The only value of a medical officer being in a first-line trench was to help the morale of the men. I remember going in the first night we ever went to the trenches, and one fellow who thought I couldn't hear said to another chap, 'Good God, the MO's come up with us – that makes you feel better, chum, doesn't it?' Then I realised that I was doing some good by being there. Medically I felt I was doing no good at all.

Paths Of Glory
C R W NEVINSON

LIEUTENANT MONTAGUE CLEEVE

ROYAL GARRISON ARTILLERY, 1916

Before the wireless was invented we had to do the whole thing by telephone lines. We put them in the trenches for protection, but you can just imagine the confusion. In some trenches there may have been up to twenty lines all mixed up. Occasionally I think they may have been coloured, red, blue and yellow, or something like that, but not always. And whenever a shell burst in a trench, as thousands did, they bust all the lines and there'd be complete confusion, with mud and lines and debris everywhere.

The signallers, who were marvellous in our battery, had a terrible job to find all the bits and pieces and to join them together again. It was absolutely hopeless in those seven days before the bombardment of the Somme, because the Germans knew exactly what was going to happen and shelled the place to blazes, so nobody had any communications after that. So the telephone system was a complete failure.

CAPTAIN TOM ADLAM

7TH BATTALION, BEDFORDSHIRE REGIMENT, 1916

We always felt that someone up above was ordering things, and that they probably knew more about it than we did. We just carried on. I mean, we used to criticise them, saying, 'What the hell are they doing this for?' or something of that kind. But we always took it. It was being good soldiers, I suppose.

LIEUTENANT CHARLES CARRINGTON

1/5TH BATTALION, ROYAL WARWICKSHIRE REGIMENT, 1916

When you came out of the line you were mentally and physically tired and hoped you were going to get a rest. But you didn't get much of a physical rest because almost every night you had to go on working parties up to the front line. The worst part was that for the last mile or two everything had to be carried by hand – somehow or other you had to get up all the food, drinking water and necessary equipment.

This included rifle ammunition, machine-gun ammunition

and trench-mortar ammunition, which was very clumsy, awkward stuff to handle. Then you had to carry enormous bundles of sandbags, balks of timber, planks, ready made-up duckboards and, worst of all, coils of barbed wire. Barbed wire is the most damnable stuff to handle. It was made up in coils that weighed half a hundredweight that we carried on a stick over two men's shoulders. You were very likely to cut your hands to ribbons before you got it there.

Although people talk about communication trenches and duckboard tracks they generally weren't there, and if they were, there was every probability that the enemy were going to shell them. The nicer-looking they were the more dangerous they were, because the enemy spotted them. So going along a trench meant stumbling along a dark wet ditch with an irregular floor and a right-angled turn every few yards so that you can't see where you're going. To manoeuvre these cursed things round a corner was something so fatiguing it can hardly be described.

One has to remember too that the men who did it were physically tired out when they started. But it had to be done. The ammunition had to get there, the barbed wire had to reach the Front to protect the soldiers who were fighting, and if you were going to get any comfort at all you had to have the planks and trench boards. So you'd go cursing and stumbling along in the dark, slipping into holes and tripping over wires. And you knew that if you made the least noise the enemy would open fire. Worst of all was the traffic problem, because there would be several parties of this kind going through the labyrinth of trenches, and you could have a jam as bad as a London traffic jam.

Then somebody would have to get out on top, and if it was you you'd stand there, exposed, with the feeling that the whole German Army was looking at you. Then you'd struggle down again and perhaps get your stuff to the front line and hand it over without disaster. But then it was two or three miles back again, stumbling through the trenches, then perhaps five or six miles back to your billet, where you'd finally arrive at dawn.

Sergeant-Major Richard Tobin

Hood Battalion, Royal Naval Division, 1917

There was no chance of being wounded and getting a Blighty one at Passchendaele. You could either get through or die, because if you were wounded and slipped off the duckboards you just sank into the mud. I don't know how far the duckboards extended because it was such slow going up to the Front, but there were hundreds and hundreds of yards zigzagging about. At each side was a sea of mud, and if you stumbled you would go in up to the waist, and literally every pool was full of the decomposed bodies of humans and mules.

Then, when you got up to the Front, there was no front line to speak of, just a series of posts scraped in the mud. A machine-gun crew here, a few riflemen there, further on a Lewis-gun crew. In some cases the battle depth of your battalion was 1,000 yards of these posts bogged down. You couldn't get food or ammunition to any of them in daylight because the Germans were shelling the whole time. When shells started dropping you ran to the right or you ran to the left to get some cover, but if you were on the duckboards you couldn't run anywhere. You just had to face it and go on.

The men found the relief was hopeless. The battalion

came from ordinary trenches but the men struggled back in twos and threes, some a day late. I have seen men going out covered in mud, they just scraped it away from their eyes. They carried in their hands what looked like a muddy bough of a tree – but it was their Lewis gun. Their only thought was that the Germans were in as bad a position as we were. In fact, there was one place where a little party of men was trying to make their hole more comfortable by scooping it out, and some hundred yards away the Germans were doing exactly the same, but both, in their miseries, didn't take any damn notice of each other.

MAJOR PHILIP NEAME

15TH FIELD COMPANY, ROYAL ENGINEERS, 1918

Just before the end of the war we attacked with an American division on our left, and we reached our objective and took thousands of German prisoners. The British divisions on our right – we were on the left of the British line – the British divisions again succeeded and got all their objectives. The two American divisions on our left were very slow in advancing and didn't get their objectives until long after we did. Then we were told to be ready for the next attack within forty-eight hours; we were ready and the people on our right were ready – the Americans weren't ready. The whole thing was delayed for four days because the Americans had got their rear area leading up to the captured trenches in such a congestion and muddle that they couldn't get their reserve troops up, they couldn't get their fresh ammunition up.

We heard afterwards that they'd got their food supplies mixed up – in fact ahead and blocking all the roads. This meant they couldn't move their artillery forward. It was a complete muddle.

SERGEANT-MAJOR RICHARD TOBIN

HOOD BATTALION, ROYAL NAVAL DIVISION, 1918

On March the 26th we dropped into a trench. It was a trench we knew of old. We had started to retreat on the 21st of March, 1918, and here we were back in the trench we had started to attack from on November the 13th 1916.

FLIGHT LIEUTENANT PETER BROTHERS

32 SQUADRON, RAF, 1940

When we went into action for the first time, on the 10th May 1940, we were told to ground-strafe an airfield in Holland, which had been captured by the Germans. I was leading the squadron because the commanding officer was new, and flying number two to me. We left 'A' flight up above to protect us whilst we went down to ground-strafe, but to my surprise the airfield was covered with Junkers 52s, troop transport aircraft. They were all burnt out in the middle, but the nose, tail and wing tips were still there. We thought this was very odd, so we didn't fire at them because it was a waste of time. Then we found one undamaged aircraft parked between some hangars. We set that on fire and came back to base. It was some months later before we discovered that the Dutch had recaptured the airfield just before our arrival. They'd destroyed those aircraft on the ground, leaving one in which to escape to England. And that was the one we'd set on fire.

Major Martin Hastings

2nd Battalion, Devonshire Regiment, Italy, 1943

We were struggling up a ploughed field which had vines in it, and I met two Americans – paratroopers – sitting under a vine. I said, 'What on earth are you doing here?' 'I don't know,' they said, 'we dropped.' And I said, 'I see you have, but I think you must be something like fifty miles out of your proper place.' I said, 'You'd better go down to the beach.' I think it gives some idea of the chaos that the paratroopers had, of being dropped in various different places, because I think the same chaos happened to our own paratroopers.

I went on with my two platoons and company head-quarters, and eventually we came to where an Italian battery was supposed to be. I couldn't see any Italians at all – but I could see one or two of the guns. We went charging into these guns – and there wasn't a soul. So I thought, 'Well, that's extraordinary,' and then I heard some noise coming from a dug-out, so I had a flash grenade, which made a lot of noise, didn't do much harm – so I chucked one of these down it, and all hell was let loose. After a lot of shouting, out came about fifty Italians with their hands up. So I thought, 'Gawd, what do I do with this lot?' So we sat them down and I went on a little bit, until I saw a hat sticking up on the end of a stick on the other side of a long wall. I fired my Tommy gun along the top of that, and up jumped another fifty Italians, all wanting to surrender. So I had to get rid of them, and I sent them off with a section down to the beach, and I didn't see that section for twenty-four hours – so by this time I was getting a bit thin of men.

Having captured this battery, my other platoon at last arrived – exhausted, having tried to catch up. At that moment, the Italians had some little two-seater tanks – R35s which had a little machine gun in them. I said to my chap in Company Headquarters, 'Where's the Piat?' – the Projector Infantry Anti-Tank, which we had in those days – and he said, 'The platoon's got it.' So I said, 'Well, go and fetch it.' But while he was fetching it, we lay down at the side of the road, underneath this wall. Then down the road came a small boy and girl, walking together. So I grabbed them and put them in the ditch beside me. Then down the road came two Italian civilians, so I grabbed them too and put them in the ditch. The Italian noticed these two children in there, so he got up and gave me a kiss on both cheeks, which rather startled me, to say the least. However, at that moment, one of our tanks at last had arrived and put an end to the R35s, so we had made quite sure of our final brigade objective.

Private Ike Franklin

Company C, 111th Medical Battalion – liaison agent with 3rd Battalion Aid Station, 143rd Infantry, United States Army, 1943

After I was taken prisoner, I worked with German doctors to treat the wounded of both sides. There was one American doctor, Captain Munro, but the Jerries wouldn't let him work. They had captured some American medical supplies and the German doctors used the plasma to treat the American wounded. But there were some Germans that could have used it – but they wouldn't give it to the Germans. This was because Hitler said it might have some Jewish or Negro blood in it, and they didn't want to contaminate the bloodstream. I told them, 'You are scientists – you know better than that.' And their doctor said, 'Well, Hitler says that, so I've got to go along with it.'

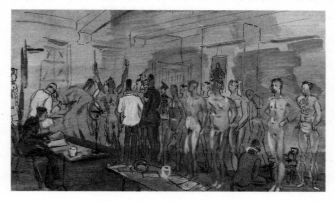

Medical Inspection of Recruits
ANTHONY GROSS

BRIGADIER ARTHUR WALTER

DIRECTOR OF PORTS AND INLAND WATER TRANSPORT, 1944

I'd been to a meeting in the morning and I was taken to lunch at the In and Out Club in Piccadilly. I had my usual black civil service case in which I had locked the papers for the meeting and I placed it under the table during lunch. Afterwards I went back to Norfolk House in St James Square but when I arrived, I realised I hadn't got the case. I'll never forget that moment. I'd left it in the In and Out Club and it contained not merely the plans of Mulberry but also information as to where we were going to invade. At that moment, I wanted to die. I wanted to be instantly shot – not that that would have helped much, but I really have never forgotten to this day my feelings of utter horror. I rang up the club and the hall porter answered and said, 'Yes sir, a case was left here and I've got it in my cubby hole,' and I galloped the whole way from Norfolk House to the club and he handed it over to me. It was still locked.

Lieutenant-Colonel Terence Otway

9th Parachute Battalion, D-Day, 1944

We arrived on time over the coast and quite suddenly, anti-aircraft fire – large and small – opened up on us. I was waiting to jump and there were some explosions near the tail and I was thrown out of the aircraft, closely followed by my batman. I saw tracer coming up and one or two tracer bullets actually went through my parachute. I realised the danger when a Stirling bomber passed under me and I wondered if it was going to hit it. It was completely chaotic. Aircraft going in all directions and levels – except the right ones. Anyway, it was clear that I was not going to drop on the dropping zone. It looked odds-on that I was going to hit a building, which I recognised as the headquarters of a German battalion. I hit it at first-floor level – my shoulder was about the level of the windowsill, and then I dropped down to the ground. Somebody threw open the window and looked out, and I was fumbling around for a grenade to throw at him, when one of my corporals suddenly appeared from nowhere and picked up a brick and hurled it up at this man who vanished from the window. We had to get away from the building, but we didn't make our way straight to the dropping zone, because if there were German troops following, we didn't want to lead them straight to the dropping zone. As we went along, we met two rather stout German soldiers on bicycles. We stopped and told them we were British troops. They replied that they were sick and tired of the SS dressing up in British uniforms and doing exercises, and could they please get back to barracks. We eventually convinced them that we really were British troops, and we took their rifles and threw them into marshy water, and told them to get on their bikes and get the hell out of it – which they rather thankfully did. I've often wondered what happened to them.

LIEUTENANT WILLIAM JALLAND

8TH BATTALION, DURHAM LIGHT INFANTRY, D-DAY, 1944

The LCIs [Landing Craft Infantry] started going round in tight circles towards the beach and when they were within striking distance, they peeled off one at a time, rammed their prows into the beach and then the next LCI would come alongside it and ram in there and so on – and it worked like a charm. The prow of our boat went into the shingle and the American sailor lowered the ramp and I knew exactly what I had to do. I was to walk off the gangway and on to the shingle and get off the beach quickly because a lot of shelling was expected. I went down, manfully I hope. I stepped off the ramp into the water. The water rushed over my head and I went straight to the bottom on my hands and knees. The prow was smashing into the shingle next to me and I watched it smashing against my legs and arms whenever it came near me. My waders were full of water and I couldn't get to the surface. I threw away the folding bicycle that I was carrying. Then I started to tear at the waders and I managed to get them off. I unfastened my webbing and slipped that off and eventually I landed on Hitler's Fortress Europe on my hands and knees, wet through, very frightened and completely unarmed.

MAJOR TONY HIBBERT

HEADQUARTERS, 1ST PARACHUTE BRIGADE, 1944

Having rocketed down from Grantham to Moor Park once or twice a week to attend briefing sessions by General Browning on a series of operations which were all cancelled, we were given the details on the 6th September of the 15th operation in this series – Operation Comet. This involved 1st British Airborne Division taking on all the tasks which three divisions failed to complete ten days later. On its own, 1st Parachute Brigade had the task of capturing and holding Arnhem. I wish to God Comet had gone ahead. It could have worked – at that stage the Germans were still demoralised, still on the run and hadn't had time to regroup and reorganise.

But Comet was cancelled. On the 10th September, the

original D-Day for Comet, we were briefed for Operation Market Garden – a rehash of Comet – but with three divisions instead of one, and with the whole of 1st British Airborne Division and Polish Parachute Brigade taking on the task of capturing Arnhem Bridge and holding it for forty-eight hours. There was a considerable gung-ho spirit and I'm sure that if somebody had offered to drop us in the middle of Berlin we'd have been as happy as sandboys. I believe Browning shared this over-optimism and was not as careful as he should have been when planning the Arnhem operation. Brian Urquhart, Browning's intelligence officer, came to see me after the briefing. He'd received confirmed reports that the 9th and 10th Panzer Divisions were in the Arnhem area, but Browning dismissed these and a doctor suggested that Urquhart was under stress and should rest. The operational plan was gravely flawed. Insufficient planes were allocated and of these something like thirty were taken to land the Corps Headquarters with Browning, south-east of Nijmegen, where they failed to influence the battle in any way. By dropping there he succeeded in putting himself out of communication with everyone in the critical first five days, and removing those planes from the 1st Division meant that we had to drop in three separate waves, which ensured that the division could be taken out in bits by the Germans. A fatal flaw. The next disastrous decision was the refusal of the Air Force to drop the 1st Division anywhere near the bridge, on the basis of faulty intelligence which suggested that there were anti-aircraft guns on the bridge. Urquhart didn't have the experience needed to overrule both Browning and the Air Force. These and other errors were leading to an epic cock-up.

4

THE FIGHTING SPIRIT

My saucepans have all been surrendered,
The teapot is gone from the hob.
The colander's leaving the cabbage
For a very much different job.
So now, when I hear on the wireless
Of Hurricanes showing their mettle.
I see, in a vision before me,
A Dornier chased by my kettle.

'SALVAGE SONG'
ELSIE CAWSER

Ordinary Seaman Jack Gearing

Benbow Battalion, Royal Naval Division, Gallipoli, 1915

We knew that the four hundred men of the East Yorks were mostly fresh from training and few had seen action, so every sailor was given two soldiers to look after. We gave them our hammocks, made sure they ate well and gave them our rum. You see, we knew that where they were going would be like Hell on earth, so we gave them all the love we could, because they were going to need it. There was all those feelings, all that silence. That's why I admire the British, they take it and they're quiet.

As we approached Suvla Bay on the night of 6–7 August, it was the darkness before the dawn. I stood on the gangway which had been fitted over the stern to allow the troops to walk down into the motor lighters. As the soldiers followed each other down with their rifles one got hit by a sniper and screamed out. I told him to shut up and put up with the pain or he would frighten the rest – that was my first scream of war.

Each day when there was a lull we'd go in and collect the wounded. Some of them were terribly badly wounded, and all so young. Suvla Bay was reasonably flat and the soldiers had made homes for themselves or taken over where other battalions had been before they moved forward. I did my best to cheer them up and encourage them. But most of the time, I was quiet because there wasn't much you could say in the face of all that horror. It was important that they had their own thoughts, they had to come to terms with it in their own way.

Every Sunday we used to try and have a service on board and we sang hymns which were heard by the soldiers on shore. They told us how much it meant to them so whenever we scrubbed the decks we sang out as loud as we could all the old hymns to inspire them: 'Onward, Christian Soldiers', 'Fight the Good Fight', anything that was rousing. It cheered us up, too.

I saw quite a lot of the Turkish prisoners on shore. They were badly dressed and always wanted our boots, they were so poor; but they were wonderful fighting men. They didn't give way. We could see them fighting from the ship; they were good. We didn't feel any anger towards them, we had a respect for them!

HMS *Queen Elizabeth* Shelling Forts, Dardanelles.
The attack on the Narrows, Gallipolli, 18th March, 1915
NORMAN WILKINSON

Reverend John Duffield

Chaplain, Lancashire Battalion, Bantam Brigade, 1916

One night I was in the line – I was helping the medical officer in his job and doing my own at the same time – when two men came in. The first was one of our men and the other was a German, and they were both wounded. Our man said to the doctor, 'Here's a job I made for you doctor, and he made this one for me.' What could you do with men like that? They were grand.

Major Jock McDavid

6th Battalion, Royal Scots Fusiliers, 1916

Out of the first car came this well-known figure dressed in a long, fine-textured waterproof. He was wearing a poilu helmet and a Sam Browne belt holster with a revolver stuck well into it. He was followed by his staff, and I could hardly believe my eyes when I saw the second car, which was piled high with luggage of every description. To my horrified amazement, on the very top of all this clutter was a full-length tin bath. What the hell he was going to do with all this I couldn't think. This very well-known figure came forward, gave a warm handshake, and introduced himself as Lieutenant Colonel Winston Churchill.

After his arrival all sorts of military and civilian VIPs came to visit us. The military types came along mostly, I think, to see if there was anything they could criticise about his duties as a battalion commander, but they didn't find much. I do remember one voice being raised. The brigadier came up late one afternoon and spotted a gap in the parapet that had been made that day. It had only been repaired the night before, and the little brigadier turned to the CO and said, 'Look here, Colonel Churchill. This is a very dangerous thing, to leave this gap unprotected.' And the colonel, turning and fixing him with his piercing eyes, said, 'But you know, sir, this is a very dangerous war.'

PRIVATE LEONARD HAINE

1ST BATTALION, HONOURABLE ARTILLERY COMPANY, 1917

It was an extremely severe winter. The gunners behind us told us there were forty degrees of frost. It made things almost impossible, because a shell bursting a quarter of a mile away could kill you. Now usually if you were in luck a shell could burst within a few yards of you and if your number wasn't on it you were all right. But at that time these shells they just hit this solid ice and they scattered. We had our colonel killed there during that February. He was a wonderful chap: Ernest Boyle. He was fifty-six years old, which for a front-line soldier was very old. He'd been severely wounded at Hooge in 1915 when we did a show there. But he was one of the few real fire-eaters I ever met. There were a few; most were unintelligent people; they hadn't got the imagination. But Ernest Boyle was a complete and utter patriot, and I remember he used to say, 'My ambition is that my bones shall be buried in Flanders' – and they were, poor chap. He got just a thing from a shell which landed, oh, two or three hundred yards away I suppose; killed him. He was taken down the line to a little village called Hamel. He was a very well-known chap because he'd got such a wonderful career, and several generals and people turned up for his funeral. But they couldn't dig a grave because the ground was completely solid.

SERGEANT ERNEST BRYAN

17TH BATTALION, KING'S (LIVERPOOL REGIMENT), 1918

We knew what the orders were; they must not break through. If retirement, and it will be necessary, retire but don't let them break through. That was all our orders, and that's what we did, that's what we did from 21st March, nine days and ten nights of scrapping and retiring, scrapping and retiring round the villages. We got to Ham eventually. That was the biggest town there was outside St Quentin. When we got into there nobody knew anybody. We were a nondescript pool of all sorts of regiments, bits and pieces, anybody at all; sanitary people, cooks, everybody, they were all in it.

SERGEANT-MAJOR RICHARD TOBIN

HOOD BATTALION, ROYAL NAVAL DIVISION, 1918

My battalion had withdrawn around the wood and now, for days, it was an infantryman's battle. Even our divisional artillery joined us as infantry, often firing alongside of us over open sights. Our major-general and his brigadiers were with us, controlling the troops, Wellington-like. It was leapfrog in reverse. Battalion went through battalion. Company through company. But always a company, always a battalion standing facing the enemy, ready to fight. And so we came back to the Somme battlefields, these old battlefields. In that trench came up Field Marshal Haig's famous message 'Backs to the wall. Every man will stand and fight and fall. No more retreating.' But still, we had a little joy in our hearts, the infantrymen, because although we had not won, we had not been beaten.

SERGEANT MELVIN KRULEWITCH

UNITED STATES MARINE CORPS, NOVEMBER, 1918

Every piece of artillery in the American Army and the adjoining French units opened up. This action produced a symphony in colour: you had the red artillery flares; orange flames coming out of the cannon; green signals indicating possibility of gas attack, and you had the shells bursting in the air creating a white colour. On top of this you could hear the thunder of the guns. It was a great support to our morale to know that this extraordinary barrage was going on behind us. On we moved in the usual way, in a long skirmish line; men five yards apart, moving along at a leisurely pace, just making sure that you wouldn't get into our own barrage fire. The artillery fire had almost wiped out the first row of trenches, so we were soon in them and taking prisoners. One or two of our boys were wounded. A great shout of triumph went up and down the line when we made the German prisoners carry our wounded back on stretchers. Then we pushed ahead. Occasionally some of the boys would kneel and take a shot at a German, but they were retreating. Then another great shout of triumph went up because we'd captured their artillery: that was about two and a half miles behind the line.

We were attacked then by long-distance machine-gun fire and we had some casualties. The fire came from the heights of Bayonville, which was part of the Kriemhild Stellung defence line. That night we moved up and took the heights of Bayonville, so there was nothing ahead of us except the retreating Germans. And we pursued them relentlessly, night after night, day after day. The Germans were losing food; losing their artillery horses and their baggage and ration wagons. They were so hungry that they would shoot a horse and cut steaks out of the rump. At first we thought the horses had been hurt by shellfire: then we saw the skilful butchering of the steaks, and we knew what they had done.

The Harvest of Battle
C R W Nevinson

Finally we reached our objective, which was to cut the Metz–Malmédy railroad on the heights looking down to the Meuse river below Sedan. We cut that on the last night of the war – November 10th – and we put a footbridge across the Meuse river under withering gunfire. We crossed the river that night and made an attack on the other side. To us the fight was just like any other fight – the fight of the 9th, the 10th. That morning we found our wounded and gassed boys lying around on the ground and we took care of them. We expected an infantry attack, but the Germans never came that night, because there was too much gas in the woods and they took a chance of being killed themselves by their own gas if they attacked. So they let go with a box-barrage of the high-explosive shelling and mustard and phosgene gas. The following morning when we collected our unit, all I had was eleven men out of a company of over two hundred.

NANCY BAZIN

TEACHER, WEST COUNTRY, AGED 18, 1940

We were told that we had to mobilise all our civilian force in Exmouth to resist the invasion that was likely to come across the Channel. Our local battalion of Devons which were organising this were going round with microphones and loudspeakers, calling us to come to the beach with spades and shovels – anything we could lay our hands on. And I went with several friends. I remember particularly the stretch of sand allotted – it was very near where our lifeboat station was. We were told to dig, and we dug a trench in the sand, and we were, at the same time as digging and getting blisters on our hands, and working for hours on this, we were looking out to sea, expecting to see these flotillas of German invading troops come. On this whole two-mile stretch of beach we were digging this trench, and it was so obviously hopeless because, with the wind and the rain and the high tide, all our work would disappear. But we did it, in this extraordinary way, believing that somehow we were defending. That was a futile operation. There was a sergeant or an officer every hundred yards, saying, 'Keep digging!'

Lieutenant Bruce Junor

On leave from HMS *Ajax*, 1940

The Commander rang me up to report at once with my boots and gaiters on and prepare to go overseas. I dashed back to Chatham where I and another officer went in an Admiralty car to Ramsgate and boarded an old destroyer, HMS *Wolfhound*.

We crossed the Channel under heavy attack by bombers but we landed on the jetty at Dunkirk. A British naval officer was giving the orders but Captain Tennant was in overall charge from a dugout at the landward each of the jetty or mole which was roughly 400 yards long.

For the first 48 hours I was never off my feet. Soldiers came from scattered units and in small groups under command, all shattered and dispirited from fighting and marching with no food or rest. Montgomery, the Divisional Commander, marched the troops by night and handled the Division so well to manage to evacuate so very many soldiers.

The Admiralty got hold of Dutch schoots which were robust, petrol-powered, large, open barges with powerful engines designed to carry cargo in the Dutch inland water-ways. For the evacuation they were manned by British naval personnel and, of course, were so useful because of their very shallow draft which enabled them to get up to the root of the pier. The destroyers could only safely reach the end of the jetty and then only at high water.

The evacuation of the beaches was a magnificent bit of organisation but it has gone down in history that the whole of the British Expeditionary Force came off on Dunkirk beaches which is nonsense. Thirty to forty thousand men were evacuated from the beaches by the 'little ships' which was a magnificent effort. It was, however, a drop in the ocean compared to the evacuation, by the Royal and Merchant Navy from the jetty, of some 220,000 men.

The Return from Dunkirk: Arrival at Dover
SIR MUIRHEAD BONE

Myrtle Solomon

Civilian, south of England, 1940

At the time of the fall of France there was a good deal of British joking going on – if they come here we'll do this and that – and people were making the most comic preparations. My mother reckoned that she'd be able to keep them off with a huge log fork – a fork for sort of stirring logs, that we had at the open fire. It was a most vicious-looking instrument, it's perfectly true. There was a very patriotic woman in the village who never went about in her car without a row of pepper pots on the front. She thought she could blind the Germans when they arrived. We were told that the Germans might arrive dressed up as nuns, so every poor nun in the country went about being observed, and being looked at in a suspicious way. I remember, myself, I went on a walking holiday for a while, in Cornwall. I had a haversack on. I thought everybody was looking at me and thinking I had parachuted in. So you were a bit twitchy.

The preparations that were made by the nation – you really didn't think would keep anybody away. I mean, a bit of barbed wire on a beach – or the erection of what appeared to be sort of small concrete pyramids each side of a line – you just couldn't see how they could stop anything.

Sergeant Frederick Gash

264 Squadron, RAF, 1940

We felt we had to stop the Germans if they tried to invade. I did talk to several of my 264 friends and comrades and colleagues about that. 'What're we going to do if the Germans do get here?' And most of them said, 'We've got to stop them from getting here – so why talk about what are we going to do if they get here? We've just got to stop them.' And that was the mood of most people, and I think that was the mood of the civilian people. We would stop them.

Aircraftwoman Jean Mills

WAAF, plotter and tracer at RAF Duxford, 1940

From the little rooms, the little wireless and radar rooms behind the controller, we could hear the crackling voices of the pilots come back, and although we had headsets on and the work was quite intensive and required a lot of concentration, we used to manage to ease one earphone off so we could hear what was going on, and then we could listen out for 'Tally ho', which meant they'd sighted the enemy, and then you could hear them talking to each other, like, 'Look out, Blue Two, bandits to your right.' And things like that, which seemed to bring it right into the room. There was an indescribable tension about the whole thing. When there was something going on, the atmosphere was electric. We were all rooting for our boys to come back. They were very much our pigeon.

OTTO PETERS

GERMAN STOKER, ABOARD KM *BISMARCK*, 1941

My first ship was the *Bismarck*. After ending our training in Kiel, we were sent to Hamburg. We lived on a merchant ship where I studied diesel electrics for about six months, while the ship was built. We had to study hard but at 4.30 every afternoon, we were free and we had contact with the civilian mechanics in the shipyard and we had girlfriends. In other words, we had a fine time. I arrived in Hamburg in autumn 1940 and the *Bismarck* was finished at Christmas. Not once during that time did the RAF try to bomb her.

I was quite proud to be posted to the ship. I was a mechanic by profession and from my point of view this ship was first class. We had four diesel engine rooms and each room had four engines and we never had any trouble at all. My superior was a petty officer named Stich who still lives near me in Hamburg. He was 'correct' – by that I mean he was kindly when necessary and hard when necessary. I was never punished. We had very little to do with the officers of the *Bismarck*. The captain was a very fine man but the first officer was strict and unpopular. I was very confident about the strength of the *Bismarck*. The first voyage was through the Kiel Canal to the Baltic Sea. We expected British aeroplanes – but they didn't come and we entered Kiel Harbour the same night. Then we had four months' training in the Baltic Sea. Shortly before we left, we had a visit from Hitler. I didn't see him and he didn't speak to the crew, but we knew this meant that something was going to happen. In fact war with Russia was about to begin.

We left the harbour and soon afterwards, we were told

by radio that a Swedish cruiser was following us. The British knew that we were heading for the Atlantic. We went to Norway and stayed there for one night and we saw a Spitfire, which we later discovered had photographed us. Then, we headed into the Atlantic and we knew that the British Navy were aware of us. I remember the action with the *Hood* and the *Prince of Wales*. The first officer told us by ship's radio that we were being followed by British ships – but we were not told whether they were merchant ships or warships. The captain came on the radio to tell us that we had sunk the *Hood*. Where I was in the engine room, we couldn't see anything. We just heard the news on the radio. All we could hear were the guns shooting. Nothing else. I couldn't feel the *Bismarck* had been hit by enemy shells. When we heard that the *Hood* had been sunk, there was no cheering but we did feel pride. Then our captain said that we were being followed by the British Navy. We felt a torpedo strike our rudder – but we didn't know where it had hit. The ship jumped a little bit. I was still in the engine room and I had to stay there for the rest of my shift – but afterwards while carrying out other duties, I went out on deck. It was rainy and windy. The captain came on the radio at about 2000 hours on the 26th May and told us that all the *Bismarck* could now do was sail in a circle and that there was no escape. I was frightened, but as a youngster I didn't quite believe it.

The following morning at about 0700 hours, we were informed that we would have a fight with the British Navy and we were alone, while the British had plenty of cruisers and battleships. A little later, I could hear that we got hit. I had to stay at my battle station and do my duty, but luckily my engine room was not hit. Then the order came from the first officer that we were free and could leave our battle stations. We had to try to get on to deck from the engine room. It was not easy, we had to open all the doors, and when I reached the deck below the main deck, all the lights were out and the water was up to my chest. I felt a hit while we were on this deck. There was another man there and we managed to force the last door open 10 inches. I had to take my leather clothes off to get through the narrow gap.

Finally we arrived on deck. I looked around and the devastation was awful – everything had been shot away and masses and masses of dead comrades lay around. I decided to stay on board as long as the ship stayed afloat so that I could keep my strength. It was windy and stormy. The ship was half submerged. A huge wave washed over the ship but I managed to grip something and I wasn't knocked overboard until a second wave threw me into the water. I was wearing a life jacket and I was a good swimmer and I tried to swim away. The sea was very cold but I was so excited that I didn't feel it. I was thinking about my girlfriend in Hamburg and how I had to stay alive to see her again. There was no wood or wreckage around me to cling to – which was lucky because in areas where there was a lot of wood and wreckage, there was also a lot of oil. There were shipmates nearby and we called to each other that whichever of us survived should tell the other's parents what happened. I was near one guy I knew well who wasn't saved, and afterwards I wrote a letter to his parents.

After a couple of minutes, I turned around and I saw the ship turning upside down and going right down. About fifteen minutes later, I saw a ship ahead of me through a rainy wall and I swam towards it. The ship was the *Dorsetshire* but I didn't know it at the time. I saw a Union Jack on the ship and I thought that I was going to be killed. As I got closer, I saw ropes on the side and I realised that they were going to rescue us. I grabbed a rope, but the waves kept pulling me back into the water. I tried to get the rope in between my legs and keep it tight. Finally, I came up with a wave and when the wave was high on the side of the ship, the British sailors grabbed me and pulled me on board. They rescued seventy-eight of us.

We sailed towards Newcastle and it took us three days. On the second day, the British captain spoke to us and said, 'Well, boys, I was a prisoner of war in Germany during the First World War and I was treated well, so give us your names and I'll send them over the radio so that the Red Cross know the names of survivors.' My brother was a wireless operator in the army and he picked up my name and he told my parents that I was safe.

CAPTAIN ROBERT MONTGOMERY

ROYAL ENGINEERS, ATTACHED TO NO. 2 COMMANDO, SAINT NAZAIRE RAID, 1942

The shooting started rather slowly, but pretty soon all hell broke loose. There was banging and crashing and lights and tracer. The bridge was hit and the coxswain was killed, so another naval rating took the wheel and then he too fell away. I seemed to be the next in line, so I grabbed the wheel but I wasn't very certain what to do with it. I desperately tried to remember which way to turn it for port and starboard, but luckily at that moment someone else took it away from me.

The searchlights came in handy because they showed us we were fast approaching the lighthouse on the old mole and we were able to change course right away. If we hadn't seen that, we might well have rammed the mole rather than the gate. Soon, we hit the gate with an almighty crunch which threw me back against the bridge. The assault parties immediately began clambering off the front end. It was quite a game climbing down the ladder as there was a fire blazing in the fo'c'sle. Corporal Calloway's trousers caught fire as he climbed down and he had to take them off. He carried out the whole operation in his underpants.

I followed Chant, who'd been hit in the hand, and when he got to the door of the pumping station he found it locked. I had a six-inch-long limpet mine, which I slapped on to the lock. I lit it and we blew it in. In order to control the demolitions, Sergeant Jameson and I tried to get on board one of the two tankers in the dry dock, but there was a machine-gunner on board. We threw a couple of incendiary devices at him but I don't think they did any good. Then Chris Smalley came up and asked permission to fire the winding house. When he tried, nothing happened because his igniters failed and he had to go back in to sort that out. Then Chant showed up, having laid his charges in the pumping house, which went up almost immediately. That was wonderful. Chunks of concrete the size of a bench came off the roof. We went inside and saw that two of the motors which pumped the shaft had fallen through the floor. The other two were leaning drunkenly. Two of the men destroyed the switchboards and dials, cut the transformer pipes and threw in a couple of incendiaries. They had a fine time. I then sent Chant and his boys back and went up the dry dock.

While I was on my way up there, there was a splendid explosion came from the winding house, and that was obviously a write-off. Coming back, I met the party on the caisson gate who had had a bit of trouble. Gerald had been wounded early on and Burtenshaw had been killed while trying to lay the demolitions. They hadn't been able to get into the caisson because the Germans had covered the hatches and built a road on top. Eventually, they put underwater charges on the dry side and it was reported that water had been heard going into the dock at either end of the caisson, so we reckoned it was off its seating and wasn't going to be much good. That completed the operation very nicely and successfully.

On the way back, I found a railway truck and lit an explosive and hurled it in. The truck disintegrated in flames. It was lovely. I then came to a bridge, held by Donald Roy, who told us not to cross but to go over on the seaward side, using the girders underneath, because it was under heavy fire from the basin. I reported back to Newman, thinking everything was marvellous. Our operation had gone 95 per cent according to plan. I asked Newman whether I should go to the embarkation point or go off to see how Pritchard was getting on. Then, the adjutant, Stan Day, told me to look out in the river, and that was when I realised we were unlikely to get home because all the little motor launches were burning all over the river. We fired the signals for rallying but none of the other demolition people came in. It was very depressing.

Newman decided that we would have to fight our way into the open country. He put us into parties of about fifteen or twenty and off we set. I was in the front, quite by accident. I promptly came up against a brick wall which forced us to turn round. After that I was at the back – a much happier situation. We moved along the edge of the submarine basin, when suddenly a grenade burst just beside me and I got a tiny bit of metal in my bottom, and it was just as if you'd shot a rabbit. I went head over heels, thought 'O Lord, I'm dead,' and then got up and realised I wasn't. By that time, we'd got into the old town square and we had to get across a bridge if we were going to get out of the town. So Newman assembled us again and we decided to charge. George Hands, the troop sergeant-major, gave covering fire with a Bren gun as we ran across the bridge. From the amount of fire that was coming at us, we should have been absolutely massacred, but Newman had a theory that they'd been firing at us from long range and they forgot to drop their sights. Everything was going over the tops of our heads. There was clanging against the girders on the bridge but we got through.

We found a truck which Bill Copeland tried to get going, but all he managed to do was turn on the headlights and that caused a lot of screaming and shouting from us about black-outs. As we went on, an armoured car came down the street firing at everything, so we had to clear off the street. We split up into parties and so began the St Nazaire obstacle race. We were over walls, into people's gardens, through houses, and when another armoured car came along, we decided to stay where we were. We were in a house with an air-raid cellar so we went to ground and gave some of our wounded chaps morphia and tried to bandage them up and make them comfortable. Someone operated on me with a fighting knife and cut a small chunk of metal out of my bottom.

Then the Germans began searching the house. They searched upstairs and found nothing and were just about to leave when there was a cry in German from upstairs – whether it was from a Frenchman or not I don't know – 'Have you looked in the cellar?' At that stage, Newman surrendered. I don't know why the Germans didn't just chuck a hand-grenade into the cellar – I'm sure that's what I would have done – but they pulled us out and took off our tin hats and moved us about a bit and there was a lot of shouting and screaming. One of us pulled out a fighting knife and another chap pulled out a hand-grenade and they lined us up against a wall and trained a machine gun on us and I thought that was it. But Newman explained to them that we were just trying to get rid of our weapons.

An officer came and took us into the house opposite which was the German headquarters – we hadn't really chosen our hiding place very well. We were there for quite a long time. More and more chaps were brought in. We were a bit worried because the *Campbeltown* hadn't yet gone up. It was supposed to have gone off at 4.30 in the morning and it was now half-past ten. Then suddenly, it did. There have been all sorts of stories about why it was so late. I believe that it got so hot that some of the acid in the acid pencil fuses distilled away and it took rather longer for the acid to eat through the copper and set off the fuse. Just before the *Campbeltown* exploded, Sam Beattie was being interrogated by a German naval officer who was saying that it wouldn't take very long to repair the damage the *Campbeltown* had caused. Just at that moment, she went up. Beattie smiled at the officer and said, 'We're not quite as foolish as you think!'

LIEUTENANT MICHAEL MARSHALL

4/5TH ROYAL GURKHA RIFLES, ARAKAN, 1943

It was the first time I had heard Gurkhas actually shouting 'Ayo Gurkhali!' (The Gurkhas are coming!), a fearsome noise at close quarters, which undoubtedly scared the Japs. It was also the first time I had seen them using their kukris at close quarters. They mostly went for the throat. The Japs ran.

The next morning I was told to take two platoons back to this position to bury the dead. I instructed the Jemadar to carry on, and went off. I returned to find that instead of digging graves, the Gurkhas were using the foxholes dug by the Japs. The bodies had rigor mortis, and would not fit, so the Gurkhas were cutting them up and stuffing them into the holes. I stopped this, but they thought I was being pernickety. The Gurkha has all the nicest characteristics of the British soldier – he likes sport, drinking, women and gambling. However, he has little feeling for the dead, either the enemy or his comrades. Once gone they'd gone, and there were no feelings of sadness nor remorse. When killing the enemy he is elated, and Gurkhas' eyes become bloodshot when going into action at close quarters. The Jap was a very courageous opponent and suffered enormously – but the Gurkhas were better. I was glad I was with them not against them. My battalion took no prisoners until well into 1945 and none of our men were taken prisoner – neither side took prisoners. At this time in the war, the Japs were thought to be invincible by some people, including many British troops. This was not the attitude of my Gurkhas.

Chins at War: Gurkha Commandos overlooking
Japanese Territory from Bacha Hill
ANTHONY GROSS

GROUP CAPTAIN FRANK CAREY

267 WING, RAF, BASED AT MAGWE (BURMA), 1943

The Japanese aircraft were considerably more manoeuvrable than ours were. If we got down and mixed it with them at low altitude we were in trouble, because we couldn't accelerate away from them unless we had a bit of height to dive away and they could run rings around us. The Japs at that stage were flying fixed-undercarriage monoplanes called Army 97s. They were extremely light and, for their weight, had very powerful engines, but not much in the way of gunfire. They also didn't have any armour plating behind them. If you got a good squirt at them they used to fold up.

They really worked, those Japs. One Jap that I shot down had deliberately crash-landed, trying to dive into a revetment with a Blenheim there. He missed it. We got the whole aircraft and body and everything else – he'd got 27 bullets in him and he was still flying that thing round the airfield looking for a target. They always used to try to dive into something. That was what we were up against. We also had to deal with an appalling lack of facilities – no spares, no tools, no equipment. Sometimes, to get an engine out, we wheeled a plane under a palm tree, pulled the tree down, tied it to the engine and slowly released it. Often we cannibalised one aircraft to keep others going.

When we made our first advance against the Japanese down the Arakan border with Burma, I flew to a recently repaired airfield at Cox's Bazaar to test its suitability for operations. On the return journey I had to refuel at Chittagong, which had only emergency fuel supplies on it. The refuelling party were in the process of finishing their job, and I was sitting in the cockpit waiting to start up, when I noticed a number of fighter aircraft appear from behind a cloud – about twenty-seven in all. I knew they must be Japanese, because we didn't have that many aircraft in the place.

Being without radar cover or any other warning was always a hazard, and here it was in large lumps! I started my engine, yelled to the ground crew to get under cover, and then had to taxi a long way to get to the end of the runway. I opened up, but long before I was airborne the bullets were flying and kicking up the dust around me. I got up in the air and immediately began to jink and skid to make myself an awkward target. I was helped by my own fury with myself for having been stupid enough to take off into such a suicidal position! However, luck was with me again and I led the Japs on my tail up the river at absolutely nought feet between the river boats, finally working my way up into the hills and leading them away from their own base at Akyab. Eventually they had to break off – I suppose their fuel was getting low. I thought I saw one of them crash behind me, but that was never confirmed. I really lost a lot of weight on that sortie.

Lieutenant-Commander Roger Hill

HMS *Jarvis*, D-Day, 1944

We watched them going ashore. From the bridge of my ship, they looked like little models – moving forward, stopping, firing, and moving forward again. Coming in from the big ships were the flotillas of the landing craft, and as we watched, the guns still blazing away, they formed in line abreast and were rushing for the surf line of the beach. I found myself banging the bridge with my clenched fist, 'By God, we're ashore in France, we've done it, we're back in France again.'

Manoeuvres: a Bren Gun outpost
ANTHONY GROSS

BRIGADIER JAMES HILL

3RD PARACHUTE BRIGADE, NORMANDY, 1944

In the days following D-Day, I experienced some of the hardest fighting I had seen in the war. Involved were the 9th Parachute Battalion, 1st Canadian Parachute Battalion and 5th Battalion Black Watch. Imagine what it was like for a 9th Battalion soldier. These men had never seen a shot fired in anger until forty-eight hours before. Their average age was twenty. They had suffered an appalling night drop on D-Day. They had stormed the Merville battery and attacked Le Plein. They arrived on the ridge on the 7th June, ninety strong, having set off from England with over 600 officers and soldiers. They were minus their equipment and not exactly fresh. In the first eight days of the Battle of Normandy, my brigade, which started around 2,000 strong, lost about fifty officers and 1,000 other men.

A narrow road ran along the ridge. We had to hold this ridge at all costs. If the Germans had secured it, the bridge-head at Ranville would have been untenable. Alistair Pearson and his 8th Battalion were denying the enemy the approaches to the ridge from the south. The 9th Battalion, whose numbers fluctuated during the battle, held the wooded area and the road adjoining Château St Côme. Brigade HQ and their defence platoon were in the middle. The Canadians held the Mesnil crossroads area immediately to the south. My Brigade HQ with their strong defence platoon, numbering some 150, and the Canadians with some 300 men were concentrated over a front of about one mile, astride the Bréville-Troarn Road, running north to south on top of the ridge.

Enemy attacks concentrated first on the Canadian battalion at Le Mesnil then swung against the 9th Battalion after the Germans had occupied Bréville on D+2. It was then that I realised we were up against a first-class German infantry division – 346 Grenadier Division – supported by tanks and self-propelled guns. During this period, some six attacks were launched against the 9th Battalion from Bréville and the east – three of which were coordinated with attacks on the Canadian positions at Le Mesnil. There was constant patrolling activity and on one occasion, my defence platoon accounted for nineteen Germans.

My room was on the top floor of a barn with access only from the outside staircase. I sat on the top step with my left backside overhanging the steps which was good as I smelt of gangrene poisoning – I had lost most of my left backside during a mortar attack on D-Day. From my position, I had a bird's-eye view of the German break-out from Bréville on D+4 and their attack on Peter Luard's 13th Battalion holding the north-east perimeter of Ranville. The 13th held their fire until the last moment and then mowed them down. For the next two days the Germans filtered back through the rear of our positions. I knew it was irregular to see Germans creeping about, but we had neither time nor resources to chase them.

It was about this time that we were strafed by our own Typhoons. Unfortunately the lady of the château, walking in the garden with her husband, was hit and killed. Our doctors tried to save the baby, to no avail, and we buried her in a shroud in her garden with what dignity we could muster under such circumstances. Soon after that, the husband and housekeeper left and my Brigade HQ occupied the château.

Sitting on my steps, looking down on the bank below, I saw the adjutant of the 9th Battalion, Hal Hudson, lying on the bank looking like a shrivelled parchment, waiting to be operated on by my Field Ambulance unit in the adjoining building. His story was unusual. He received some eighteen shrapnel wounds in his stomach during the capture of the Merville battery. He thought, 'I must kill one German before I die.' He imagined he saw a figure looming up and he shot it with his Sten gun. It was in fact his foot. The pain was such that it took his mind off his much more severe wounds and thanks to that and the treatment he received from the Field Ambulance, he lived to tell the tale.

On D+5, the 5th Battalion of the Black Watch were put under my command to capture Bréville. The attack went on in the early hours of the morning and was repulsed by the Germans with heavy losses. I then told them to hold the Château St

Côme itself and coordinate their defence with the 9th Battalion. At this juncture, the German Divisional Commander decided that our positions at St Côme and Le Mesnil must be liquidated for once and for all and a major attack was launched on D+6 on both the 9th Battalion and Black Watch positions and the Canadians. This attack was in strength, preceded by a heavy bombardment lasting some three hours, and it went on supported by tanks and self-propelled guns. The Black Watch were driven back and came back through the 9th Battalion and my defence platoon positions.

At 1600 hours, I received a message from Terence Otway commanding the 9th Battalion to say that he was doubtful whether he could hold out much longer. I knew that he would not send me this signal unless things were urgent and that something must be done about it. I had no bodies to spare so I went to Colonel Bradbrook, whose HQ was 200 yards away at the end of our drive, and asked him to help. At that moment, German tanks had overrun the road to his right and were shooting up his company HQ at close range. To his eternal credit, he decided that he could deal with this problem and he gave me what was left of his reserve company under Major Hanson, a very tough commander, together with cooks and any spare men, and we set off to the 9th Battalion area.

CORPORAL DANNY MORGANS

1ST PARACHUTE BATTALION, 1944

We literally had to wreck a beautiful house. First the windows had to be smashed, so the glass couldn't be blown in on us. Then the furniture was piled into barricades inside the room. Everything that was watertight, from the bath to buckets, vases and jugs, had to be filled with water, as the Germans were using incendiary ammunition to burn us out. Very soon the place was an organised shambles. Suddenly the old gentleman who owned the place appeared in his wrecked lounge. He was carrying a tray with glasses and a bottle of Advocaat. He solemnly filled up the glasses and handed them round to the men who'd just wrecked his home. I apologised for what we had done and he replied, 'It is not you, my son, it is the war.' And he returned to his cellar. To this day, if I am taking a drink and get sentimental, I call for an Advocaat and think of that marvellous Dutch gentleman.

Herbert Holewa

German soldier, 1944

The fighting on the Volturno was very tough. We had paratroops, some remnants from the Afrika Korps and units from the infantry. We were opposed by very good British forces, including some from the Eighth Army, who we had fought against in North Africa. The terrain was hard and the Allied fighter-bombers were very effective. You couldn't walk on the road. Even if you were on a bicycle, they would come down and shoot at you. The firepower of the Allied forces was enormous. Even to this day, I can't understand why they didn't achieve more at that time. They were far superior to the German forces. We were positioned forward on the bend of the river and during the night, the Allies bombed and strafed the roads. We needed it to defend ourselves, but we needed every bullet. We still had a very good fighting force. A lot of the old ones were still around and the young ones looked up to them. We had very little contact with the Italian civilians and they were actually very hostile to us. I remember we were stationed at a vineyard where they never used to look at us and doors were always being shut in our faces. I remember just one occasion when an Italian man went down into the wine cellar and fetched up a dusty bottle of wine, covered in cobwebs. He opened it and poured it out for us. That was nice.

CAPTAIN 'DICKY' RICHARDS

50TH INDIAN PARACHUTE BRIGADE, BURMA, 1944

Supply drops were a serious problem at Sangshak. The mountainous nature of the ground and the low-lying cloud made air supply hazardous, even if you could identify the target upon which to drop the supplies. Naturally, at base, if supplies were dispatched, they assumed that they had arrived, but communications were so bad that at times they had no idea that two-thirds of them had arrived or fallen elsewhere or got into Japanese hands.

We continued to fight by day and night. The position became utterly gruesome and macabre. The perimeter was littered with corpses which could not be buried and there were mule carcasses everywhere. Some went into the cooking pot, but others very quickly rotted in that climate – and there were Japanese bodies, our own bodies, and excreta everywhere. It was impossible to construct properly dug-down trenches, dysentery became rife and the situation was almost intolerable. We were getting weaker by the hour – our men were getting killed off one after the other, we were running out of ammunition and food and some men were almost delirious after many days without sleep. Some of us would drop off for a few minutes in mid-conversation. The situation was desperate, and by the 25th March, none of us expected to get out alive. But somehow that didn't seem to mean anything, either – we just went on, relentlessly. I never heard a single man complain.

Shortly before dawn on the 26th, the Japanese actually penetrated our position in the Church area, and set up machine guns in the trenches which had been occupied by the brave men of 152 and 153 Battalions. Things got incredibly intense – they were now only 100 yards from Brigade Headquarters and we'd run out of grenades. But our men became even more ferocious and daring. Every man was fighting for his life and there seemed no limit to their endurance – everyone, everywhere, was pleading for more ammunition and grenades. By 0730 hours the situation was desperate, but the brigadier was determined to regain complete control of the Church area. He sent a party from the Brigade Defence Platoon on a frontal counter-attack. This was led by young Lieutenant Robin de la Haye, nicknamed the 'Red Shadow' by the men because of his habit of doing the rounds at night wearing exquisite Jermyn Street red silk pyjamas under his webbing equipment. Robin and his men made a spirited attack but were cut to pieces by enemy fire from West Hill. Again and again we counter-attacked, now led by Lieutenant-Colonel Hopkinson, later by Colonel Abbott – but each time we were beaten back. At last, at 0930 hours, Major Jimmy Roberts with his A Company of 153 Battalion was successful and restored the situation, accompanied by deafening blasts from our own howitzers firing over open sights.

Just before six that evening there was a shout from one of the Brigade HQ signallers for everyone to keep quiet –

a message was coming through from Major General Roberts. His shout was so urgent and excited that everyone fell silent. The signaller listened hard to the crackling set and scribbled on his pad, talking into his handset. It seemed to go on for ever. Then he suddenly shouted into the microphone, 'You can stuff your bloody thoughts, General! What about the bloody reinforcements?' He was beside himself with rage as he handed over the message. It read, 'Fight your way out, go south then west. air and transport on the lookout,' and ended with the words, 'good luck. our thoughts are with you.' This had prompted the signaller's reply. Our reactions resembled a 'Bateman' cartoon. For a moment we were horrified by his audacity, but seconds later broke the tension with spontaneous laughter – and that was a sound not heard at Sangshak for quite some long time.

A conference of unit commanders was called and, as night was about to close in, we heard the familiar sound of the air-supply Dakotas in the distance. Our initial euphoria at this last-minute chance of survival was soon dampened by the enormous problems of evacuating the seriously injured, who would have to be carried, and the walking wounded, bearing in mind the sheer mountainous jungle slopes between us and Imphal. I cursed when I found that the bulk of our supply drop had fallen straight into the hands of the Japanese. As the night darkened, the Japs lit fires and sounded overjoyed at this unexpected bonus. Brigade Commander Tim Hope Thomson decided that there should not be any movement before 2230 hours that night. Units were to give top priority to pairing off walking wounded with their comrades, using every able-bodied man to help carry and protect the stretcher-cases. Our greatest concern was the plight of the wounded – many were within an hour or two of death and others so serious that death would occur if they were moved. It was the worst dilemma to face any man and we were stunned by the selfless courage of our Indian Medical Services senior officer, Lieutenant-Colonel 'Bobby' Davis, who pleaded to be allowed to remain behind, after the evacuation, to tend to the dying men who could not be moved, and anyone else who might not have been found in the utter shambles we were to leave behind.

Tim Hope Thomson gave it much deep thought, but knew that on past records of the Japanese, neither the gallant doctor nor his patients would have any chance of survival. We should try and take those who were considered to be mortally wounded, no matter how slim their chances of survival appeared to be. At Brigade HQ our cook, Swami, excelled himself, keeping his cauldron on the boil well into the evening. We were amused to see him adopting the role of a Brahmin high priest, which was hardly his status, giving dispensation to the Hindu to accept the possibility of corned beef within the cauldron, and the Muslim not to reject the infamous American-made 'soya link' sausage and gallons of rum included in the pot!

As the 2230 hours start-time approached, tension mounted. That evening Japanese fire had been limited to sporadic shots and a few bursts, but we wondered whether they would strike. If they did, our chances for survival would have been slim – but they didn't. Colonel Abbott ordered me to channel the few remaining exhausted men of 152 Indian Para Battalion through the 4th/5th Maratha Light Infantry position, which was the safest of the lot. The former had taken a terrible hammering with over 350 killed. Few had properly eaten or rested for well over a week and they were now practically without ammunition or grenades, or senior ranks to guide them, with a tortuous journey facing them through the Jap-infested jungle to Imphal.

As the break-out got under way, I felt surprised at the

quietness and orderliness as parties with makeshift bamboo stretchers and walking wounded vanished from sight into the jungle below. It was a painful and heart-rending experience, particularly for the medical men, whom I saw patching up and attending to anyone showing any signs of life.

Nearly a week later I arrived back at HQ 23rd Indian Division in Imphal. We had survived walking into an armed Japanese supply column heading for Sangshak by throwing ourselves or rolling into the thick elephant grass and lying 'doggo', whilst they passed within feet of some of us – we had no grenades and hardly a round between us. Days later whilst intelligence officers were debriefing us, I had a quiet cup of tea with Ouvry Roberts, whom I knew well. He left me in no doubt about the value of the stand which we had made. He said that the brigade, with its attached units, fighting under the most appalling conditions, had undoubtedly saved both Kohima and Imphal from the danger of being immediately overrun by the Japanese spearhead troops. This was later to be confirmed in a Special Order of the Day by General 'Bill' Slim himself.

As we were taking our leave, I asked him off the record whether he had heard the British signaller's comments on his personal message – 'You can bloody stuff your thoughts, General!' His reply was just an enigmatic smile.

5

ENDURANCE AND DEFIANCE

I have a rendezvous with Death
At some disputed barricade,
When Spring comes back with rustling shade
And apple-blossoms fill the air—
I have a rendezvous with Death
When Spring brings back blue days and fair.

It may be he shall take my hand
And lead me into his dark land
And close my eyes and quench my breath—
It may be I shall pass him still.
I have a rendezvous with Death
On some scarred slope of battered hill,
When Spring comes round again this year
And the first meadow-flowers appear.

God knows 'twere better to be deep
Pillowed in silk and scented down,
Where love throbs out in blissful sleep,
Pulse nigh to pulse, and breath to breath,
Where hushed awakenings are dear . . .
But I've a rendezvous with Death
At midnight in some flaming town,
When Spring trips north again this year,
And I to my pledged word am true,
I shall not fail that rendezvous.

'RENDEZVOUS'
ALAN SEEGER

Mrs M. Hall

Munitions worker, 1914

I'd never been in a factory before, but the crisis made you think. I thought well, my brothers and my friends are in France, so a friend and I thought to ourselves, well, let's do something. So we wrote to London and asked for war work. And we were directed to a munitions factory at Perivale in London. We had to have a health examination because we had to be very physically fit – perfect eyesight and strong. We had to supply four references, and be British-born of British parents.

We worked ten hours a day, that's from eight in the morning till quarter to one – no break, an hour for dinner, back again until half-past six – no break. We single girls found it very difficult to eat as well as work because the shops were closed when we got home. We had to do our work and try to get food, which was difficult. I remember going into a shop after not having milk for seven days and they said, 'If you can produce a baby you can have the milk' – that was it! I went into a butcher's shop to get some meat because we were just beginning to be rationed and I said, 'That looks like cat.' And he said, 'It is.' I couldn't face that.

It was a perfect factory to work in: everybody seemed unaware of the powder around them, unaware of any danger. Once or twice we heard, 'Oh, so and so's gone.' Perhaps she'd made a mistake and her eye was out, but there wasn't any big explosion during the three years I was there. We worked at making these little pellets, very innocent-looking little pellets, but had there been the slightest grit in those pellets, it would have been 'Goodbye'.

We had to do a fortnight on and a fortnight off. It was

terribly hard, terribly monotonous, but we had a purpose. There wasn't a drone in that factory and every girl worked and worked and worked. I didn't hear one grumble and hardly ever heard of one that stayed home because she had her man in mind, we all had. I was working with sailors' wives from three ships that were torpedoed and sunk, *Aboukir*, *Cressy* and *Hogue*, on the 22nd of September 1914. It was pitiful to see them, so we had to cheer them up as best we could, so we sang. It was beautiful to listen to.

After each day when we got home we had a lovely good wash. And believe me the water was blood-red and our skin was perfectly yellow, right down through the body, legs and toenails even, perfectly yellow. In some people it caused a rash, and a very nasty rash all round the chin. It was a shame because we were a bevy of beauties, you know, and these girls objected very much to that. Yet amazingly even though they could do nothing about it, they still carried on and some of them with rashes about half an inch thick but didn't seem to do them any inward harm, just the skin. The hair, if it was fair or brown it went a beautiful gold, but if it was any grey, it went grass-green. It was quite a twelve-month after we left the factory that the whole of the yellow came from our bodies. Washing wouldn't do anything – it only made it worse.

Each day we really and truly worked as I've never seen women work like it in my life before or since. It was just magic, we worked and we stood and we sat and we sang. If anyone had come into that factory they would never have believed it could have gone on, because we were such a happy band of women working amongst such treacherous conditions. And there was the cold. I am certain I'd never known brass to be so cold as it was in those factory nights.

But we were just one big happy family. It was amazing and I shall never forget it as long as I live, the way those women worked and talked and chatted about their ordinary everyday experiences, their boys at the Front, but mind you, it was the boys at the Front that we worried about and thought about and that's what made us work like that.

I used to be in Kent quite a lot and I used to see all the troop trains coming – the Red Cross on them, non-stop night and day. I went to Chatham Hospital to see a brother of mine, who was there, from the Front and I saw all the soldiers come in from Hill 60. Never shall I forget the sight as long as I live. They were unhealthy, they were verminous, and they used to say, 'It's Hell.' That was their words, only a few more adjectives with it, but that's their words, 'It was Hell.' But I know that they were glad to see women at home and the nurses who looked after them. There they were, soldiers lying in Chatham Hospital from that battle scene, and how grateful they were for a kindly word from their womenfolk.

Shop for Machining 15-inch Shells.
Singer Manufacturing Company, Clydebank, Glasgow, 1918
ANNA AIRY

Private Reginald Haine

1st Battalion, Honourable Artillery Company, 1914

As far as sandbags are concerned, the first time I saw a sandbag in France was when we were paraded one evening at Kemmel, a small town about half a mile behind the lines at Wytschaete. We didn't take these sandbags up empty, as Kemmel had been knocked about, there were lots of broken bricks and that sort of thing. The Pioneers had filled these sandbags and we carried them up one by one to the line. A whole line of us had one sandbag; that's all we could carry because of the conditions of the road.

Of course, going up on a trip like that one was bound to have a few casualties. Sometimes it was a quiet night and you only got one or two fellows wounded, but sometimes you were not so lucky if you'd got a machine-gun on you. They'd got this road taped to an inch and they knew we used it, just as we knew they had to use the road on the other side of the line. But we took these sandbags up to the line and it seemed to me stupid at the time that we had to do a thing like that. Well, of course, that attitude only lasted a very short time.

We used to hump these sandbags at night, chiefly, because we couldn't show our noses in the daytime, we were so close to the Germans. And then they did make a tremendous difference. Instead of just living in a ditch one could take rather a pride in building a decent sort of trench, and we got extremely good at improvising these trenches. Of course, one problem was that directly Jerry spotted we had got sandbags we were shelled to blazes straight away as he tried to knock the whole thing to bits. But that was the luck of the game.

The shelling was not the big stuff which we had later on in the war, it was chiefly what we called whizz-bangs. They were equivalent to our 18-pounders, they were little chaps. But they were frightening enough, especially when they knocked the sandbags to bits. And then, of course, let's face it, we got a lot of casualties with those too.

The finest training for warfare is warfare itself. In a fortnight you learn more than two years of any training can teach you. And so before the end of the year we were a very seasoned battalion and – I say it without bragging – we were as good as any regular battalion in the line. There was nobody behind except people like the Army Service Corps and suppliers. But as far as the fighting troops were concerned we were all very near the front line the whole time. Practically the whole time you had to sleep with your boots on in case things went wrong anywhere. Even if one was in support – not in reserve so much, in reserve you could get your clothes off – but if you were in support you had to sleep in your clothes. The winter of '14 was extremely hard because we had no amenities whatsoever. It was just ditches, the trenches were just waterlogged ditches, and one was often up to one's knees in frozen mud. You could do nothing about it except stick there. The actual fighting was nothing like it was in the later years of the war, the years I know most from a fighting point of view, and, of course, the casualties and everything then were terrific. But in '14 there were many casualties through sickness and shelling. There was shelling every day but nothing like the intensity of later on.

We had not been trained for any of the tasks we were asked to undertake. It was all improvisation really. The ordinary infanteer, he shot his rifle. And we had a couple of Vickers guns in the battalion, that's all the machine-guns the battalion had in those days. And there were specially trained people who used to have to hump up their ammunition for them, which was a hell of a job. That was because sometimes one had marched two or three miles to get near the firing line, and then we would have to carry not only our own kit with 250 rounds of ammunition, but sometimes they'd ask us to, between two people, carry up 1,000 rounds of machine-gun ammunition as well. And in those conditions in the winter of '14, when everything was as muddy as it could be and there was really no drainage or anything, it was a terrific task. From a physical point of view it was a killing job but we most of us got through it.

PRIVATE HUBERT TROTMAN

ROYAL MARINE LIGHT INFANTRY, 1917

It was time for leave. We travelled in a boxcar to Calais. We were as lousy as cuckoos. When we got to Calais we had to head for the fumigator. But there we saw a queue a mile long. We were told the boat sailed in half an hour and if we didn't make it we would lose a day of our leave. So those of us at the tail end of the queue broke off, went down to the docks and, damn me, we just walked onto the boat. We hid down below until it had sailed. So we disembarked unfumigated. That night I got as far as Paddington and the next day I caught the first train to Didcot. When I got home, just to take it in and breathe the familiar smell of the bakery again, I stood outside the shop for a while. Then I opened the door and shouted, 'Mother I'm outside. I'm home.' What a sight I must have been. I hadn't changed my clothes for months. I had a beard and I was in a hell of a state. She took one look at me and tears rolled down her face. She said, 'I'll clean you up.' 'No,' I said, 'you can't do that yet.' I put my hand in my armpit and took out a handful of lice. 'Look,' I said. 'Lice, hordes of them, I can't come in like this.' I put them back where they came from and went up to the hospital to see the matron. She knew me well, because I had visited her on my rounds when delivering bread to the hospital. She said, 'Hubert, we will soon fix you up.' She put a large sheet on the ground outside. 'You stand on that. Empty your pockets and then take all your clothes off.' Then she put me in a big bath. When I got out I asked about my clothes. She told me she had put them in the copper, lice and all. I had to spend my leave in civvies.

Heinrich Beutow

German schoolboy, 1917

Black and white posters went up showing a man putting a hand to his lips and saying, 'Be careful, don't talk too much, the enemy is listening in.' Nobody took them very seriously. Not we as schoolchildren, anyway.

Food was getting scarce, queues were getting longer and soon going to a soup kitchen became one of the features of everyday life. Meat was particularly scarce. Butter was quite scarce and we had the famous German turnips again and again because there were so few potatoes. The winter of 1916 to 17 was called the Turnip Winter.

Schoolboys were taken out of school, and we had to go into houses and count everything – rabbits, for instance, and goats and sheep. Everybody seemed to be keeping rabbits because of the shortage of meat. Then they took us out in whole classes and sent us into the country to help the farmers. We liked that, but it meant we didn't get much teaching. All the teachers were out as soldiers anyway, and generally the whole life of the country was becoming grimmer.

There was a strong sense of people saying, 'This war is lasting too long.' Some became quite outspoken. The feeling was that the war was lasting too long and that Germany didn't have much chance of winning it, because the conditions within the country were getting so very difficult.

Lieutenant Ulrich Burke

2nd Battalion, Devonshire Regiment, 1917

It had rained and rained and rained. We even had to cease the battle for a few days before continuing on, while the ground we went over became more and more broken up. All this gave the enemy time to reorganise and reinforce, so it became even more difficult. And there were no trenches at all at Passchendaele. There were just a series of shell-holes that had been reinforced with sandbags so that you could hide inside them. If, for instance, you wanted to urinate and otherwise, there was an empty bully beef tin kept on the side of the hole, so you had to do it in front of all your men then chuck the contents, but not the tin, over the back.

I had to go round my sector once a night with the sergeant-major. And when we left one shell-hole we'd have to ask which way to go next, because each night the ground would have absolutely shifted. One night the people on our left were planning an attack and we were going to give them heavy covering fire. It was a night attack due to start at 10 o'clock, but at half-past nine an order came through that the attack was off. So my sergeant-major and I had to go round twenty-four of these front-line shell-hole posts, quickly and in the dark, to stop the men firing when there was nothing to fire at. It was awful. We didn't really know when we were going towards the enemy and at one point, when my sergeant-major was within about ten yards of them, a Very light went up behind him. Because of the kind of Very light it was, he knew damn well he was out in front. So he quickly doubled back and managed to find the post.

But the conditions were miserable. You lived cave-like. You can imagine a man after being in one those holes for a week, where he couldn't even wash. Each day he got a two-gallon petrol tin of tea given him, delivered in a small box of hay which was supposed to insulate the tin and keep the tea warm. Well those tins were baked, boiled – everything was done to them – but whenever you put a hot substance in them you still got petrol oozing out, and that gave the men violent diarrhoea. But they had to drink it because it was the only hot drink they had.

Troops had to go overland to all these shell-hole posts every day, the first time to deliver rations and ammunition and the second time, at night, to bring the tins and hayboxes back, because there wasn't room to keep them in the little shell-holes. You couldn't chuck them over the top because they were needed again.

It was a terrible experience for the ration parties to make two journeys. The troops were from other battalions, because it was realised that the battalion on the line couldn't possibly do it. And they couldn't care less how they did it. The butter came in a round flat tin but bread was just bread and some-times, when the fellow had fallen about a dozen times, there was a thick paste of dirt and mud all the way round it. Well, chaps started cutting this crust off and throwing it away, but then they found they had no bread left, so they had to eat it.

Oh, the conditions were terrible. You can imagine the agony of a fellow standing for twenty-four hours, sometimes up to his waist in mud, with just a couple of bully beef tins or his mess tin trying to get the water out of this shell-hole. And he had to stay there all day and all night for about six days, that was his existence. And when he got a hot drink it was tainted with petrol, so he knew that for the next four or five hours he'd be filling a bully beef tin.

The men were hardened, but the life was terrible. Another extra chore was that lime had to be spread on the back of the posts because open excreta was being chucked out and if you didn't put down lime then when you came crawling out you'd be covered in it. A further great problem was trench fever and trench foot. When a fellow got a very high temperature, you could tell he'd probably got trench fever. It wasn't dysentery exactly, but it was constant diarrhoea and left him weak and listless. Trench foot was owing to the mud soaking through your boots and everything. In many cases your toes nearly rotted off. We lost more that way than we did from any wounds or anything.

A Group of Soldiers
C R W Nevinson

Sergeant Perry Webb

7th Battalion, Dorsetshire Regiment, 1918

The NCO would look up and say, 'Here's so many biscuits for you.' We used to put it all together, and if you had six men you knew that was a sixth each of everything that was there. If there was, say, a pot of jam, you had your part issued to you when you had a meal in your billycan. That's what the Americans couldn't understand when they came with us. They said, 'How on earth can you have rations dished out like that? Our fellows would eat the lot.' I said, 'Well, our fellows don't.' They all had their proper rations and it was up to the NCO to see to it that they had, because they were in trouble if you didn't.

Bread was very, very scarce. You might not see bread for two months, so mostly it was just big square biscuits, like dog biscuits. They were nutritious no doubt, but we'd have to break them up with a trenching tool handle to make them small enough to eat.

There were potatoes though, and Maconochie vegetable rations. I don't know if it was a form of greens, it was concentrated. You'd get a round tin each of sliced potatoes and a little lump of fat pork in the middle, and you'd just jack-knife it open and eat them as they were. Then there was bully beef, which was more or less plentiful. I think everybody had a fair share of bully beef. I did see bacon once or twice, but it was very rare. You might get a bit of cheese occasionally, but not often, and you got margarine but never butter. I only ever had hot food once or twice in the trenches, and that was when we were on a very quiet front and our kitchens were able to get right up to the reserve line.

Captain Desmond Gordon

1st Battalion, Green Howards, 1940

We were fighting a losing battle from the time that we arrived in Norway, so morale was not high – it couldn't be expected to be – though discipline was remarkably good. Most of the men in my company were recalled army reservists who'd served in India with me until being demobilised – so they were seasoned soldiers, and they behaved magnificently.

The Germans had about a dozen tanks which could only be deployed one behind another on the road. They had come up against almost no opposition until they met the leading elements of the 15th Infantry Brigade near a village called Kvam. There the 10th Company commander had deployed forward four of his anti-tank guns, and concealed them astride the road, hidden in the gardens of the houses. That company destroyed the first German tank of the war, and that had a remarkable effect in slowing down the German advance. Not only did it block the road – and everything hinged on road movement – but it was an indication to the Germans that they were up against a force better equipped than what they had experienced so far.

Unknown to me, the higher command had decided that we had got to be evacuated back to Aandalsnes. A train had been assembled in the tunnel at Dombaas which was to take the battalion back. By that time, the Germans had caught up with us, and we were told to hold our position until I got the signal that the rest of the battalion had entrained in the tunnel. For the first and only time in this short-lived campaign, my company was given the support of a troop of Norwegian 25-pounder guns. The effect on morale of having these shells going over our heads in the direction of the enemy was incredible. With their help, we literally ran to the train and I staggered into the very last carriage, completely exhausted. By that time it was late evening. We came to a halt when the engine hit a bomb crater. We at the back of the train were ordered to get out and get on to the road which ran parallel with the railway line.

The commanding officer got hold of the intelligence officer – who'd got a bicycle from somewhere – and said, 'Go to the nearest village and find out if there is a tunnel where we can hide.' His one thought was that we must get some protection from German air attack when daylight arrived. He came back and reported that there was one eighteen miles away. We marched through the night and we had just about reached it when the first German aircraft spotted us. We had about 700 men in the tunnel – and there was also a bloody train, which had to keep steam up – so we were practically suffocated. All that day we sat there, with the Germans air-bombing us, trying to hit the tunnel – which they failed to do. We stayed there until darkness appeared, then we got into this train and finally ended up in Aandalsnes – which by this time was virtually an inferno. The whole of the fjords around us were just lit up with flames of this little town burning. It was an unforgettable sight. Those aircraft that were bombing us in the tunnel went on to bomb Aandalsnes.

I found myself on a cruiser – the *Calcutta* – who hadn't got a single shell left to fire. She'd tucked herself in under one of the fjords throughout that day, and had fired every single round of ammunition she had to protect herself. I shall always be very grateful for the way the crew received us on board and looked after us during our trip back to Scotland.

We weren't in frightfully good shape by that time. We got very little sleep and we were very, very tired from being continually on the move and withdrawing. You can sustain yourself when you're advancing and achieving success – you can sustain yourself on short rations – but that's not so easy when you are retreating.

CORPORAL HENRY PALMER

1/7TH BATTALION, QUEEN'S ROYAL REGIMENT (WEST SURREY), DUNKIRK, 1940

The beach was one vast sea of bodies. I had never seen so much dejection. Soldiers felt that they had been left there. Some seemed to have given up, but personally I didn't. There was one place I was going, and that was back to England.

There was panicking, but most of us managed to keep our heads. One chap scrounged a tin of bully beef and laid it out like a picnic, tucked his napkin in, then apologised he couldn't supply the wine because the butler happened to be away that day.

FREDERICK DELVE

LONDON FIREMAN, 1940

There was a short, sharp message sent by Winston Churchill to the fire services in London (which was not received until 11 o'clock), saying that St Paul's was to be saved at all costs. Now it was interesting because every fireman, without being told, knew that the target was St Paul's – that St Paul's was to be destroyed that night. And without telling anyone, they almost lined their backs to St Paul's and pointed their jets outwards to make sure that no fire would reach St Paul's – and generally they were successful. There was slight damage, but it was not destroyed – and yet the whole of the area around there was just devastated.

DOROTHY HONT

TEENAGER IN LIVERPOOL DURING 'MAY WEEK' BOMBING, 1941

It was night after night. Your life rotated around the sirens. You'd go to work and you'd close the shop early or come home a bit earlier, have a fast tea, get yourself into something warm, gather little bits of specials that you wanted to save, down to the shelter and that was it. And we used to knit in the shelter or play cards or guessing games, or just doze. Half the time you were up to your ankles in water because water used to seep in. Every day you'd have to go down and bail out. So we used to put bricks on the floor to put our feet on – cold, miserable and horrible. I wouldn't wish it on anybody.

In the very bad times, such as the week of a bright moon or early dark nights, you would have the sirens practically every night. And then if you went a few days without, that was as nerve-racking as the others, because you were waiting for them. But after we had a bit of a respite, you tended to get a little bit cheeky. You'd go to the pictures or something like that. I only went to two dances and one cinema during the whole session of the war. That was the extent of my social life.

Captain John Sim

12th Parachute Battalion, D-Day, 1944

My company commander asked me to see if there were any Germans in four houses nearby, where we were going to establish our Battalion Headquarters. I took a sergeant and two soldiers and when we got to the first house I noticed there was a light on inside. I knocked, and after probably about a minute, a middle-aged lady in her day clothes opened the door. At two o'clock in the morning this was a bit unusual. Behind her, her husband and two kids were also dressed in their day clothes. I said, '*Bonjour Madame, nous sommes soldats d'Angleterre; nous arrivons ici par avion, parachutistes. L'heure de libération est arrivée. Où sont les soldats allemands? Les soldats allemands restent ici?*' She looked blankly at me. I was a dunce at French at school, but I thought I'd done quite well. I had another go but now she looked dazed and terrified – we were all camouflaged up with blackened faces. I then asked my sergeant, a right raw Yorkshireman, if he could speak French – he couldn't and neither could the other two, so I tried again. I'd barely started when she burst into tears, embraced me and said, 'You're British soldiers, aren't you?' So I said, 'Yes, I've been trying to tell you this for the last three or four minutes. You can speak English well, can't you?' 'Yes,' she said, 'I am English, born in Manchester, and I married a French farmer before the war and settled here.' I asked her why it took her so long to come out with it. She explained that there had been Germans masquerading as British commandos or parachutists in the area to test them out. Then she said, 'It wasn't until I heard your frightful schoolboy French and your backchat to your sergeant that

I realised that no German could possibly have acted the part!' She told us there were no Germans in the area.

Lieutenant Michael Marshall

4th Battalion, 5th Royal Gurkha Rifles, Burma, 1945

We got the word that the advance into Burma was to take place. We went from Tamu to Kalewa, down Kabaw valley, and news came that we were to march down Gangaw Valley at night as the whole movement of the division was to be kept secret. The Gangaw Valley we found to be one of the most unhealthy places in Burma. It was very hot even at night – dry and dusty. We marched 300–400 miles, which took the whole of January 1945. Marches generally started at 2200 hours and lasted for eleven to twelve hours. It was tiring for the British officers because Gurkhas have short legs and march at between two and three miles an hour, whereas the British Army marches at between three and four miles an hour. So it takes longer. By the time we had finished this march one could say that everyone was fit.

6

GRIM REALITY

What passing-bells for those who die as cattle?
Only the monstrous anger of the guns.
Only the stuttering rifles' rapid rattle
Can patter out their hasty orisons.
No mockeries for them from prayers or bells,
Nor any voice of mourning save the choirs –
The shrill, demented choirs of wailing shells;
And bugles calling for them from sad shires.

What candles may be held to speed them all?
Not in the hands of boys, but in their eyes
Shall shine the holy glimmers of goodbyes.
The pallor of girls' brows shall be their pall;
The flowers the tenderness of silent minds,
And each slow dusk a drawing-down of blinds.

'ANTHEM FOR DOOMED YOUTH'
WILFRED OWEN

Heinrich Beutow

German schoolboy, 1914

After the initial enthusiasm and patriotism came a wave of quietness, because then the first death lists were published in the papers. And my mother – she was English – was suddenly surrounded by women of the regiment, the wives of the other officers of course, and most of them – because my father's regiment was one of the first to march over the border into Belgium – were widows. And even as a child, I must say, it gave me a great shock to see that most of the officers were dead and killed during the first weeks. A lot of the younger soldiers were dead and the whole feeling of enthusiasm faded away very quickly, in my opinion. The world became grey after that.

Private Charles Ditcham

2nd Battalion, Argyll and Sutherland Highlanders, 1914

On the night of the 25th at one in the morning my battalion went into a factory in the village of Le Cateau. And at 4 o'clock we moved out hurriedly because the German Uhlans were at the other end of the village. So we took up our position to do a rearguard action for the Expeditionary Force. All this meant was that the company was put in a cornfield and we were told to dig ourselves in. So we just made a bit of a hole in the ground with your trenching tool and then took up a position. Then the party started when the Hun came along. It was what made me realise what war was about. We just lined up in the cornfield, one company on the right, one company on the left, Middlesex and other people, all mixed up. And these Germans came in their hordes and were just shot down. But they still kept coming. There were sufficient of them to shove us out of the field eventually. And then, the realisation what war meant – when I saw my company sergeant-major for instance, a fellow called Sim, who was wounded in the mouth. He was going back dripping blood. And there were various people getting killed and wounded.

What I shall never understand is what I was supposed to do with a bugle in the front line during the battle, except to blow if my platoon officer, who incidentally became a prisoner of war, had told me to. But what he would have asked me to blow I wouldn't honestly know. I mean I couldn't blow cease-fire because it didn't mean a thing. And afterwards, according to later accounts, it was an orderly retreat. Well, as one who took part in the orderly retreat, I didn't think it was very orderly. On my way out I met another drummer and on our way back we met the corporal of the drums, a fellow called Balfour. And this chap had been very badly wounded so we took him back to the aid post in a church in the village of Le Cateau.

When we arrived, it gave me the shock of my life to see all the badly wounded people there – there were stretcher cases and walking cases, the church was full of them. So we left this wounded fellow and just followed the tribe, I didn't know where it was going. The only thing that I am very thankful for was seeing an old soldier who had served with my father, who was driving the ammunition wagon in my company. He was taking back two Clydesdale horses – the wagon had been dumped – and he dragged me onto the back of one of these Clydesdales. And I sat on that thing half asleep till I arrived at St Quentin the following morning. When I fell off it, I could hardly walk.

Wounded in the Chest: 'Just out of the trenches near Arras'
SIR WILLIAM ORPEN

Private Clifford Lane

1st Battalion, Hertfordshire Regiment, 1914

We'd all got these long, thick woollen underpants and vests on and we were soaked right through. When we got back to the trench it was dark, and we tried to get around this little brazier fire, but of course only two or three men could get near anyway so we didn't really get dry. And then they brought us 'Princess Mary's gift box'. And in this box was cigarettes, tobacco and a bar of chocolate, which was very much appreciated. And then we had what the English newspapers called Christmas Dinner. This consisted of cold bully beef and a cold lump of Christmas pudding, that was our Christmas dinner. The English newspapers said the British troops in the front line 'enjoyed' their Christmas dinner.

Sergeant Charles Lippett

1/8th Battalion, Queen's Royal West Surrey Regiment, 1915

We arrived at Béthune, where we stayed the night. We went off on the line of march headed by our band, moving up to attack Hill 70. We hadn't the faintest idea where we were going, but we sang the usual soldiers' songs – 'Tipperary', and all those sort of things – we were thoroughly enjoying ourselves. We had the usual stops, which were supposed to be ten minutes every hour, but actually we halted far more than that because of the chaos on the roads – traffic going up and down, ammunition limbers and walking wounded.

Our first shock was when we met the walking wounded. They said when we were laughing and talking, with an eager to get at 'em sort of attitude, they said, 'You'll laugh on the other side of your ruddy faces when you get up there.' Of course, that didn't mean very much to us at that time, we were members of the Queen's you know, and as Kitchener had said, we were going to do as well as those who had gone before, so we didn't bother very much about that.

Our baptism of fire was our attack on Hill 70 in the Béthune area. We advanced in short sharp rushes and everywhere men falling. I began to get really anxious as I moved forward because I could see men disappearing and didn't know quite what was happening to them because you couldn't see the bullets. My biggest shock, in advancing up that hill, was to come across my own platoon officer, Lieutenant Cressy, who was either dead or very badly wounded. I remember shaking him and telling him to come on, but of course he was dead, so he couldn't.

Then I realised that we had to get on and do something, but there was no one to give us orders – they had all been killed or wounded. The thing that worried me most was the fact that on my back was about 60 lb of weight and I just couldn't carry it very much further. So I got the man next to me to get out his jack-knife and cut it off, and I did the same for the remainder of the fellows who were there.

In the meantime we were still firing, and as we approached this wire I could see the bodies of men hanging on it, obviously dead or badly wounded, and there were no gaps in it at all. Our artillery had not cut the wire, even firing 18-pounder shells at it. The shell could land in a certain spot and instead of cutting a neat swathe through the wire to allow the troops through, it just lifted great lumps of it up and made the confusion worse. So there was no way of getting through the wire at all. I couldn't even see where the enemy trench was, the barbed wire was so thick and so deep.

Well, we laid down, and how many men there were at the time I don't know, but it was very few indeed. We lay there wondering what on earth to do until some bright spark said, 'We've got the order to retire.' Now I didn't fancy going down that hill again with my back to them, it was bad enough coming up in front. But I knew there was a sunken trench to the right of us, so I got the few men that were around me back into this trench, and temporarily at least we were out of fire. Well, how long we laid there I don't know, but I realised that we had made a mess of the thing, or at least, someone had.

Private R. Richards

Royal Engineers, 1915

When we finally got to France we went straight up to Dickebusch, and of course it being the latter part of November, it was pretty filthy weather. The Germans were only about fifty yards away and they had highly specialised snipers, which made life pretty unbearable. We could never retaliate properly because this sort of warfare had taken us completely by surprise – we had nothing to lob back at them.

But then all of a sudden there was a violent explosion, and I was blown back about twelve yards. When I finally got up all I could see was smoke, and I could hear the cries and screams of the survivors. As I crawled towards them I could see what remained of the section that had been making these bombs. Some had been cut in two, some in three parts, legs and arms were strewn all over the place and there was that acrid smell of explosion. Well, all my romantic ideals of war completely vanished with that episode. The following day when I was given the job of going round with sandbags, collecting the pieces, we had to rescue some bits from telegraph wires where they'd been blown at great velocity, and we buried them in the common grave.

LIEUTENANT STEFAN WESTMANN

GERMAN MEDICAL OFFICER, SOMME, 1916

For a full week we were under incessant bombardment. Day and night, the shells came upon us. Our dugouts crumbled. They would fall on top of us and we'd have to dig ourselves and our comrades out. Sometimes we'd find them suffocated or smashed to pulp. Soldiers in the bunkers became hysterical – they wanted to run out, and fights developed to keep them in the comparative safety of our deep bunkers. Even the rats became hysterical and came into our flimsy shelters to seek refuge from this terrific artillery fire.

For seven days and seven nights we had nothing to eat and nothing to drink while shell after shell burst upon us.

PRIVATE NORMAN DEMUTH

1/5TH BATTALION, LONDON REGIMENT, 1916

One thing I found when I eventually got home was that my father and my mother didn't seem in the least interested in what had happened. They hadn't any conception of what it was like, and on occasions when I did talk about it, my father would argue points of fact that he couldn't possibly have known about because he wasn't there. I think his was probably the approach of the public at large They didn't know – how could they? They knew that people came back on leave covered with mud and lice, but they had no idea of what kind of danger we were in. I think they felt the war was one continual sort of cavalry charge; that one spent all day and all night chasing Germans or them chasing us. Had they realised the strain of sitting in a trench and waiting for something to drop on one's head, I don't think they would have considered it was just play. And of course the general idea was that England couldn't possibly lose.

MABEL LETHBRIDGE

MUNITIONS WORKER, 1916

When my father and brothers, uncles, relatives and friends came home on leave and were staying at or visiting our house, I noticed a strange lack of ability to communicate with us. They couldn't tell us what it was really like. They would perhaps make a joke, but you'd feel it sounded hollow, as there was nothing to laugh about. They were restless at home, they didn't want to stay, they wanted to get back to the Front. They always expressed a desire to finish it.

Reliefs at Dawn
C R W Nevinson

Private George Hancox

Princess Patricia's Light Infantry, Canadian Army, 1917

At Vimy Ridge the weather wasn't too good, it was threatening rain and we had a certain amount of drizzle. The trenches themselves were nothing but unconnected ditches, there was no traversing and no revetment, and just a sandbag parapet in front with loopholes. There were a number of flares going up, which gave a very eerie effect, and quite a bit of rifle fire, but not too much machine-gun fire. On the whole we found it more depressing and disillusioning than frightening. We weren't so much frightened of being killed and wounded as we were depressed by the conditions. We had thought we were going to fight a glorious war, but the reality was so different.

PRIVATE RAYNOR TAYLOR

WELCH REGIMENT, 1917

I was just eighteen years old and I'd been doing a bit of courting. My girl worked at the cotton mill, same as me, and lived nearby, so after I'd been home for dinner we'd walk back together. I thought she was wonderful and when I went in the Army I used to get some very nice letters from her. When I came on leave I'd go out with her every night and I was even invited to their house for my tea, which was a step forward. I think it was because I was in uniform.

I thought I was in love with her, I really did. I treasured those letters. I was so sentimental I felt like a music hall star. Try and imagine this: a full moon. Not a sound. You're on sentry duty in the front line. It's peaceful. You're thinking about home. Thinking about this girl. I'm thinking that the same moon will be shining on her. I can remember this, I was really moonstruck.

We came out of the line and I got a letter from her and one from my mother. I remember I didn't open my mother's, I opened hers first to see what she had to say. It was devastating. In the nicest possible way she said she didn't want to go out with me again because she was going out with somebody else. It was a lad I knew, who I thought was a good friend, but he wasn't, he pinched my girl. Honestly, my world fell apart. I was eighteen and this was the first girlfriend I'd had, and she ditched me. Of all the experiences that I've had, even today, I can't think of anything that upset me more than that did.

SERGEANT CYRIL LEE

LONDON REGIMENT PASSCHENDAELE, 1917

I remember trying to help a lad in this copse about a hundred yards from our jumping-off trench. There was no hope of getting to him, he was struggling in the middle of this huge sea of mud. Then I saw a small sapling and we tried to bend it over to him. We were seasoned soldiers by then, but the look on the lad's face was really pathetic – he was only a mere boy. It pricked my conscience, I felt I should try and do something more for him, but I couldn't do a thing – had I bent it a little more I should have gone in with him, and had anyone else gone near this sea of mud they should have gone in with him too, as so many had.

PRIVATE DI LUCCA

US 42ND DIVISION, 1918

When we finally reached our trenches it was raining a deluge. So we had to form a line by holding each other by our rain-coats, to get through the trenches, and we marched through, during a terrible barrage which had started fifteen minutes earlier. Everything was coming down – trees, stones, rocks, everything came over our heads: it was a dangerous spot to be in. We came forward until we reached our dugouts, where we rested for two or three hours.

At dawn we got the order to go over the top. We had to get out of our trenches and meet the enemy, who was only twenty feet from us. We didn't know this. They come out of their trenches; we come out of our trenches. We met one another, faced one another like a bunch of animals. We lost our senses; we charged them with our bayonets. I saw a German, a six-footer, coming towards me – why he picked me I don't know. Anyway, I saw him coming. I don't know what gave me the idea, what gave me the strength, but as soon as he came near me, I turned my rifle by the butt, broke his thrust and I hit him on the chin. All of a sudden he was bleeding. He let go his arm, put his hand towards his chin to find out where the blood came from. That gave me a clear spot: I turned the rifle and I hit him in mid-chest with the bayonet. I left the bayonet there till he fell down. Looked at him, pulled out my bayonet – I know what happened to him, I know the conditions – and I just left him, and I kept following my other friends – they were going ahead of me. We chased the enemy, which was in full retreat, from trench to trenches, from place to places, all the way down the embankment from the hill of St Mihiel.

When we reached the city of Château-Thierry I joined my division. The place was littered with dead. Only a few days before, the marines had met the onslaught. The ground was full of holes: dead all over the place; dead mules, dead horses – everything was putrefied. The place smelled terribly. The rain, it rained constantly, which never helped any, didn't help decompositions of the body. I had never had any training for this. I never expected to find anything so gruesome.

Captain Paul Hawkins

Royal Norfolk Regiment, 1939

Our duties were to guard ammunition dumps which were laid out along the sides of a network of roads about seven or eight miles from Arras, and also to try and dig fresh emplacements by the side of the road to put in shells and ammunition. I always remember that time of digging out one particular piece by the side of the road, which would only come away in large chunks because the frost was in the ground to a couple of feet deep. We found the skeleton of a First World War German soldier whose jackboots were still reasonably intact, and a Canadian soldier whose identification disc was still there. They were taken away and buried elsewhere.

Sergeant William Harding

2nd Regiment Royal Artillery, France, 1940

The roads were absolutely jammed solid with civilians of all ages – mostly very young and very old. The old people I shall never forget because it's something I've never seen before – never thought I'd see. Some of them must have been in their eighties, with huge bundles on their backs, bowed right over, walking along these hot roads.

There were mothers pulling prams piled up with belongings, little children hanging on their skirts crying. They weren't walking – they were just trudging along in the heat, virtually worn out. We all responded straight away. All the

lads rummaged in their pockets, everywhere. The cookhouse
– it was just the field kitchens – started making loads of tea
with what water we had, and dishing it out. We felt so sorry
for them. I was so fagged out, my legs felt like lead. So all
I could do, shells or no shells, was just amble along. I just
trudged along, carrying this old Bren gun and all this ammunition stuck in my blouse, in the boiling hot sun. Sweat was
pouring off me.

On the 23rd the Germans must have got nearer, because
this is where the mortars really took hold of the situation.
The mortars came over thick and fast. Nearby there was a
Vickers pom-pom on blocks of wood, manned by three
gunners. A mortar bomb hit it and the three blokes were just
shattered. I ran over to them, and I looked at one poor fellow
– his face – his eyes staring up at me. And I thought, 'Well,
I can't do anything for him.' I ran back again, and there was
this chap, dragging himself on his elbows. He was sobbing,
and there were two lines in the sand from his legs – but there
was no feet on the end of his legs. I thought. 'God what a
terrible thing to happen to anybody!' I looked away because
there were more explosions all around us. Then I saw this
rifleman running in front of me. One minute he was there
– there was a terrific explosion – next minute he was in bits.
How can a man, fully clothed in webbing, uniform, a belt
round his waist, gas mask, boots and everything else, within
seconds be lying there without a stitch of clothing on him?
He was totally in pieces with his head lying on his neck, eyes
open. The skin of his belly was taken right off – and there
was his intestines, just like you see in a medical book, undisturbed. How can something like this happen?

Then a rifleman next to me shot an old woman that ran
out of a house – and I cursed him for what he'd done. I
thought it was unnecessary to shoot an old lady – but he said,

'I'm sorry, that was my orders. Anybody dressed as old women, nuns or priests or civilians running about, gets shot. Five of my company have been shot by Germans dressed as nuns.'

SERGEANT LEONARD HOWARD

210 FIELD COMPANY, ROYAL ENGINEERS, DUNKIRK, 1940

I saw a regimental sergeant major in his knee breeches and his service dress jacket and cap – and the tears were streaming down his face. He said, 'I never thought that I would see the British Army like this.' And I always remember him. Poor man was absolutely shattered. He was a regular soldier and the tears were streaming down his face.

Dunkirk – Embarkation of Wounded, May 1940
EDWARD BAWDEN

ORDINARY SEAMAN DICK COPPEARD

ROYAL NAVY DUNKIRK EVACUATION, 1940

At Portland we were given a night's leave, so we went ashore, picked up a couple of WAAFs and took them to the pictures. While we were there they flashed on the screen for all personnel of the ships in harbour to return to their ships immediately.

Eventually we found out that we were going over to France to pick up the troops. We were told to carry on to Fécamp and embark as many people from the jetties as we could. Most of them were stretcher-cases and walking wounded. They looked like a beaten army – they weren't really, but they looked it. Some were from the 51st Highland Division, a few French, and a regiment from the Midlands.

We cleared the mess decks to make room for the stretchers. The walking cases were pushed into corners. There were two or three hundred of them on board, plus about sixty of us crew. We tried to feed them but ran out of food. At one point we had to take bread off some French soldiers who didn't want to share it around. They seemed shocked and were very, very quiet. I don't think they realised what was happening to them. A lot of them had never seen warfare. We got the chaps off at Portsmouth. Those that could walk marched off the jetty, heads up and shoulders back.

Sergeant Rosemary Horstmann

WAAF, RAF Hawkinge, 1940

It was very dramatic, because several of the girls who were working with us had boyfriends who were pilots, so they would find themselves monitoring a battle in which their brothers and fiancés were fighting, and we were writing down what the German pilots were saying – things like, 'I've got him,' or 'He's down!' and sometimes you would hear the pilots screaming.

Aircraftwoman Jean Mills

WAAF, plotter and tracer at RAF Duxford, 1940

We were all pretty young – girls of only nineteen or twenty – when we got assigned to Duxford, and for a lot of us it was the first time we'd been away from home, so we were laughing and joking, because it seemed like an adventure. Suddenly we reached the brow of a hill and we could see Duxford, stretching out in front of us. It was a beautiful sunny day. As we looked, we could see that something had happened. There were lots of planes – one plane seemed to hover and was nose-diving to the ground with smoke trails rising. The noise of our chatter stopped instantaneously and the mood changed. We realised it wasn't a great lark and that we were in for serious business. We were reminded of this because the pilot who was killed had an Alsatian, which kept roaming the camp looking for him. It was very sad.

Major Henry Cree

2nd Battalion, West Yorkshire Regiment, Burma, 1943

Nobody thought that a dressing station would be attacked – but it was. The Japs got into it and did the most appalling execution there amongst the wounded and sick in this hospital. We could hear it going on – shouts and screams and shooting. I was asked by the CO of the Indian hospital to counterattack the hospital and take it, but I said I couldn't. It was pitch dark by that time, and I said it was impossible for us to attack. You couldn't tell friend from foe, and we should only end up by shooting all our own men if we tried to attack it by night. We didn't know the ground, anyway. It was impossible to put down any sort of covering fire with mortars or guns, or anything – we'd only have made matters worse. So I said, with great reluctance, 'I don't think I can do anything about it tonight.'

Early the next morning, A Company went in and counter-attacked the main dressing station. The Japs were still there in full force and had to be just winkled out, inch by inch. We lost fifteen men ourselves in that attack – but we eventually got them all out of it – booted them out.

It was horrid – they'd shot men lying in their beds. They just shot them. They shot several doctors too, they just lined them up and shot them. It made everybody very furious and determined to get the better of them – which we did. What happened was that the whole of the 9th Brigade, B Echelon was in the position, just a little way from us on both sides of a deep chaung. This chaung ran up into the main dressing station area, getting much narrower as it went up, but it was a well-defined channel. That night, Japs started passing down this chaung on the way from the main dressing station. Both sides of the chaung were held by our B Echelon personnel, muleteers, orderly room staff, sanitary men, quartermaster's storemen, chaps like that – nearly all old soldiers, including the regimental Sergeant-Major. They twigged what was happening. They just let the Japs have it. They killed an enormous number of them in that place, which became known as Blood Nullah afterwards. These were the chaps who had raided the main dressing station, so we felt we avenged that one.

ABLE SEAMAN KEN OAKLEY

ROYAL NAVAL COMMANDO, D-DAY, 1944

On the evening prior to the D-Day landings, the senior arms officer gave us a briefing and I will always remember his final words. 'Don't worry if all the first wave of you are killed,' he said. 'We shall simply pass over your bodies with more and more men.' What a confident thought to go to bed on.

SERGEANT WILLIAM SPEARMAN

NO. 4 COMMANDO, D-DAY, 1944

There were bodies – dead bodies, living bodies. All the blood in the water made it look as though men were drowning in their own blood. That's how it looked.

Private Eric Collins

1st Battalion, East Lancashire Regiment, 1944

The day after the bombing of the Canadians by the RAF, we started off through the Falaise Gap, and at either side were devastated Tiger tanks and horses that had drawn the gun-wagons blown up like balloons. What people tend to forget is that the German Army was largely supplied by horse-drawn supply columns, so it was horses and carts, and dead horses, and dead men and dead equipment – an absolute horror. The appalling smell and stench – it was a terrible sight to see.

Corporal Eric Lord

5th Battalion, Coldstream Guards, Germany, 1945

Once we were across the Rhine and progressing through Germany, we came across lots of Germans fleeing. Once, we passed a convoy of horses and carts and a young girl was sitting on top of one cart with all her possessions on the cart behind her. She stared at me with a look of cold hatred. I knew a bit of German so I called at her, 'Denken sie an . . .' to tell her to remember Poland and France and Russia and the terrible things the Germans had done. She carried on staring at me, full of hate.

Captain Richard Smith

2ND BATTALION, OXFORDSHIRE AND
BUCKINGHAMSHIRE LIGHT INFANTRY, BELSEN, 1945

The first thing I saw was a whole collection of German guards, stripped to the waist, barefooted, with no belts, carrying corpses from the pits where they'd been flung into a newly formed burial ground on the other side of the road. The Germans were being beaten by the British guards with their rifle butts. I went into the headquarters established by the provost who was in charge of the camp, and the major who was there said, quite honestly, 'I have no control over my troops.'

We were taken in to see the camp commandant, Kramer, who was known as 'the Beast of Belsen', and that woman Irma Grese. He was eventually hanged. The woman had obviously been given a beating. It was the most extraordinary few hours and I've never forgotten it.

It has to change your attitude to the Germans. I remember a day or two later, in Celle, in the market square, the British authorities had taken these photographs of Belsen and had put them up on the notice boards to show the population what had been going on under their very noses. An old woman was looking at these photographs – she'd come out to get a few potatoes or whatever it was. She didn't know I was behind her, and when she was looking at these photographs showing the corpses in these communal graves and skeletons, and God knows what, she said, 'Ah – propaganda.' I just seized her by the back of the neck, pushed her face into the photographs and said it wasn't propaganda. I lost my temper. Yes, you're bound to be affected by things like that. You can't possibly escape being affected. The thing that everybody asked was how on earth could a massive camp of that type be fed and watered without the population nearby knowing? It's almost unbelievable. But when you asked any German, they said they didn't know what was going on. It was a stock answer.

LIEUTENANT DOMINIC 'NICKY' NEILL

INTELLIGENCE OFFICER, 3RD BATTALION, 2ND GURKHA RIFLES, BURMA, 1945

With orders to procure a Japanese captive, we patrolled the village of Lambagunaon in the Arakan. As we were moving through the northern part, the villagers said the Japs were occupying the south. We took up a position overlooking a strip of paddy between the two halves of the village. From there we saw three Japs stand up from behind a small mound seventy-five yards away. We watched them fascinated as we had never had the chance to study Japs at leisure before. We made the most of this opportunity and then we killed them.

The next day, we learned from villagers that a Japanese patrol was approaching the base. There were nine of them, bunched up in single file, with rifles with fixed bayonets slung on their shoulders. They were moving idly and talking among themselves. I was surprised at such laxity. It was very unusual. I grinned at the soldier alongside me and he grinned back. When the Japs were about seventy-five yards away, a long burst of Bren fire shattered the silence. Excitement had obviously got the better of the left-hand section's gunner. The Japs took cover behind the bund like lightning. Everybody fired without any control orders from me. The sight of our enemy pinned down in front of us drove us berserk. We fired and fired until the barrels of our weapons became red hot, raking the bund. I had fired nearly three out of my five magazines, and hit nothing before changing to single shots. I saw one Jap trying to crawl away so I fired quickly two or three times. I saw hits on the wet shirt on his back. A wet rump poked up for a moment, and I fired three quick shots at that. One of them hit and the Jap was flung backwards into the flooded paddy.

Battle of Arakan, 1943: Overlooking Japanese Positions at Rathedaung
ANTHONY GROSS

As I hit him with another shot, I remembered that our mission was to take a prisoner, and if I didn't act soon, all candidates for the POW cage would be dead. I screamed above the din to the left-hand section to give me covering fire and ordered the section with me to cease fire, fix swords, draw kukris and charge. Over the bund we leapt, and plunged into the water of the rice field, yelling blue murder. I could see the strike of the shots from the supporting section hitting the field ahead.

Suddenly two enemy broke cover and tried to make a dash for it. I fired at one – too short – magazine empty. I knelt and guiltily changed magazines, switched to automatic, determined to kill the Jap. The other fleeing enemy stopped and flung up his hands in surrender. I was not gaining on the other man, my chest was heaving, my Tommy gun muzzle was going up and down, my eyes full of sweat. I fired three bursts and could see the rounds hitting the man's back, flicking away pieces of shirt and flesh. I had not realised the hitting power of a .45-inch bullet before. The Jap shot forward like a rag doll hit with a sledge-hammer. I went over to him and took his rifle. I told my men to check the remaining seven bodies for signs of life, and that I wanted to search each one for documents. The Japs were great ones for keeping diaries, which disclosed useful information.

I started on the body of the man I had been chasing. His documents told me that he was a private of the 143rd Regiment. He was about my age – we had come a long way from our respective homes to meet under such violent circumstances in a flooded field on the remote coast of Arakan. In his wallet there was a photo of a young girl and his two tiny children. In the years since, I have often thought of the young woman I made a widow and the children I made fatherless. Then I think what he would have done to me had our positions been reversed.

WALTRAUDT WILLIAMS

CIVILIAN IN BERLIN, 1945

By the 26th April – my birthday – the fighting was getting nearer and nearer to Berlin. We were beginning to hear it and we also heard of street fights over areas we knew by name that made us realise it was only a matter of time. Little bands of German soldiers and SS and tanks were trying to join together to continue the fight or perhaps to get away from it. I knew some who were trying to escape and they were asking for civilian clothes – which we gave them. By this time, we had no water and had not had a thing to eat for ten days and all we could do was sit in our cellar and wait. It wasn't safe to be in the house as the Russian planes were strafing.

I remember a German army lorry standing right outside where we lived. An elderly German lady who was one of the tenants had spent all night praying on her knees and she rushed into the house shouting, 'Meat! Meat! They've brought us meat! I've seen it in the lorry outside!' Some of us went out to look and we saw her meat. It was a lorry full of dead soldiers and what she'd thought was meat was the blood dripping through the floorboards of the lorry. At the time, we felt that Berlin should surrender but we knew they wouldn't. Goebbels had been quoted as saying, 'When we bang the door behind us, the whole world will hear.' We knew that wasn't an empty threat – that they could carry it out, they could finish us all. They tried to turn all sorts of people into soldiers – they gave men over seventy Belgian rifles and they issued children with the Panzerfaust. That's a terrible weapon for a child to carry on his shoulder and be sent to immobilise tanks. The Russians made good their promise to get to Berlin on 1st May, but they didn't reach us until the next day. Some of us had ideas of ending it all, but I was too much of a coward.

My Uncle Arthur came to find out whether we were still alive just after the Russians had set fire to our house. We had no way of putting the fire out, so Arthur herded us along the road to his house where there was food to be had – not much, but a little. The Russians seemed largely oblivious to the plight of the civilian population, perhaps because their own people had had far worse. Whatever food they found, they ruined deliberately. They filled bath tubs with edible food and defecated all over it. They didn't want us to have it because they didn't think we were entitled to it.

7

BROTHERS IN ARMS

When you are standing at your hero's grave,
or near some homeless village where he died,
Remember, through your heart's rekindling pride,
The German soldiers who were loyal and brave.

Men fought like brutes, and hideous things were done;
And you have nourished hatred, harsh and blind.
But in that Golgotha perhaps you'll find
The mothers of the men who killed your son.

'RECONCILIATION'
SIEGFRIED SASSOON

Private Frank Sumpter

London Rifle Brigade, 1914

After the 19th December attack, we were back in the same trenches when Christmas Day came along. It was a terrible winter, everything was covered in snow, everything was white. The devastated landscape looked terrible in its true colours – clay and mud and broken brick – but when it was covered in snow, it was beautiful. Then we heard the Germans singing 'Silent night, Holy night', and they put up a notice saying 'Merry Christmas', so we put one up too.

While they were singing our boys said, 'Let's join in,' so we joined in and when we started singing, they stopped. And when we stopped, they started again. So we were easing the way. Then one German took a chance and jumped up on top of the trench and shouted out, 'Happy Christmas, Tommy!' So of course our boys said, 'If he can do it, we can do it,' and we all jumped up. A sergeant-major shouted, 'Get down!' But we said, 'Shut up Sergeant, it's Christmas time!' And we all went forward to the barbed wire.

We could barely reach through the wire, because the barbed wire was not just one fence, it was two or three fences together, with a wire in between. And so we just shook hands and I had the experience of talking to one German who said to me, 'Do you know where the Essex Road in London is?' I replied, 'Yes, my uncles had a shoe repairing shop there.' He said, 'That's funny. There's a barber shop on the other side where I used to work.'

They could all speak very good English because before the war, Britain was invaded by Germans. Every pork butcher was German, every barber's shop was German, and they were all over here getting the low-down on the country. It's ironic when you think about it, that he must have shaved my uncle at times and yet my bullet might have found him and his bullet might have found me.

The officers gave the order 'No fraternisation' and then they turned their backs on us. But they didn't try to stop it because they knew they couldn't. We never said a word about the war to the Germans. We spoke about our families, about how old we were, how long we thought it would last and things like that. I was young and I wasn't that interested, so I stood there for about half an hour then I came back. But most of the boys stayed there the whole day and only came back in the evening. There were no shots fired and some people enjoyed the curiosity of walking about in no man's land. It was good to walk around. As a sign of their friendliness the Germans put up a sign saying 'Gott mit uns' which means 'God is with us' and so we put a sign in English saying 'We got mittens too'. I don't know if they enjoyed that joke.

Private Clifford Lane

1st Battalion, Hertfordshire Regiment, 1915

I can remember that one of my comrades got wounded and this induced in me a sense of desolation which would normally only come if you lost very close family – a member of your family really, that sort of feeling, for quite a time, you felt absolutely, completely desolate. There is that feeling of comradeship which can't be understood by anybody unless they were actually in the front line in the War. It was the sort of trust between men that rarely occurs.

Fraternity
AUGUSTUS JOHN

PRIVATE HENRY BARNES

4TH AUSTRALIAN BRIGADE, 1915

We were so close to the Turkish front line that we were constantly on good terms with them, even though we were officially fighting them. We regularly exchanged bully beef and biscuits for strings of figs and oranges. You see instead of throwing a bomb, you could throw a tin of bully beef over, and when they discovered that, you got a string of figs back.

One day I sat on the parapet and after a while walked over and offered bully beef to one Turk, and he smiled and seemed very pleased and passed me two whole strings of dates.

Jack – as we called this Turkish soldier – was very highly regarded by me and all the men on our side. I never heard him decried, he was always a clean fighter and one of the most courageous men in the world. There was no beating about, they faced up to the heaviest rifle fire, and nothing would stop them, they were almost fanatical. We came to our conclusion that he was a very good bloke indeed, we had a lot of time for him.

CORPORAL CHARLES QUINNELL

9TH BATTALION, ROYAL FUSILIERS, 1916

My home town of Woolwich was a very busy place with all the munitions workers, and the place just hummed with activity. There was plenty of money about, some of them were getting four, five and six pounds a week. All my old friends had joined up, so I was very lonely.

One thing I really noticed was that after being with the young fellows in the Army, we were a race apart from these civilians. You couldn't talk to the civilians about the war, you'd be wasting your time. They hadn't got the slightest conception of what the conditions were like and so forth. So after a time you didn't talk about it.

You went home on leave to forget. I know that one of the most pleasurable things at home was mother's cooking, and after army cooking it was very nice indeed. Father was a good scrounger and I lived like a fighting cock for seven days.

It was a life apart from anything that you'd done in civilian life. You'd become a gypsy, you'd learned to look after yourself, you'd learned how to cook for yourself, to make do, to darn your own socks, sew on your own buttons and things like that.

Corporal William Skipp

Western Front, 1916

We had a sniper's post, which was just a sheet of metal two inches high and a foot wide – just a hole big enough to put the end of a rifle through. Well, we had two boys who were orphans, they'd been brought up together, joined up together and been all the way through together. They were standing in the trenches and one said, 'What's this, George, have a look through here,' and he had no sooner approached it than down he went with a bullet through his forehead. Now his friend was so flabbergasted he too had a look, and less than two minutes later he was down the trench with his friend.

Lieutenant Edmund Blunden

11th Battalion, Royal Sussex Regiment, 1917

One or two signallers and I had to walk in the open straight in front of the Germans, who were perhaps two or three miles off. But they could see us all right and they did some beautiful shooting, they made rings round us. One of the lads, a tall handsome youth, said, 'I never did see such shelling!' It was exactly like applauding a conjuring trick, or something in the halls, or a piece of fast bowling in a test match. It struck me even then, what self-control. But he was really looking at a remarkable feat of skill on the part of some other human being, and I thought a lot of that.

Lieutenant E. W. Stoneham

Royal Artillery, 1917

The comradeship among men was really most extraordinary and very difficult to describe. On one occasion I was offered a safe job behind the lines if I would care to join Brigade Headquarters. It was very tempting but I didn't want to go. There was something about the relationship with the men that one didn't want to break. One would somehow have felt rather a traitor to them, so I refused it and stayed with them. Somehow one had a very strong sense of belonging – to the men and to the job. Even when I got back to England on leave, it seemed to me that I really belonged at the Front, that the leave was only an interlude. In a way I was quite ready to get back. That was reinforced by the fact that my family didn't understand what was happening out there, and I didn't really want them to know about it. So when I was talking to my parents or my sisters, I had to pretend that it was all very nice out there, and I had to describe a world that wasn't real at all. The real world was the one that I had to get back to, and I felt no compunction about getting away when the leave was over.

SERGEANT-MAJOR RICHARD TOBIN

HOOD BATTALION, ROYAL NAVAL DIVISION, 1918

When we were out of the line we used to stand by the road and watch the fresh, strong, plump and new American battalions swing by. They waved and laughed and shouted. Our boys stood by the side of the road and grinned back – but we wondered, 'Did they know? Could they do it? Would they do it?'

MAJOR KEITH OFFICER

AUSTRALIAN CORPS, 1918

Nearby there was a German machine-gun unit giving our troops a lot of trouble. They kept on firing until practically 11 o'clock. At precisely 11 o'clock [on November 11th] an officer stepped out of their position, stood up, lifted his helmet and bowed to the British troops. He then fell in all his men in the front of the trench and marched them off. I always thought that this was a wonderful display of confidence in British chivalry, because the temptation to fire on them must have been very great.

Private Edward Watson

BUGLER, 8TH BATTALION, KING'S ROYAL RIFLE
CORPS, FRANCE, 1940

As we were going along, walking along the road, I remember seeing English tanks blown to pieces. These lovely English tanks. We'd been told that the Germans only had cardboard tanks, and I couldn't believe it.

We shared the food out, with some wine that we had found. I don't think I'd ever drunk wine before – I didn't like it very much, this red stuff – tasted very bitter, but some of the fellows were really gushing it. Banbury, the officer, said that if he found anyone drunk he would shoot them. 'You can drink as much as you like', he said, 'but if you're drunk, then I'm going to kill you.'

We were finally taken prisoner. They were outside and throwing hand-grenades into this house and calling – what was the phrase? 'Tommy, for you the war is over.' They could all say this – they must have been taught to say this.

I remember being very impressed with these German soldiers at the time – how bloody tough they looked. How efficient they seemed, relative to us. They were so businesslike and how very smart the officers seemed by comparison. Everything seemed so much better than what we had. They were professionals by comparison to us. I'd never seen anything like them.

Flying Control Room Bringing Halifax Aircraft
HAROLD WILLIAM HAILSTONE

SERGEANT RAY HOLMES

504 SQUADRON, RAF, 1940

We built up a sort of synthetic hate against them, which was a bit artificial. I wanted to shoot an aeroplane down, but I didn't want to shoot a German down. I really did not. We did hear stories of Germans shooting our fellows in parachutes, and we used to think that was pretty horrible – but we weren't sure whether it was true or not. I know I had an experience of a German aircrew getting draped over my own wing – he bailed out of a bomber and got caught on my wing with his parachute, and I was jolly careful to get him off as easily and as quickly as I could, manoeuvring the aeroplane and shaking him off. And I was very glad when I heard he'd dropped down in

Kennington Oval safely. So I had no feeling of wanting to kill that fellow personally.

SERGEANT JAMES A. GOODSON

AMERICAN PILOT, 43 SQUADRON, RAF, 1940

Once you got used to the Spitfire, you loved it. It became part of you. It was like pulling on a tight pair of jeans, and it was a delight to fly. I used to smoke a cigar sometimes – against all rules and regulations – and if I dropped my cigar lighter, instead of groping around on the floor, I would move the stick a fraction of an inch, and the Spitfire would roll over, and I would catch the lighter as it came down from the floor. That was the kind of plane it was. Everyone had a love affair with the Spitfire.

Even the Germans got to respect it. I remember Peter Townsend went to see one of the German pilots which he had shot down, close to the base. The German pilot said to him, 'I'm very glad to meet the Spitfire pilot who shot me down.' And Peter said, 'No, no – I was flying a Hurricane. I'm a Hurricane pilot.' The German kept arguing with him, and Peter kept saying, 'No – you were shot down by a Hurricane.' The German pilot said, 'Would you do me a favour? If you ever talk to any other Luftwaffe pilots, please tell them I was shot down by a Spitfire.'

PILOT OFFICER FRANK CAREY

43 SQUADRON, RAF, 1940

On one particular sortie, the human angle predominated for a while. The formation in which I was flying came upon a rather lonely Heinkel 111 way out in the North Sea which we naturally proceeded to deal with. After a few shots, a fire was seen to start in the fuselage and the flight commander immediately ordered us to stop attacking it. The enemy aircraft turned back towards Wick and we escorted it on its way with me in close formation on its port side where the fire was. Being only a few feet away from the Heinkel it was all too easy to become sympathetically associated with the crew's frantic efforts to control the fire and I even began to wish that I could jump across and help them. I suddenly converted from an anxious desire to destroy them to an even greater anxiety that they survive. We had got to within a few miles of the coast and had really begun to hope that they would make it, when we were all outraged to see a Hurricane from another squadron sweep in from behind and without a single thought about us all around, poured a long burst of fire into the Heinkel which more or less blew up in our faces and crashed into the sea without any survivors.

PILOT OFFICER HAROLD BIRD-WILSON

17 SQUADRON, RAF, 1940

On the 24th September we were flying at about 16,000 feet and suddenly, when we were south of the Thames area, a

Spitfire came down through our formations – which worried us a bit, because we hadn't realised that they were being chased by 109s. The next thing I experienced was a terrific bang in the cockpit and there were flames coming from the fuel tank. There was no Perspex left in my hood, and it was getting fairly hot, so I bailed out immediately.

One notices the quietness, having bailed out. The battle was still going on. I could hear the rat-a-tat of the guns going off in the distance, and my fellow pilots circling above me, making sure I got down safely. I was slightly wounded with shrapnel, but I was floating down peacefully. It was then that I saw a navy torpedo boat coming out to intercept me.

Forty-two years after the event, I read in a book that I was the fortieth victory for Adolph Galland – the famous German fighter ace who was made Lieutenant General of the Luftwaffe.

MYRTLE SOLOMON

LONDON CIVILIAN, 1940

We had a very big basement, and my mother said, 'We'll just open it up.' So people came in every night, for, I believe, years – long after the blitz. There were people we didn't know – because you know how it is in London – how little you know your neighbours. But there were many families there, including two Italians and Austrians. Their husbands got taken away to the internment camps, which was a very grim experience for the wives, who came every night to the shelters. I remember trying desperately to help get their husbands out. The other one was a Jewish-Italian doctor, whose wife was nearly going mad without him.

It was not required at that stage, but several of us in the road went voluntarily to take a short course in what to do when incendiaries dropped. We were equipped with stirrup pumps, water and sand – nearly all of which seemed to be totally useless. Because the stirrup pump didn't work, I remember kicking incendiary bombs off the roof with my feet, or the end of a broom, just to get them into the garden away from the roof of our house. I remember throwing sand on a bomb for ages. I kept doing exactly what I'd been told to do – and throwing this sand on, and it just flared up again. The planes were still overhead, and you thought they could see you – and thought if they saw a fire going, they would drop another bomb on you. So you were absolutely petrified.

In the morning, you felt good to be alive – but with this awful sense of guilt that other people weren't – and shouldn't it really have been you?

Demolition: Sorting and Chipping Bricks
ETHEL LEONTINE GABAIN

JOHANNES ZIMMERMANN

GERMAN STOKER, KM *BISMARCK*, 1941

We were in action against HMS *Hood* – she was the biggest ship in the British Navy and we were the biggest ship in the German Navy. It was the biggest against the biggest. From one end of the deck of the *Bismarck* to the other was nearly 200 yards. We received two or three hits but couldn't feel them – I was in the middle of the ship in the boiler room. The radio said there was an artillery action going on and six or seven minutes later we were told the *Hood* was sunk. Everyone was jubilant.

We had won a victory over the mighty *Hood* – but soon we were hit by a shell from the *Prince of Wales*. We were hit on the port side in Section 20 over the waterline and Section 21 underneath the waterline. So the front part of the ship filled up with water and the electric pump didn't work any more. Another shell hit the front electric turbine room which filled up with water straight away. The second boiler room on the port side was broken up and water flooded in.

At about eleven in the evening, we got attacked by an aircraft from HMS *Victorious* and its torpedo hit the armoured plate on the starboard side and exploded in the bottom of the boiler room. Then the second boiler room on the port side filled up with water. During the night we left the British fleet behind us but the Admiral sent a message that we were heading straight to the French coast. This gave the British a chance to find us again.

On the 26th May at about 10.30, I was on the upper deck and we got the aircraft alarm. On the port side we saw a seaplane, and by now, the Mediterranean fleet was on its way to block our escape route. At 1600 hrs I went to the boiler room and that was the beginning of the end. I didn't come out for 16 hours.

At midnight, destroyers attacked us. As we left the boiler room next morning, heavy artillery fire started up from the port side. We were told to go back the way we had come so we went on to the lower deck to where the boiler rooms are and we heard explosions on the water pumps and the sea valves. Ten minutes later I went back up and saw the *Dorsetshire* and the *Norfolk* on the starboard side. Some of us thought they were firing gas shells, as we saw what looked like green smoke coming from the shells.

The first lieutenant was standing in the doorways to Section 9 when a shell hit him. I was told to go another way. I opened the door to the upper deck and right in front of me was the turret of the first 150 mm gun. The sight of it was terrible. Blood and pieces of comrades. You couldn't tell what came from one man and what came from another. Suddenly, as the ship turned over, I slipped off the deck into the sea. It was very rough. We were all being tossed up and down by the waves. The waves were ten metres high. Nobody was powerful enough to swim in this water.

I was swallowing a cocktail of seawater and oil. I came up close to the *Bismarck* and it was easy enough to put your hand on the upper deck but it was harder staying there – you slipped off again each time. I was swimming alongside a friend of mine who was a neighbour from home. We had gone to the same school. He died in that water.

Finally, I was pulled on to the *Dorsetshire*. A small sailor boy gave me a big bottle of gin. I took it and started to drink. Suddenly all my insides came out – all salty water, everything. Since then I've never touched gin. I was taken down below, where they took my clothes and gave me a blanket. They put me in the library where all I did was try to read an English book I found in there – *The Last of the Mohicans*. I was treated very well. The crew made us all feel like shipmates.

MARINE EDWARD HILL

ROYAL MARINES, CRETE, 1941

We were very much rookie soldiers. I had only actually fired five rounds on the rifle range. As we landed on the quay, a German sniper shot the tallest man in the outfit – he was about six foot four – plumb dead centre in the forehead. This had a very demoralising effect on the men at that time.

We'd no sooner arrived, too, than we were heavily bombed by German aircraft. I realised that our potential as a fighting force was practically nil. We eventually, in our panic and hysteria – or rather our ack-ack boys – shot them down ourselves, because we'd been so used to the German aircraft coming over and bombarding us, that we just used to shoot anything that flew. My first impression of Crete was being stuck in the olive groves around Suda Bay where we were – and just being bombed to blazes all the time.

As the battle began to manifest itself, we were very lucky to have with us the Maori Regiment from New Zealand. Now, these were classic warriors of the type that would rather use knives than automatic weapons, and my first real memory of absolute fear was being in a trench, thank God with them, where when told to advance upon German positions, they would stand on top of the trenches and do their Maori tribal war dance.

We were positioned on a hill, only about a quarter of a

mile from the beach, and I had a twin Lewis gun with very little ammunition – and the rest of my boys were in front of me in trenches. The Germans were laying down a creeping barrage of mortar fire, which would creep up the hill – and eventually annihilated everybody in front of me – but it took about six of these mortar shells to creep up the hill, and I can remember thinking quite clearly as I watched the creeping barrage, that the seventh one definitely had my name on it. They were coming straight up the hill, and the seventh one would obviously drop straight on my head. I was sitting at the time behind a rock, which is why I survived. We were being well raked with machine-gun fire at that stage.

Anyway, the seventh one did come, but somebody must have moved the gun – I don't know who it was – but it just went to the side and behind. I got mortar and shrapnel in the back, and although I wasn't seriously wounded, it must have hit some nerves, because my legs were paralysed. I sat there for the rest of the day while the whole hill was being raked by machine-gun fire. Then to my amazement, as it got towards evening, coming belting across this ridge calling out, 'Is there anybody there?' was an Australian.

I called out to him and he picked me up. I said to him, 'My God, you're not going to make a run for it with me on your shoulder, because they're raking the hill with machine-gun fire.' He said, 'We won't worry about that, cobber.' I thought, 'This is it – we've definitely had it.' I've always had a very high opinion of the German soldier, and in this case, they were mainly Austrian mountain troops. They must have respected this man's great bravery, because they didn't fire. He carried me down to the beach, and that's when I saw the last boat going out.

Private Ralph Jetton

HQ Company 504th Parachute Regiment,
US 82nd Airborne Division, Salerno, Italy, 1943

On the fourth night on Hill 414, I was sitting there in the hole, dark as pitch. Things had been quiet all evening. The Germans had pulled back, and I was sitting there thinking of home, and wondering about my brother. A lieutenant out of the 141st came by and he asked me where the Command Post was, and I told him. But first I said, 'What outfit are you out of?' and he said 141st — so I said, 'What battalion?' and he said, 'Third,' so I said, 'Do you know a fella the name of Jetton?' and he said, 'Yes. He was, a few minutes ago, sitting down on the side of the hill, waiting to come up here and relieve you.' I jumped out of my hole and ran down that hill — it was pitch dark, you couldn't see anything — and I got down to the little hacked-out road and started calling his name quietly.

I was walking down the road with the guys laying down on each side of the road. I couldn't really see them, but I knew they were there in the dark. He didn't say a word until I got up close, and he said, 'Yeah, what the hell do you want?' He didn't know who I was — he thought he was going to get detailed out on a patrol or something — and I said, 'This is Dub,' and he said, 'You little sonofabitch!'

Everyone was delighted, and they gathered around and we were beating on each other and hugging. Best moment of the war for me.

CAPTAIN RUSSELL COLLINS

16TH BATTALION, DURHAM LIGHT INFANTRY, ITALY, 1944

In Naples I went into a little bistro place and had some spaghetti, and sitting at the next table were a couple of American troops – American Negroes, who had come straight over from the United States – from their speech they must have been from the Deep South. Presently, one of these chaps, who was sitting only a few feet from me, turned and sort of beamed, sort of jovially, and said, 'How do?' And I said, 'How do you do?' and he said, 'Nice day,' and I said, 'Yes, lovely weather here, isn't it?' 'Gee,' he said, 'you sure do speak American very well – you speak it almost as well as I do.' And I thought that was lovely – and he'd never been outside the States before – and I'd never met an American Negro before – but a nice little illustration of how people are thrown together, you know, from different parts of the world.

PRIVATE JOHN STANLEIGH

21 INDEPENDENT PARACHUTE COMPANY, 1944

We didn't really think that we'd have to retreat. We felt we'd done well on our particular front, so it came as quite a surprise. As we got away, we marched down to the river. I was marching next to a bloke who was wearing a German helmet. 'Why are you taking that home?' I asked. 'Vass,' he seemed to reply. I looked at him and the penny dropped.

'Are you German?' 'Yes.' 'What are you doing in this column?' 'I've had enough of this war, thank you. I want to be a prisoner.' So he got evacuated on the boat along with the rest of us.

CAPTAIN JOHN MACAUSLAN

INTELLIGENCE OFFICER, 5TH RECONNAISSANCE REGIMENT, 1945

After the war ended, I was surprised that I wasn't all that elated. I just felt a slightly lost feeling – relieved a little bit that one was safe now – but not very happy. I didn't know what to do. I knew I'd have to be a solicitor but I didn't want to be a solicitor. What I knew about was all finished. I'd only had one leave at home in two years and I hadn't enjoyed it very much. It was rather depressing with blackouts and bad food and one thing and another. And now, what I'd known for such a long time vanished and there was nothing to take its place. One day I saw one of our corporals digging up the road in Chancery Lane when I was walking over to the Law Society. We talked and I was glad to see him. I think he was glad to see me. But there was really nothing to say. It was all gone.

8

FEARS, TEARS AND LAUGHTER

A bomb, last night, fell close by Radlett.
The pulsing engine stopped right overhead.
Four minutes to the crash. Slowly we counted;
One girl cried, 'Oh God! dear God!'
The tension grew to bursting point; the blast
Shattered the windows. We breathed again.
Always the bombs come over in early evening
Just before we go on shift. We talk of rush-hour traffic
But underneath the fear remains. Death can come
From so many angles. Tomorrow, next week, next month
It may not pass us by.

'DOODLEBUGS'
GRACE GRIFFITHS

Private William Chapman

Royal Army Medical Corps, 1915

Next morning the new draft – fifteen or twenty of us – had to parade with a sergeant-major and a sergeant in command. Their purpose was quite a noble one – to find out what we had been in civil life so that we'd be suitably placed in the Army. So they started:

'And what were you in Civvy Street?'

'Oh, I was a butcher, Sergeant-Major.'

'Sergeant, send him to the quartermaster's stores.'

'What were you in Civvy Street?'

'Well, I was a clerk, Sergeant-Major.'

'Send him to the orderly room.'

Then he came to me. 'And what were you in Civvy Street?'

'I was a theological student, Sergeant-Major.'

'What?'

I said, 'I was a theological student.'

He said, 'What's that?'

I said: 'Well, just I was a theological student.'

'Sergeant,' he said, 'come and ask this fellow what he was.'

So the sergeant came and I was beginning to enjoy it then.

'What were you in Civvy Street?'

I said, 'I was a theological student, sergeant.'

They then walked away and had a little conference. Right, Chapman, Royal Army Medical Corps. They didn't know the difference between theological and biological!

LIEUTENANT RICHARD TALBOT KELLY

ROYAL FIELD ARTILLERY, 1915

I think you are chiefly afraid, you know, of how you will behave when you really meet the worst things that war can produce, and I became afraid of seeing my first dead man. I'd never seen a dead man and was very afraid of seeing anybody killed in front of my eyes. Well, now this bit of line had been fought over a few weeks previously in the battle of Festubert, and some of the old German trenches that we had captured were left lying in a derelict mess. Between our trenches we had dug new ones beyond them and I knew that there was an old stretch of German trench between our first and second line where there were a lot of German and Canadian corpses. One afternoon when things were slack – we were only allowed to fire three rounds per gun per day – I thought I would go and have a look at these corpses and see what I felt. I went along the communication trench and slipped over the side into this German trench. It was very impressive. To begin with, the Germans had run short of sandbags when they had built their trenches in this part of the world, and they had looted the cottages round about and made sandbags out of curtains, counterpanes and tablecloths and any other material they could lay their hands on. So these trenches were the most varied and coloured affairs you could imagine, and faded wonderfully into the wild flowers and cabbages and everything else of the landscape – in fact they produced a camouflage excellence that we never achieved again in the war.

I wandered along this old German trench for a bit and was very interested in the way it was made. I found the odd German cowhide pack, a round cap and bashed pickelhaube.

Then suddenly round the bend in the trench I came to a great bay which was full of dead Germans, but they weren't a bit horrible. They had been dead for about six weeks and weather and rats and maggots and everything else had done their stuff. Now they were just shiny skeletons in their uniforms held together by the dry sinews, that wound round their bones. They were still wearing their uniforms and still in the attitude in which they had died, possibly from a great shell burst. It was a most weird and extraordinary picture and I was absolutely fascinated. A skull, you know, grins at you in a silly way, it laughs at you and more or less says: 'Fancy coming here all terrified of dead men, look how silly we look.'

GUNNER GEORGE COLE

3RD NORTHUMBRIAN BRIGADE, ROYAL FIELD ARTILLERY, 1916

I can remember going past the church in Albert, with the madonna. There was a legend that on the day this madonna fell, the war would finish. I was a bit of a comic, like, so I said, 'Let's knock it down now and the war will finish.'

PRIVATE NORMAN DEMUTH

1/5TH BATTALION, LONDON REGIMENT, 1916

Almost the last feather I received was on a bus. I was sitting near the door when I became aware of two women on the other side talking at me, and I thought to myself, 'Oh Lord, here we go again.' I didn't pay much attention. However, I suppose I must have caught their eye in some way because one leant forward and produced a feather and said, 'Here's a gift for a brave soldier.' I took it and said, 'Thank you very much – I wanted one of those.' Then I took my pipe out of my pocket and put this feather down the stem and everything and worked it in a way I've never worked a pipe cleaner before. When it was filthy I pulled it out and said, 'You know we didn't get these in the trenches,' and handed it back to her. She instinctively put out her hand and took it, so there she was sitting with this filthy pipe cleaner in her hand and all the other people on the bus began to get indignant. Then she dropped it and got up to get out, but we were nowhere near a stopping place and the bus went on quite a long way while she got well and truly barracked by the rest of the people on the bus. I sat back and laughed like mad.

First Study for Staff Train at Charing Cross Station
ALFRED HAYWARD

LIEUTENANT CHARLES CARRINGTON

1/5TH BATTALION, ROYAL WARWICKSHIRE REGIMENT, 1917

The Australians suggested that as we were having a few days without any particular battle going on, it was surely the moment to have a test match. They found a bit of unshelled ground within reach of their positions and ours, we got some bats, balls, bales and stumps – and we played cricket. What the Germans could have thought was going on I can't imagine. But it must have been reported by some German because unfortunately next morning, when the Australians were assembling on the pitch and we were on our way, they were heavily shelled. Some were killed and others were wounded and the ground was ruined. There was never going to be a return match.

LIEUTENANT CHARLES CARRINGTON

1/5TH BATTALION, ROYAL WARWICKSHIRE REGIMENT, 1917

The noise would grow into a great crescendo and at a certain point your nerve would break. In a flash of time, in a fifth of a second, you'd decide that this was the one. You'd throw yourself down into the mud and cringe at the bottom of the shell-hole. All the other people around would be doing the same.

Sometimes you miscalculated and this wasn't a shell for you, and it would go sailing busily on and plonk down on somebody else four hundred yards away. When a shell arrived it would drop into the mud and burst with a shattering shock. The killing splinters flew off and might fly fifty yards away from the point of impact. You could find a fragment of red-hot jagged iron weighing half a pound arriving in your shell-hole.

They'd take another second or two before they would all settle down in the mud. Then you'd get up and roar with laughter, and the others would laugh at you for having been the first one to throw yourself down. This of course was hysterics! It becomes a kind of game in which you cling on and try not to let the tension break. The first person in a group who shows a sign of fear by giving way and taking cover – he'd lose a point and it counted against him. The one who held out longest had gained a point – but in what game? What was this for?

DORIS SCOTT

CIVILIAN, CANNING TOWN, EAST LONDON, 1939

I was terrified of what would happen, since I had been through the First World War, and had had to take shelter in a chapel on the corner of the street where we lived. The air power of the First World War wasn't anything like that of 1939, but those raids were frightening enough. The possibility of war was really frightening, especially with two young children.

We were told that we all had to go to the local town hall and receive gas masks. My baby had to be issued with a sort of diving helmet with horizontal wires, totally encasing her. My other daughter was three, and had this Mickey Mouse gas mask which wouldn't scare her. My mother, being asthmatic, was given another contraption, which was right for her breathing – and I had the normal mask that everyone else did. So we had four different types of gas mask in one family.

DOROTHY WILLIAMS

TEENAGER AT OUTBREAK OF WAR, 1939

It was a very anxious time. My parents followed the events very closely, so when we knew that war could break out – I think it was 11 o'clock in the morning – we were really keyed up. I was frightened. We didn't know what was ahead. We had relatives who had been badly gassed. Father said if the Germans ever landed, he would kill us all rather than us ever fall into their hands. That frightened us a little bit too – we didn't know which was going to be the worse of the two. Oh yes, he meant it. He had been right through the previous war and he had seen a lot.

FLYING OFFICER ALEC INGLE

605 SQUADRON, RAF, 1940

The first flight you made in the morning, you would get a sinking feeling in the pit of your stomach, until you saw the enemy and the minute you'd made your first interception, for the rest of that day it didn't matter what happened. The adrenalin was flowing and certainly, as far as I remembered, it flowed in reasonable quantity. Once you pressed your gun button, then for the rest of the day, you could take on the complete Luftwaffe. That's the reaction I had to it.

Senior Aircraftman James Merrett

Ground gunner, RAF, 1940

I went in the pub the first night I came back from France, and the landlord said to me, 'Oh, we thought you'd been took prisoner.' And old Bill, the postman, took one look along the bar. He said, 'I told you if there's only one bugger come back it'll be him.'

Flight Lieutenant Al Deere

54 Squadron, RAF, 1940

We were frightened. On the way out there was an awful gut fear. When you sighted them it really was – it was quite a frightening sight. But once you got into combat there wasn't time to be frightened. But we were frightened – of course we were – the whole bloody time. But if you're in combat, you're so keen to get the other guy and, if you like, save your own skin, that your adrenalin's pumping and there's no room for fright.

Aircraftwoman Jean Mills

WAAF, plotter and tracer at RAF Duxford, 1940

I remember coming on for a night shift and seeing a great glow in the south-east, like the biggest sunset you ever saw, and we said to the guard, 'What's that?' and he said, 'Oh, that's London burning.' That was the first time, really, that I felt it in the pit of my stomach.

EVELYN WHITE

NURSE RELOCATED FROM BIRMINGHAM TO HELP IN LONDON, 1940

On night duty we would have to put the beds into the centre of the ward to prevent flying glass from coming in from falling bombs. The patients, who were nearly all cockneys, were wonderful. Great sense of humour. No matter how ill they were feeling, they'd always get out of bed and help us to push the beds into the middle of the ward.

There was great fellowship. The air-raid shelters in the hospital grounds filled with water, so we couldn't use them, so they converted the X-ray department into a large air-raid shelter. They sand-bagged it, they put in wooden pillars. If we were on duty at night, we would bring our mattresses over from the nurses' home, spread them out on the floor and spend the night in the X-ray room, which was well protected, we hoped, except from direct hits.

I can't ever remember laughing so much as I did in those days. I think perhaps it was a reaction, but it was great fun. There was a great sense of fellowship – 'we're all in it together – we've got to pull together'. When we used to walk back from the X-ray department, you could tell by sniffing the air where the bombs had fallen. I can remember we were crossing over to the nurses' home and we could smell burning sugar and fat, and we knew the docks had got it.

I can remember when the City got it – the infamous

night of bombing – standing on the roof with others and seeing the dome of St Paul's ringed by fire. That's a memory that stays vividly in my mind.

PILOT OFFICER HAROLD BIRD-WILSON

17 SQUADRON, RAF, 1940

I was both worried and frightened at times. We were praying for bad weather – probably the only time anybody in England prayed for that! Somehow during the battle we had beautiful weather – sunshine and blue skies most of the time – and we did pray very hard. Fatigue broke into a chap's mentality in most peculiar ways. My chaps had the jitters and facial twitches. I had nightmares and used to wake up in the dispersal hut about twenty-five yards from my aircraft. I was night-flying my Hurricane.

SQUADRON LEADER FRED ROSIER

229 SQUADRON, RAF, 1941

Life in the Western Desert was tough and demanding. We had to put up with the extremes of heat and cold – the sand-storms which got worse and, even more depressing as time went on, the flies (particularly where the Italians had been), the shortage of water, the monotony of the daily diet of bully beef and hard biscuits – and the fear . . . that feeling in the pit of the stomach before going on operations.

Henry Metelmann

German soldier, 22nd Panzer Division, 1941

To be honest, I had a little bit of fear – of course, one never admitted it. We were in our railway compartments there, and everyone was happy. 'Now we are going to do some fighting with our division, and we do some great things.' One said these things, but I had the feeling of fear, and I am sure that others had that too, because at several places we saw the result of the fighting, and we saw the Russian tanks standing there, incapacitated of course, and buildings blown up. We saw the people in the villages – it was a very strange experience, and one sensed somehow the strength of Russia.

Wing Commander Lucian Ercolani

159 Squadron, RAF, Burma, 1943

On one occasion, I dropped into the mess to have lunch. We had only just had our first glass, when a distraught villager burst in. Would we help? A leopard had just mauled a child in their village and it was still there.

Armed with rifles we set off in a jeep with Frank Carey – a distinguished Battle of Britain pilot – with the villager to show the way, and us not quite knowing what we were going to find.

We saw this poor child with a great lump torn out of her side, which they had filled with a cow pat. Apparently they had healing properties! The womenfolk were in a terrible state and the men were going in all directions, armed with spears, bows and arrows, and an assortment of quite fearsome weapons!

There, in the branches of a great mango tree, in this tiny collection of huts, was this lovely creature, draped out along a branch. The two valiant gentlemen took careful aim and fired, obviously wounding the animal but, unfortunately, not killing it. It came bounding down the tree, scattering us all as it went, and disappeared. We realised that honour was at stake and we were duty bound to track it down, but didn't quite know where to go.

The Headman then took charge and pointed to the eaves of one of the huts where it had taken refuge. We were pushed forward by all the villagers, they were all around us, until we were only about ten yards away. There was a great roar and out leapt the leopard. We couldn't even lift our rifles properly with everyone crowding around us and by great good fortune, the leopard didn't touch any of us, but bounded right through between us all. Unwisely for him, he again took refuge up this tree and this time we didn't make a mistake.

When the leopard skin was returned from the curers in Calcutta, the skull, which had been sent with the skin in order to give the appropriate savage appearance to the ultimate fireside rug, had not been properly cleaned. The head of the rug had rotted, to become a hairless, flat and wrinkled grey mass. This prompted the story that Frank hadn't actually shot the leopard at all, but had paid some local lads to club it to death.

Group Captain Frank Carey

267 Wing, RAF, based at Magwe (Burma), 1943

A group of us – all pilots temporarily off ops in Eastern India – formed a club called the Screechers' Club. There was a tendency for the young to hit the bottle when the pressure let up, myself included, I must admit. The idea was, you were allowed drink only as long as you remained amusing. The club also had ranks. At the bottom was Hiccough, then Roar, Scream, and Screech at the top. Everybody but me had to start as a Hiccough. I permitted myself one grade up at the beginning, since I was running the thing. Everybody else started at the bottom. You had to behave yourself because, if you went over the top, you were downgraded. The only way to move a grade up was to hang around at the bar and buy drinks for one of the higher grades. When we had graduation night – about once a week – if a chap had bought me four drinks, he was certainly worth a grade higher. Chaps would hang inverted from the ceiling punkahs and things like that, which would gain them a higher ranking as long as they weren't stupid and injured themselves.

Somebody gave us a grand piano there. We used to have singsongs and I started to compose two pieces of music. One was called the 'Prang Concerto' and the other was the 'Symphonie Alcoholique'. I could play the symphony all ways – you didn't necessarily have to use your hands! The 'Prang Concerto' had three movements, and the last movement demanded the complete demolition of the piano. I had to go through and play the third movement on my last day there, before being posted to the Middle East. It cost me quite a lot to replace that darned piano. Actually, I never did really complete the third movement, because it's almost impossible to break the heavier wires of a piano, even using a broken-off piano leg! Humour relieved everybody's feelings.

SERGEANT IKE FRANKLIN

111TH MEDICAL BATTALION WITH 3RD BATTALION AID STATION, 143RD INFANTRY, UNITED STATES ARMY, ITALY, 1943

It was one long nightmare, really. I remember one time, a buddy of mine and I got pinned down there at Altavilla between artillery crossfire. The Americans were over-shooting and the Germans were undershooting, and we were pinned down between the two. My pal said, 'Ike, what are we going to do?' and I said, 'We're going to stay right here.' And he said, 'What about the shells?' And I said, 'Well, they're going to kill me the same if I'm asleep as I'm awake. I'm going to have some sleep.' And that was the only damn sleep I got from the time we landed until after I got captured.

CAPTAIN J.H.B. HUGHES

ABOARD HMS DANAE, SCOTLAND, 1944

When HMS *Danae* was nominated as a member of the In-Shore Bombardment Squadron for Operation Overlord, the commander addressed the ship's company on a freezing quarterdeck in Greenock. His comment that we had the honour to be expendable was smartly countered by, 'Fuck that for a lark,' from the ranks of the stokers' division.

SERGEANT-MAJOR WILLIAM BROWN

8TH BATTALION, DURHAM LIGHT INFANTRY, D-DAY LANDINGS, 1944

The water filled the gas trousers. We could feel it sloshing around inside and we stood on the beach, like idiots, in trousers full of water.

MAJOR JOHN HOWARD

2ND BATTALION, OXFORDSHIRE AND BUCKINGHAMSHIRE LIGHT INFANTRY, 1944

The flight at about 6,000 feet over the Channel was very, very quiet – so much so that for the first time in a glider, I wasn't sick. It was a sort of company joke that I was going to be sick and some bright lad at the back of the glider would always shout through, 'Has the company commander laid his kit yet?' which of course caused a lot of mirth amongst the rest of the men, but that night nobody used their brown-paper bag.

MAJOR IAN TOLER

GLIDER PILOT REGIMENT, 1944

There were endless delays and cancellations leading up to Operation Market Garden – order and counter-order and the consequent disorder were the order of the day. We spent the whole of one day loading and unloading our gliders – when the order changed for the sixth time that day, we just sat back and laughed. It was a good job we had some sense of humour.

MAJOR PETER MARTIN

2ND BATTALION, CHESHIRE REGIMENT, 1944

I spent the winter on 'The Island' – the Nijmegen Bridgehead between the rivers Waal and Rhine. It was very monotonous there and very wet. The slit trenches were filled with water. We had to get empty 44-gallon oil drums for people to stand in to keep themselves dry. The people in the local farm were very friendly and very upset to hear that we were to leave before Christmas. We were told this was because they were fattening up their cat to give us in lieu of a Christmas turkey. For that reason I was quite glad we did leave.

FLYING OFFICER KEN ADAM

609 SQUADRON, RAF, 1944

There was a Canadian pilot called Piwi Williams who went to his death, fully aware that he was going to die. It was unbelievably touching.

We were flying an operation over France and I could see his aircraft gradually losing height and I called on my radio, 'Piwi, what are you doing?' He called back and said that he was hit and paralysed, and he went slowly down for several minutes. I'll never forget his last words, just before he hit the ground. 'Order me a late tea.'

SERGEANT BERT 'WINKIE' FITT

2ND BATTALION, ROYAL NORFOLK REGIMENT, BURMA, 1944

Colonel Scott wasn't a man who just went and got in a dug-out and stayed there. Oh no, he went round his positions to make sure that everything was covered and he spoke to people as he went round. He was a great soldier – one of the finest soldiers you could ever meet. I always said that he should have had the VC. When he got scalped, he shook his fist at the Japanese. He said, 'The biggest bloke on the damn position and you couldn't get me. If you were in my bloody battalion, I'd take away your proficiency pay.'

COMPANY SERGEANT-MAJOR WALTER GILDING

2ND BATTALION, ROYAL NORFOLK REGIMENT, FAR EAST (BURMA), 1944

I saw Scott go down and the stretcher bearers come to try to pick him up. They cut his trousers open to put a field dressing on his wounds. This uncovered his bottom and through all the noise that was going on, I could hear Scott shouting, 'Cover my bloody arse up!'

John Brasier

Child in Stevenage, 1944

One Sunday morning in 1944, I was doing a Sunday paper round when I heard a noise which I later understood to be a V-1 doodlebug. I ran into a side of a house and pressed myself against the wall. Dogs were barking – I had no idea what it was. I had no idea that it was a pilotless vehicle with a bomb in it. It was a cigar-shaped thing with a fin and a flame belching out of the back and a terrible humming noise. To see it so low, literally a hundred feet up in the air – I'll never forget it as long as I live.

Sergeant William Spearman

No. 4 Commando, D-Day, 1944

The planners might have gone through a lot of campaigns at a very high level but nobody can know what it's like to be on a beach where you can do nothing. Where you're under severe fire and you've got to get off. And it's only a person who's been through it a number of times who can know – you stay and die or you get off and live. People doing it for the first time – no matter how many times you tell them – they don't realise it. And people didn't get off the beach. They were so transfixed with fright, they couldn't get off. I was transfixed with fright but I had the certain knowledge that you either stopped and died or you got up and got away. So I took the coward's view and got out of the bloody place.

Lieutenant Nick Archdale

7th Parachute Battalion, D-Day, 1944

Just before I jumped, I threw out a stuffed moose head which we'd purloined from a pub in Exeter, and was planned to put the fear of God into any German it hit. Then out we went.

9

COURAGE

I did not see Lannes at Ratisbon
nor MacLennan at Auldearn
nor Gillies MacBain at Culloden,
but I saw an Englishman in Egypt.

A poor little chap with chubby cheeks
and knees grinding each other,
pimply unattractive face –
garment of the bravest spirit.

He was not a hit 'in the pub
in the time of the fists being closed,'
but a lion against the breast of battle,
in the morose wounding showers.

His hour came with the shells,
with the notched iron splinters,
in the smoke and flame,
in the shaking and terror of the battlefield.

Word came to him in the bullet shower
that he should be a hero briskly,
and he was that while he lasted
but it wasn't much time he got.

He kept his guns to the tanks,
bucking with tearing crashing screech,
until he himself got, about the stomach,
that biff that put him to the ground,
mouth down in sand and gravel,
without a chirp from his ugly high-pitched voice.

No cross or medal was put to his
chest or to his name or to his family;
there were not many of his troops alive,
and if there were their word would not be strong.
And at any rate, if a battle post stands
many are knocked down because of him,
not expecting fame, nor wanting a medal
or any froth from the mouth of the field of slaughter.

I saw a great warrior of England,
a poor manikin on whom no eye would rest;
no Alasdair of Glen Garry;
and he took a little weeping to my eyes.

'HEROES'
SORLEY MACLEAN

Corporal Alan Bray

We took up positions near Kemmel Hill. It was foggy and the attack was delayed two hours, which didn't do our spirits much good. Then the time came for us to go over. We had to run forward about fifty yards, up some planks over our own front-line trenches, and then across a meadow where it was almost impossible to run, we could only stagger along. As we were going over these planks about half of us were knocked out – either killed or wounded – and going across the meadow there were a lot more killed.

When we finally stopped and lay down, trying to get what shelter we could from the tremendous rifle fire which was coming over, a sergeant just in front of me jumped up and said, 'Come on men, be British.' So we jumped up again and followed him. He ran about six yards and then he went down too.

Well, then there were about a dozen of us left and we ran on another twenty yards towards the German trenches. Those trenches were literally packed – the men were standing four deep, firing machine-guns and rifles straight at us, and the only shelter we could see was a road which ran up at right angles to the trench with a bank on the left-hand side. We managed to reach this bank but found ourselves looking straight up at the German trenches while they were firing straight down, gradually picking us off. Eventually there was only myself and another chap that weren't hit.

Private Walter Stagles

3rd Battalion, 1st Australian Division, Gallipoli, 1915

It was pitch dark then all of a sudden the coast, a dim outline of the coast, loomed up. As we got closer, we were all beginning to get tensed up, nervous, wondering what was going to happen as everything was so quiet. Then a single shot rang out and a yellowish light flared up in the sky, and from then on the Turks let loose, machine-gun and rifle fire at the boats. The pinnaces cast us off, the muffled oarsmen took up the row. As soon as the boats grounded it was every man for himself, it was out, do the best you could.

As we scrambled ashore, those that were lucky enough to get there, we found what cover under the cliff we could. As we lay there for a few moments gathering our wind, we slipped off our pack, fixed our bayonets and someone in the crowd – there was no officer – shouted, 'Right lads, after the bastards.'

Wounded at Montauban
SIR WILLIAM ORPEN

SERGEANT CHARLES LIPPETT

1/8TH BATTALION, QUEEN'S ROYAL WEST SURREY
REGIMENT, 1915

The men in the line tended to despise conscientious objectors, but it was not until I was appointed regimental policeman that I came in contact with them.

There were, of course, different varieties of conscientious objectors – there were the political ones, the religious ones, and those who just didn't want to bother. But it was not until I had actual contact with them that I could see that there was something at the back of this thing, that neither I or anyone else around me had realised.

One morning it was my job to go into the cell where these people were put prior to their appearance before the commanding officer, and this fellow had scrawled across his cell wall, which was whitewashed, a slogan which I now know well. 'Workers of the world unite, you have nothing to lose but your chains.'

I wondered what it meant and I asked the fellow all about it. He proceeded to explain, and I think that was the start of my political education. But the thing I must emphasise is the treatment we were forced to mete out to these poor blighters because they thought as they did. I remember one man in particular, who absolutely refused to have anything to do with the Army at all, and refused to put on khaki.

Well, we were instructed to take measures to remedy this state of affairs, which included taking him to the baths, stripping him and forcing a suit of khaki on him. We took him to the open compound, and as it was very cold at night we thought he would be forced to wear this khaki to keep himself warm, but he had other ideas. During the night he stripped himself of this khaki and shredded the whole of the suit up and hung it around the barbed wire, and that man walked about all night long without a shred of clothing on him. That was the type of treatment we had to mete out, and I am bitterly ashamed that I was forced to take part in it.

Another fellow I well remember, a great big strapping fellow with a black beard, and we had the lousy job of taking this beard off this man, and I shall never forget now his eyes as he looked at us, to think that we fellow men were doing this to him. We had to do it, I suppose that was our excuse. But ever since then I've admired these men intensely. I would take off my hat to them any time, because I realise that what they did in defying the British military might – and they defied it in every way possible – they had far more guts than we did who were doing these things to them.

CAPTAIN REGINALD THOMAS

ROYAL GARRISON ARTILLERY, 1918

It was a magnificent sight as the French cavalry came out of the forest at Soissons. Their uniforms were all new, bright blue, every bit and spur-chain was burnished and polished; their lances were gleaming in the sun; and as the bugler blew the charge the horses went into the gallop in a fan attack – two regiments of French cavalry. They went along beautifully, magnificently, through the wheat field in the afternoon sun, until they hit the German machine-guns which had just come up and unlimbered. The machine-guns, they opened on them at close range and aimed high enough to knock the riders off the horses. Riderless horses went all over the field for two or three hours. At the end of that time there was practically nothing left of those two cavalry regiments.

PILOT OFFICER GEORGE BENNIONS

41 SQUADRON, RAF, 1940

I was very concerned and very upset. I was annoyed at myself for having been shot down so decisively, and I felt terribly isolated. I couldn't see or hear very well, and so I couldn't recognise people. I felt so very sorry for myself, which is not a good situation for anybody. I felt so deflated, that half of my life had been taken, and half wasn't worth bothering with. It was, I think, the worst period of my life.

There was one person in particular who put me on a much more even footing. He had been shot down by a Hurricane. He had sent a message to go and see him. I was on crutches at the time, and I managed to get over to where he was with a hell of a lot of struggle and self-pity. As I opened the door in Ward 3, I saw what I can only describe now as the most horrifying thing I have ever seen in my life. This chap had been really badly burnt. His hair was burnt off, his eyebrows and his eyelids. You could just see his staring eyes, with only two holes in his face. His nose and lips were also badly burnt. Then I looked down, and saw that his hands and feet were burnt. I got through the door on my crutches with a struggle, and then this chap started propelling a wheelchair down the ward. Halfway down, he picked up the back of a chair with his teeth – and it was then that I noticed how badly his lips were burnt. Then he brought this chair down the ward and threw it alongside me and said, 'Have a seat, old boy.' It was then that I cried – and I thought, 'What have I got to complain about?' From then on, everything fell into place.

Corporal Jack Sharpe

1st Battalion, Leicestershire Regiment,
Far East Prisoner of War, 1941

Before I was captured I remember the dead and dying men we were forced to leave behind as the Japanese forced us to retreat up the Malay Peninsula. I remember the hundreds of dead I saw on the streets of Singapore. We were marched to Changi and then moved to a barracks in Singapore town and ordered to sign a paper saying we would not escape. We all refused. But the conditions were like the Black Hole of Calcutta and our senior officers agreed to sign under protest because they were worried about an epidemic.

I was then transported to Thailand to the base camp at Ban Pong. The latrines there were full of great big maggots. I'd had enough. Because the Japs thought no one would escape the guards were thin on the ground. I got out of the camp and headed north but after two days I was captured by a local Thai who had a large gun like a blunderbuss.

I was handed over to a Japanese lieutenant who lined me up in front of a firing squad. They cocked their rifles. I knew for certain I was going to die. Then all of a sudden a Japanese colonel arrived and struck the lieutenant in charge. They were jabbering in Japanese and I was wondering whether they were going to shoot me or not.

In the end the colonel came across and beat the living

daylights out of me with his scabbard. Every time I fell he booted me and told me to get up. My hands were then tightly strapped and I was marched back to Ban Pong and handed over to a guard. He had been a frontline soldier himself and respected me. He loosened the straps, which certainly saved my hands. He gave me a puff of a cigarette. It was the last act of compassion I was to get. I was sent to the House of Cages in Bangkok. It was a stinking place full of wooden cages, about five feet by eight feet. The Japs were forever interrogating a Chinese lad in my cell. He returned from one grilling to say he'd overheard that I was to be court-martialled for trying to escape.

At the court martial I was sentenced to two years' imprisonment. I had heard before about the place I was to be sent to, and you knew no one could survive two years there. The president of the court asked me if I had anything to say. Then I told him just what I thought of the Japs and cursed them. I was sentenced to four and a half years. The president then insulted me by saying that no Japanese soldier with a body as strong as mine would allow himself to become a prisoner.

That was it. I told him that I was going to live, not only to see him surrender, but the whole of the Japanese nation – and that I would walk out of that prison on my own two feet. His insult gave me the will to live. I was then clamped into shackles and taken down by train to Singapore where I was put in Outram Road Jail. I was put into solitary confinement for fourteen months.

Corporal Frederick Birch

No. 7 Commando, seconded to No. 11 Commando, 1941

In November 1941 we learned we would be carrying out a raid on Rommel's headquarters – the idea being to take him prisoner. The local German headquarters was at this place called Bela Littoria.

We went out in submarines – the Torbay and the Talisman. When we came to get off the submarines, we were landing in small rubber dinghies – two men in each – the first dinghy away was Colonel Keyes's, and I was in the next one. All the explosives and ammunition were sealed in four-gallon petrol tins. Ammunition and food were all in these tins, sealed around the top with solder and strapped into these dinghies.

We were put over the side off a hydroplane, and then paddled away. A couple of dinghies got washed away, and apparently, on the other submarine, only two dinghies got away. For some reason they put all the dinghies on the super-structure of the sub, and she hit a very heavy wave. They all got carried away, so there was no way that the rest of the group could get ashore.

We pulled our dinghy up the beach, and Colonel Keyes said to me and this other chap, 'Go and keep an eye for anybody approaching.'

It wasn't until it started to get light that we set off inland, and we ended up in a cave where everybody got quite warm. The next night we were due to do this raid, but during the day it started to rain – rain, and rain, and rain.

As we'd approached this cave, we were travelling in dry

wadis – little gullies which were all dry. When we went outside, these things were like raging torrents, there was that much water. We were hard pushed to hold on to one another. We were walking along in single file, holding on to the back of the fellow in front.

The idea had been that we should travel to the German headquarters and leave the main party to deal with that while we blew a communications pylon a couple of miles away. We would blow our target at midnight, at the same time that the other party would be going into the headquarters. Then there would be no sort of flashback of information through the telephones.

The pylon, when we eventually got to it, was a great big, four-posted, pyramid-shaped construction with hundreds and hundreds of telephone wires on it. We'd been delayed so much that we had less than half an hour to get to this pylon before the main body went into the headquarters. We just had a small chance of making it.

We put these blast charges round the four legs and linked them all together. Then we found the one thing that was a problem – our matches were wet.

So we'd got our charges all set up and we couldn't think of a way to get them to go. Then one of the fellows said, 'What about using an incendiary bomb?' I banged one of these on a stone, and when the fire started to spout out of it, I lit the fuses. I had a big bunch of fuses, and I'd covered the lot about four times – I had far too many fuses, but to do the job, because of the wet, I had a bunch of fuses in one hand and this incendiary bomb in the other. I waited until I saw the spark coming out of the fuses, then I dropped the incendiary – and I was off.

There was so much light from this incendiary bomb, I could see my own shadow as I was running away – my shadow was running ahead of me. I eventually got behind some bushes – and then the thing went. We heard a groan, and it fell over sideways. When we come to walk away, we found that a lot of the wires hadn't broken. So I had to set the lads to cut all the wires using wirecutters.

When daylight came, we found ourselves in a cemetery. We found a tomb which had an opening which was easy to get into, and inside there were several chambers. We tried to dry ourselves, and we had our iron rations.

As soon as it got dark, we started off again towards the coast, but we were picked up by the Italians while we sheltered in a cave. We learned later that Colonel Keyes had been killed on the raid on the HQ and that in any case, Rommel wasn't there. The colonel got a posthumous VC.

SERGEANT RONALD BUCKINGHAM

RAF PRISONER OF WAR IN STALAG LUFT III, 1943

At Sagan we had in the camp one of the most celebrated RAF escapers who never got back to this country, and whose final end had never been established completely. That was a chap named Grimson. I saw a bit of the escape – but obviously, we just carried on walking. One didn't stand and stare, but it was the most fantastic daylight escape, in that he was dressed as a German civilian, carrying a ladder, which had been taken from the theatre block. He worked his way across from the centre of the camp, up against each electricity pylon, with a box, purporting to test the connections – and so he came until he got to the warning wire. Whereupon, he shouted to the postern in the box – he spoke perfect German, and had false papers, of course – and took his ladder over the wire. He put it up near the postern box, twiddled around with his box of tricks and dropped them down between the two main wires, into the coils of wire.

I am told that he swore for a good three minutes in German, and then said to the postern, 'Well, you know, I'll be in the dirt for that. I'd better go and get another one and continue the job. I don't want to go all the way round there and out through the Kommandatura, and so on. I'll just nip over . . . all right?' He showed his papers to the postern, who said, 'Ja, ja, ja,' then Grimson just went over the wire, I'm told, and away. Then, of course, there was a ladder up against the wire. The guards changed, so there was a different guard in the box, and a ladder against the wire, and our blokes got hold of a Jerry officer in the camp and said, 'Hey, one of your blokes pinched our blooming ladder out of the theatre block, and left it against the flaming wire. We want it back, please.' So the officer went with a group of our blokes – called to the postern – got the ladder back and put it in the theatre block. There was no evidence at all that he'd gone. That's the coolest escape I know.

FLIGHT LIEUTENANT BILL REID

61 SQUADRON, RAF, 1943

On the night of my tenth raid, we'd set off as usual – we were heading for Düsseldorf. As pilot, I got the full briefing, whereas the rest of the crew only had a specific briefing for their particular section – navigation, wireless operator, etc. All pilots made sure they knew the courses roughly anyway, for safety's sake, because it sometimes happened in training that the navigator would put Red on Blue – meaning an error of 180 degrees, and give you the wrong heading. That's how I knew the rough headings after the navigator in my aircraft was killed.

We had just crossed the Dutch coast, when, suddenly, there was a great bang in my face. I thought it was predicted flak. We lost about 2,000 feet, and I felt blood running down my face. I pulled the plane up and then I felt this pain . . . something had hit my shoulder too, it was just like a hammer blow. The crew were all right, except for the engineer – I think he'd been hit in the forearm. I didn't see any point in saying I'd been hit, in case they panicked. So I checked that everyone was OK. I trimmed the plane and we flew on. I still thought we'd been hit by predicted flak, but Cyril the mid-upper said, 'No, it was a Focke-Wulf 190.' But the first instruction I received was, 'Dive starboard.' I think his guns had jammed, but we flew on. We were at about 19,000 feet when – wham – again. We were really hit this time, and we started to spin down.

At about another 2,000 feet below, everything went dead in my ears. There was no intercom, nothing. My hands were a bit bloody, skinned, really, when the windscreen had shattered. So I pulled on my silk gloves, then my leather ones, and put on my goggles because the windscreen was out. Then Jim Norris was hit in the arm, and the port elevator damaged, so there was only half an elevator holding the aircraft straight and level. Together, we held the stick back and I trimmed off as much as I could. I asked Jim to get me another heading from the navigator and he came back and signalled that Jeff was unconscious, but I felt that it was not a permanent situation.

I looked out and got the pole star and knew we were heading about 120, south-east. And I thought, 'Well, we'll just carry on like this.' That night we were actually aiming towards Cologne, dropping spoof flares there, and then turning at the last minute for Düsseldorf. I thought we were all right for timing, and I could see other planes beside me, so I knew we were still fairly well in the stream. Then on time I saw these flares come down ahead of us, obviously Cologne, and I turned up on to 060, the bombing run. As for Les, the bomb-aimer, he didn't really know what had happened yet, because we had been keeping things going, but let him know that we were now heading for the target and he set up the bombsight and switches. I opened the bomb doors and looked for the three target indicators which I aimed at and kept her straight and level, and held it until I felt the bombs go off. Held it for the photograph, then turned and headed back to base. I just kept going. The oxygen supply had been hit, so Jim fed me little bottles of oxygen. I occasionally slumped forward on the way back and he would change the oxygen bottle. We came down to about 12,000 feet by then.

Stirling Bomber Aircraft: Take-off at sunset
CHARLES ERNEST CUNDALL

When I saw water I went down to 7,000 feet and that was below our oxygen height. Then all four engines cut. The engineer usually kept the tanks fairly level, in case they got hit, so you didn't lose your petrol, but he'd forgotten about it in all the hubbub. He just turned them on and they started up again. My biggest problem, actually, was how to hit England. Then I saw some beacons flashing, and it was a wee station, EEH or something, and we couldn't get down. We headed off, and I spotted a big canopy of searchlights further north, and headed for that. But on the way there I saw this big aerodrome with a Drem system of lighting, and it was big enough for us to land on. So I circled there, reduced my height, and said, 'Stand by for a crash landing.' And, of course, we'd no hydraulic pressure, because the bomb doors had stayed open. But we used the emergency air-bottle and let down the undercarriage, then I flashed my landing lamp on and off, and kept circling. They put some big sodium flares out because it was a bit foggy, and we took a low approach coming in. As we touched down, the undercarriage legs collapsed – they'd been shot through. We went along on our belly for about fifty yards, and it was only then that I realised Jefferies was dead, because he slid forward down beside me.

We'd landed at an American aerodrome, Shipdham in Norfolk. They took us into their hospital – the only thing I remember is that I was as dry as a bone, dying of thirst, and they gave me a drink of water. They stitched me up, and I went off to bed. The next morning they took us to Norwich Cottage Hospital, and two days later we were shipped down to the RAF hospital at Ely. Jim Mann, the wireless operator, died the next day.

Air Vice-Marshal Cochrane, the Base Commander, came to see me that first week. He said he'd heard my story from the rest of the crew, but he wanted to hear it from me. He asked me why I didn't turn back, and I said that I'd thought it was safer to go on, rather than turning back among all the other planes; I mean eight or ten miles of aircraft all flying in the same direction. I said if one of the engines had packed up I'd have turned round right away, but the plane was still flying. It wasn't that I was determined to drop the bombs or anything, but I just thought it was the safest thing to do at that time. Then he said, 'You know, Reid, the returns from ops have been practically nil since your raid. It's as if they all said, "That bugger Jock, he went on even though he was wounded, so we can't turn back just because of a faulty altimeter, or something like that."'

Flight Sergeant Norman Jackson

106 Squadron, RAF, 1944

I was shot down on the 26th April 1944. Our target was the ball-bearing factory at Schweinfurt. We'd had a lot of goes at that already. Anyway, we'd got our bombs down, but the flak was coming up and there were fighters all around. We all thought we were going to make it. I was sitting in the cockpit when we were hit, and I saw flames coming from the starboard inner engine, so I grabbed the fire extinguisher and put it inside my Mae West – it was smallish. We'd decided that either the bomb-aimer or myself would have to get out if there was a fire, since we were the only ones who'd been trained to deal with that sort of thing. I released my parachute inside so that the bomb-aimer and navigator could hold on to it in case I slipped. It was my duty to get out. There was a hatch behind me. I got out and slid down on to the wing. We were doing about 140–160 knots and we were at 22,000 feet. I hung on to the air intakes on the leading edge of the wing with one hand, and tried to put out the fire with the other. I'd got it under control, but the German pilot had seen me and was aiming at the engines, so the aircraft was shaking all over the place. I couldn't even jump, because they were holding on to my chute. Then I was shot off the bloody wing, and they threw the parachute out of the plane.

I was going down and watching it burn about me. It was in flames, and the holes in it were getting bigger all the time. I hit the deck fairly hard – bushes and I don't know what else broke my fall. I could hardly walk, my hands and my eyes were badly burnt, and I got a couple of bullets and bits of shrapnel in my legs.

Anyway, I crawled to this village, picked a house and knocked on the door. The bloke opened the door and was bawling and shouting in German. Then two young girls came and pushed him aside. They took me inside and gave me schnapps and bathed my wounds. They were nurses from the hospital, and I thought, well, 'Maybe this won't be too bad, after all.' The rest of the crew had been rounded up. The pilot and rear-gunner had been killed but the others were all right, so we were taken to a police station. The others were knocked about a bit, but I was in the worst shape. I could only just see.

After the police station I went to a German hospital where they patched me up. I was in there for about eight or ten months. As a matter of fact, the pilot that shot us down later came into the hospital to say hello, which I thought was nice of him, the bastard.

Able Seaman Ken Oakley

Royal Navy Commando, D-Day, 1944

Suddenly the air was split by a piercing sound of bagpipes. Along the beach, some hundred yards away, a piper was marching up and down. There was Piper Bill Millin filling his bag up and getting his wind. Lord Lovat had asked him to play a few tunes. Lord Lovat came up behind Bill, formed up his troops and they marched off in parade-ground style, straight up into the village of Colleville. It was amazing. How could he have the pipes on the beach amidst all this battle noise? Shells screaming and fire all around. And silently, as the sound of the pipes died away into the hinterland of the beach, we got back to work bringing the landing craft in. That was a real high point in the whole landing.

Private John Stanleigh

21 Independent Parachute Company, 1944

We weren't far from GHQ dropping zone, when Major Wilson, our commanding officer, spotted some Germans. One of them was firing at him, so he walked up to them and started to shout at them. 'What the bloody hell do you think you're doing, firing at British officers?' And the Germans put their weapons down. They were rather elderly German troops, I must admit, but I still thought that was tremendously courageous. Major Wilson had won an MC at Cambrai in the First World War. He never even pulled his revolver, he just used psychological pressure and the Germans were frightened of him.

10

HOPE AND INSPIRATION

Oh I have slipped the surly bonds of earth
And danced the skies on laughter-silvered wings;
Sunward I've climbed and joined the tumbling mirth
Of sun-split clouds – and done a hundred things
You have not dreamed of; wheeled and soared and swung
High in the sun-lit silence. Hovering there
I've chased the shouting wind along, and flung
My eager craft through footless halls of air;
Up, up the long, delirious burning blue
I've topped the wind-swept heights with easy grace,
Where never a lark nor eagle flew;
And while, with silent lifting mind I've trod
The high untrespassed sanctity of space,
Put out my hand, and touched the face of God.

'HIGH FLIGHT (AIRMAN'S ECSTASY)'
JOHN GILLESPIE MAGEE JR

Sergeant W. Daniels

Royal Artillery, 1916

My first experience in the trenches concerned the padre, who we called the chaplain then. He arrived from brigade headquarters, and I was pleased to see a man of that description risking his life to come into the front-line trenches. He asked me how I felt in regard to God, and was I frightened? I said I was frightened, more than once. He asked me my age and I said I was sixteen, which was much too young to be out there. 'Would you like me to pray, or would you like to pray with me?' he then asked. I said I'd very much like to, and we knelt on the fire step – which was the step we stood on to fire at the Germans – and prayed there while the others in the traverse looked on. I was leg-pulled after that, but I told them exactly what I'd said to God, that I hoped he'd save me from death. And I really think without a doubt that praying to God did save my life.

Captain Herbert Sulzbach

German Artillery, 1916

One summer evening soon after the battle of the Somme had started, the guns were rumbling and there was a terrible noise of battle in our ears. Yet where we lay, just thirty metres from the trenches, there were mountains and peace, and hardly any shooting. We could see the French soldiers, and one night a Frenchman started to sing – he was a wonderful tenor. None of us dared to shoot and suddenly we were all looking out from the trenches and applauding, and the Frenchman said, 'Merci'. It was peace in the middle of war, and the strange thing was, that just a few kilometres northwards, the terrible battle of the Somme was going on.

TROOPER GEORGE JAMESON

1/1ST BATTALION, NORTHUMBERLAND YEOMANRY, 1916

I'd give full marks to the Salvation Army. They had one place I used to drop into often. And it was a most uncomfortable spot to be in. It was at Vimy. The main road came through Vimy and down on to the plain that way. Well, you didn't take that main road if you could avoid it, it was under constant shellfire. At night it got even worse, as the Germans reckoned that transport used it at night, so they would keep strafing it the whole time. But tucked into the side of the hill was the Salvation Army. And they used to have tea and whatever going all hours of the day. How they survived there I don't know. Wonderful people. In the middle of nowhere to suddenly walk into a place and get a piping hot pot of tea, it was a great reviver.

CAPTAIN PHILIP NEAME

15TH FIELD COMPANY, ROYAL ENGINEERS, 1916

I think what we all thought and hoped was that the war was bound to end with some form of open warfare. It could never go on for ever with this trench warfare.

Lieutenant Colonel Alan Hanbury-Sparrow

2nd Battalion, Royal Berkshire Regiment, 1917

The crucial attack of the division on the right had completely failed and we were in rather a precarious position. The brigadier came up, and whilst he was there there was a sudden stampede of our men as they were driven off the hill and they fell back. We fell back from where my temporary head-quarters were and took refuge behind an old parapet that I think had been built in 1914 – it was not thick enough really to be bulletproof. But, providentially, it was facing the right direction and about fifty of us took refuge there.

An attack started forming up against us out of Polygon Wood. At the same time there was a gun ranging on this particular trench. It had obviously seen us go there and I imagine it was one of four guns in a battery. I knew that once that battery got the range and opened fire we were done for. At the same time a machine-gun, which seemed very much closer than I liked, swept the top of our parapet and killed three in the process. They'd got the position exactly. We were in a very parlous situation.

I sat down as there was nothing to be done, and I did what I generally did on those occasions – I played chess with my adjutant. I always had with me a little chessboard with pegs. We played on, rather aimlessly it's true, but it steadied the men. Then suddenly a shell fell into the trench. I thought to myself, 'Now our time has come, you've had a long run for your money and I wonder what it'll be like to be dead.' At that moment I realised that whatever happened I wasn't going to be killed. It's impossible to describe this consciousness. It's not like ordinary consciousness at all, it's something like a prophet of old when the Lord spoke, something quite overwhelmingly clear and convincing. I wasn't very proud of myself because I didn't care what happened to the others – I was going to survive. I took a rifle and began shooting. I hit two Germans at six hundred yards and made a third skip for his life. The extraordinary part was that the machine-gun never fired again, that was the last shell that it fired, yet there was no reason why it should have stopped. It was as though for a moment I got a glimpse of time coming towards me.

Spring in the Trenches, Ridge Wood, 1917
PAUL NASH

CAPTAIN CYRIL DENNYS

212 SIEGE BATTERY, ROYAL GARRISON ARTILLERY, 1918

Well, of course, I was very young. I think that the sexual aspect worried some of the older men quite a lot. I mean, it made them jumpy. I remember there was one case where a captain who was getting on in age applied for special leave. You could get a week's special leave to go to Paris or somewhere. On his leave chit he was asked for his reason. He put quite boldly, sexual starvation. And to everyone's surprise and delight he got his leave. He went off and we hoped he satisfied his needs in Paris.

PRIVATE JOHN FIGAROVSKY

US 1ST DIVISION, 1918

When we landed, one of the first things we did was to parade through the town of St Nazaire. The French people were just delirious with joy, because in the Americans they saw hope for the future. As we marched through town, the sidewalks and even the gutters on both sides were full of people – and we felt so proud and important that such a fuss was being made over us. The mayor even proclaimed a holiday.

Most of us were young fellows, and we must have made a good impression because the French girls would jump in the ranks and throw flowers at us and scream and even kiss some of the soldiers. But we kept on, you know, with army discipline, we tried not to notice too much of that. It was such a wonderful reception – we never imagined anything like that would happen, that we'd be welcomed so warmly. They must have admired us a lot. And, of course, we were looking forward to a great adventure ahead of us. We were looking forward to the fight – we didn't know how serious it was because we'd never been to war before. But we didn't stay in St Nazaire for long, we were marched about three miles out of town where they had some cantonments.

When we trained with the French troops they were very cooperative. Most of them were short, and it seemed they'd had their clothes on for a year – they hardly ever changed their clothes. But they were very nonchalant about everything, I guess they were tired after four years of warfare. And they were surprised to see that we were so eager to get into the fight.

DORIS SCOTT

CIVILIAN LIVING IN CANNING TOWN, EAST END OF LONDON, 1940

Once, as I was leaving the park shelter and coming back to my house, those all around were bomb blasted, and I saw this woman cleaning the front doorstep of her demolished house as if it were business as usual.

Often when a place was bombed in the East End, the King and Queen would come and visit. It would give people a certain amount of heart and, in fact, if we knew that they had a hit, it made us feel better, because it brought them down to our level. Yes, they did inspire people in their own way.

Sergeant John Longstaff

2ND BATTALION, RIFLE BRIGADE, 1942

Montgomery came to the southern sector of the Alamein front at Alam Halfa, and one of the first things he asked was, when did we leave England and had we had any post? Not a single soldier had had a letter. Had we any NAAFI? We hadn't even seen the NAAFI. We were scrounging as much as we could from other units – cigarettes – and understandably, other units weren't prepared to give them away or even sell them. He wanted to know why our shirts were stained – because we only had one shirt, and there was sweat – and they were hard, like bloody cardboard. He wanted to know if we'd had any leave. Nobody had had any leave at that stage. He made sure his adjutants took note of everything. He wasn't talking to the officers – he was talking to the riflemen – he was sitting inside little dugouts with the lads.

Before Montgomery, we never knew what our role was – where we were going, what was going to happen, who was on our left flank, right flank – who were our reserves. We didn't even know who the enemy was prior to Montgomery. He gave the order that every soldier will be told who is on his left and who is on his right – who is behind him and who is in front of him, and he will be told what he's going to do. When a man is told those things, he starts getting confidence. He doesn't feel that he's fighting by himself.

Corporal Peter Taylor

2nd Battalion, Rifle Brigade, 1942

It was about the twelfth day of Alamein when the enemy really started to go. The desert was littered with Alpine boots and rucksacks with a cover which was made with the hide of a deer or elk or something – hair-covered rucksacks. We found out afterwards that this Alpine regiment had been hurriedly sent from Italy across to Tripoli and whistled down to the battlefield almost before they could pause for breath. All their Alpine boots had been hung on the outside of their packs. They'd been put straight into the front line to hold positions. This stuff was all over the place – the dross of an army, if you like – tins and cans and bullets and guns and rifles, boots, packs, hats – a hundred and one things every- where. Burnt-out vehicles and tanks – and a few graves, though not many. The dead on our side had all been taken away. They were taken away and buried. I should imagine the engineers had burial details – had graves prepared ready for the possible number of casualties. The casualty evacua- tion and withdrawal of people of ours who were killed was incredible. The wounded were got away extremely quickly in jeeps and little armoured cars with stretchers built on to the back of them – strap him down and whoosh – off. They'd have an orderly sitting on the back to see the chap didn't get bounced out. The medical evacuation was heartening because people had been told, 'If you get wounded, you'll be whipped away straight away.' We'd never had this sort of thing before.

Everything had been thought of – that was why the spirit was so good. After years of being pushed about by the Axis forces, at last we were holding our own and doing a bit better than holding our own. We were actually beating them. Everybody could see we were beating them. It wasn't because they were short of weapons – they had almost as much as we had – but we had a little bit of the edge with the Sherman and the anti-tank guns. We had a bit of the edge.

BRIGADIER ARTHUR WALTER

DIRECTOR OF PORTS AND INLAND WATER TRANSPORT, 1944

We were summoned to a cinema in Portsmouth. There were about 400 officers there and redcap police all round the place, it was all very secret and we sat down in this cinema and Monty came in. He told us something about the plans for the invasion. He said this is what we're going to do, this is what we expect the Germans to do – and this is what I'll do to the Germans. It was terribly inspiring, because I'd been planning my own little corner of the invasion, getting more and more puzzled, not knowing quite where it fitted in, and he suddenly put everything into perspective and I can only say that he raised my morale just like that. He was a leader and I would have followed him to hell.

LIEUTENANT WILLIAM JALLAND

8TH BATTALION, DURHAM LIGHT INFANTRY, 1944

As the preparations for D-Day gathered pace, I remember being open-mouthed at some of the equipment that was being assembled. Part of PLUTO that looked like an enormous bobbin floated about in Southampton Water. We didn't know what that was. We saw pieces of Mulberry, some with cranes, some without. Again, we'd no idea what they were. We saw the crabs, the scorpions, and the flails. We didn't know what any of it was, but we knew we'd be on our way very soon.

FLYING OFFICER KEN ADAM

609 SQUADRON, RAF, 1944

I had a gold ring made up of the wedding rings of my mother and father. Before I went on an op I would turn this ring three times. On one particular occasion we had to attack a Gestapo headquarters in the middle of Dunkirk. As I started my engine I went to turn my ring, but it wasn't there. I must have dislodged it when I went to grab my parachute. So I said to myself, 'Well, this is it.' I started to look for any reason to abort the mission. But the plane was behaving perfectly. I took off, and it was a particularly nasty attack in which we lost the squadron commander and three other pilots. I was hit several times, but managed to get back. As I climbed out the fitters were walking towards me, great grins on their faces, holding my ring, which they had been turning for me.

CAPTAIN JOHN SIM

12TH PARACHUTE BATTALION, 1944

Finally the evening came – the evening of the 5th June, when we got into our lorries and we were transported to the airfield. We collected our chutes and the lorries took us around the perimeter, miles away into the countryside where our aircraft had been dispersed. The aircraft we were going to jump out of was the Stirling. It was a peaceful June evening – lovely and calm.

We just sat and talked for a while amongst ourselves, and then the padre came whipping up in his jeep and we had a little prayer. He wished us well before he dashed off again to another aircraft. Then came the jeep of the RAF crew roaring up, and they got out and said, 'All right, you chaps. Don't worry! Piece of cake! We'll get you there!' It was a tremendous, exciting, light-hearted atmosphere.

Private James Sims

2nd Parachute Battalion, 1944

One morning in Stalag XIB, I saw RSM Lord of the 3rd Battalion coming towards me. He was tall, slim and immaculate in battledress, with red beret exactly an inch above the eye. His badges and buckles shone like jewels and his black boots were like glass. I automatically adjusted my collar, which was undone, and put my beret on straight. I had never met the RSM. 'What battalion are you from?' he asked. I told him the 2nd Battalion. He asked me about the other wounded men and his expression hardened. Then suddenly he gripped me by the shoulder and said, 'Don't let them get you down, lad,' and then he was gone.

RSM Lord always treated German officers and NCOs correctly, but did not bother to disguise his contempt for them, referring sarcastically to the Germans as 'the detaining power'. His task in Stalag XIB was a very difficult one. The Airborne accepted him without question, as did also any

Guardsmen, but there were men from almost every unit in the British Army, as well as some Canadians, Australians and New Zealanders. Some of them felt that now they were prisoners they should no longer come under army discipline.

Enforcing discipline was extremely difficult, as a man could not be confined to camp, or his pay stopped. Extra duties would have been no punishment, as boredom was our main problem and most of us would have volunteered for any extra work if we could have got it. For the most part the RSM had to rely on the good sense of the men, plus threats of post-war punishment. He did not hesitate to make an example of anyone who transgressed, and I remember that when one soldier refused to wash, the RSM had him stood up in a sink stark naked, and buckets of cold water were thrown over him whilst two NCOs scrubbed him down fore and aft with yard brooms, and it was below zero.

The RSM had made an office out of Red Cross packing cases, and on his door was a notice which said, 'British RSM. Knock and wait.' A German warrant officer was in front of me and he walked into the RSM's office. I heard a scuffle and the RSM shouting, 'Can't you bloody well read?' then the German warrant officer came hurtling out to land flat on his back. His cap was tossed out behind him, and the door slammed shut. As the German was armed, I feared the worst, but he got up, dusted himself down, grinned and walked to the door and knocked. The RSM shouted, 'Come in,' and that was that. This incident more than any other, as far as I was concerned, illustrated how good RSM Lord was at understanding the enemy. There was nothing the average German understood better than a good kick up the arse from someone in authority.

RSM Lord had been wounded in the right arm at Arnhem and when his arm was better he told us he had decided that he would salute any German officer he saw. He said, 'In future, when I see a German officer I shall draw myself to my full height, look him straight in the eyes and I shall salute in the correct fashion. However, gentlemen, as I do this I shall say to myself in a firm voice, "Bollocks!"' We thought this was wonderful. From that moment on, we were saluting every German officer we could find – I tell you, we were looking for them. They were as pleased as Punch – they thought we'd really come round to their way of thinking. That one word 'bollocks' summed it all up. Now we began to believe in ourselves again. We needed food, medical help, warmth, but above all we needed hope and that's what J.C. Lord gave us – hope.

A Night Scene in Normandy: La Délivrande
ALBERT RICHARDS

Lieutenant-Colonel David Warren

1st Battalion, Hampshire Regiment, 1944

What we all felt – and this was the most astonishing thing about the Normandy landings – was that everyone was 100 per cent confident that whatever happened to you or to anyone else, the operation would be successful. There was no question that it might not be. And everyone was glad to get on with it because it felt like the green light for the end of the war.

Private James Bramwell

224 Parachute Field Ambulance, RAMC, Rhine crossing, 1945

Codenamed Varsity-Plunder, you can't imagine a more unfortunate name. We called it Varsity Blunder. There was no mystery about it – it was all in the newspapers with headlines shouting about the imminent drop. It was like a sporting event with BBC commentators waiting to send the news back to London. We were to drop in daylight, right on top of the enemy, which was news to us. When Brigadier Hill briefed the brigade, there was no hint of the horrors to come.

'No doubt you will find some Germans when you reach the ground, but you can take it from me they will be bloody frightened. Just imagine the reactions of the wretched Germans cowering in their slit trenches, when lo and behold, wave after wave of you bloodthirsty gentlemen come cascading down from the sky. What would you do in their place? But let there be no misunderstanding. If anybody does shoot at you, you will ignore him completely. Your job is to hasten to the RV and not to amuse yourself by returning his fire. And if I find any of you gentlemen going to ground, I'll come round personally and kick his bottom. If you happen to hear a few stray bullets, you needn't think they're intended for you. That, gentlemen, is a form of egotism.'

This briefing had a tonic effect. It gave exactly the right tone and in such a delightful turn of phrase.

11

SURVIVAL

Lop-sided from a shrapnel wound,
he got a job as warehouseman at Twyfords,
and packed lavatory cisterns in straw.

His son Eric was pallid and fragile.
Nervous with love,
his father followed him everywhere.
Their voices matched. On Sundays,
at our house, the treble blended
with Arthur's cracked bass
which had won him, in Rome with the sixth army,
a NAAFI singing competition.

He was my famous soldier-uncle,
with real medals to show.
One-handed, he taught me to box,
easy left-hand feints and evasions
that never landed a real blow.
The new bureaucrats –
planners, managers, health officials –
schemed and struggled, as I did,
to get under that affectionate defence
and never managed it.

He is a survivor, as soft and steady
as his own slurred Longton accent.
He lives in Mawby Street,
a smoky terrace that tilts
over the hill's brow like a raisin-cake tiara.

They say a quiet victory
has stolen over this city.
New suit, crepe shoes, slow voice,
Arthur sidles through his sixties.
He is the gentlest of heroes.
He goes dancing now, at the Locarno,
is handsome
in his new grey toupee.

'ARTHUR'
GEOFFREY ADKINS

Private Frank Brent

2nd Australian Brigade, Battle of Krithia, 1915

It just went on all day. The older battleships in the bay were letting go as hard as they could, and the harder they fired the more confident you felt. So whilst it was about the most precarious position a bloke could find himself in, you sort of made up your mind that, 'Well, we're here, and the only way the enemy can get us off is by carrying us off feet first.'

The dust and the noise – it was so loud you couldn't hear each other speak – went on for a quarter of an hour, then suddenly everything was as silent as the grave. And that was when we had to hop it. The barrage had been so heavy that in the quiet we thought, 'Well this is going to be a cake-walk, there's nothing to stop us.' But the mistake we made was that after we got out of our 'hop-out' trenches our own artillery began to put down a barrage just in front of us and some of it was firing short. You could see your mates falling, going down right and left, and you were face to face with the stark realisation that this was the end.

And that was the thought that was with you the whole time because despite the fact that you couldn't see the Turk, he was pelting us with everything he had got from all sides – the marvel to me was how the Dickens he was able to do it after the barrage that had fallen on him. And sure enough we got within a mile of Krithia village when I copped my packet – as I laid there I said, 'Thank Christ for that.'

Private S. T. Sherwood

Ypres, 1917

As I slipped to the bottom of the shell-hole I took my torch out, flashed it around and to my horror found I had a German companion – that was where the terrific stink came from. I thought, 'Heavens, am I going to spend the night with you!' I knew that without help it was impossible to get out, so I shouted, screamed and did everything possible to make someone hear me. I shone my torch up in the air in the hope that someone would see the light, but nothing happened.

I wasn't one to panic, I was always one to keep cool if possible, but for the next half-hour I struggled as hard as I could to climb up the sides, and in the process my trench boots were left at the bottom. But every time I would get within a yard of the top and then slide back into this terrible filth again. I reviewed my position and realised I'd have to keep myself going until the morning. First I decided to sing, and sang all the songs I could possibly think of. I sang, I cursed, I raved and eventually I prayed. I prayed that help would come before morning.

I was sweating from head to foot with all the exertion. Then as I lay back in the trench I remembered my old pipe and tobacco and smoked pipe after pipe. Gradually I found I was sinking further and further into this mire – the water had gone above my waist, and no matter how I struggled it was impossible to get out. I knew that struggling further wasn't going to help me so I continued smoking and singing and shouting as best as I could until my voice had almost gone.

I took my rifle and jammed it into the side of the shell-hole as far as I could to give me some support, putting my right arm through the sling. Then I either dozed off or became unconscious, I don't know which, because when I woke the bottom of my body was completely paralysed by the coldness of the water, which I could feel creeping further and further up. During this period the Germans commenced shelling the area. The vibrations made the shell-hole shake from one side to the other. I was rather pleased because it gave me something to interest myself in – it kept me awake and alive. I was still sinking further into the mire. I filled my pipe again then put my hand into my tunic pocket for my matches and found they were wet through.

It was then I began to despair. I thought, 'I'd sooner be killed with a shell or a bullet than die in a bloody filthy shell-hole.' From then on I can remember no more until I thought, 'Can I be dreaming – there are footsteps somewhere.' Feebly, I tried to shout until I heard a voice say, 'Where are you?' I shouted, 'I'm here, in a shell-hole.' The footsteps went round again for a few minutes, then looking up I saw a head appear over the top. 'Oh, my God,' he said, 'hang on, hang on, chum.' I remembered no more from that 'hang on' until I found myself in hospital between clean white sheets.

FUSILIER JOSEPH PICKARD

1/5TH BATTALION, NORTHUMBERLAND FUSILIERS, 1917

I remember being in this sort of advanced clearing station. And when I come round it was dark and I was lying on a stretcher, and I didn't know what was the matter with me. It turned out there was a blanket over the top of me and I'd been left for dead. My old lady later got the number of my grave and the King and Queen's sympathy, but fortunately I didn't know that at the time. I got rid of this blanket and then I saw a light near where I was, so I shouted down an orderly, and two of them eventually came down and had a look at me. They wouldn't give me a drink of course, but they picked the stretcher up and put it straight on a hospital train.

Men in the trenches, near Hendicourt
Sir William Orpen

Flying Officer Geoffrey Page

52 Squadron, RAF, 1940

We were all sitting around, having tea on the grass alongside a tent, which had a field telephone connected to Sector Operations. At about five o'clock, they phoned through and said there were ninety bandits approaching from the South at about 15,000 feet. There were only ten of us, but we took off. We could see the usual swarm of what looked like little insects taking shape – it was a large formation of Dornier 217s, escorted by [Messerschmitt] 109 fighters. I was in the leading group of three, then I could see the tracer coming towards me from the whole formation – they had obviously singled me out as a target.

All these things which looked like lethal electric light bulbs kept flashing by, then finally there was a big bang and the aircraft exploded. The scientists reckon the temperature goes up from a cool room temperature at 15,000 feet to 3,000 degrees Centigrade in ten seconds. So, when you consider water boils at 100 degrees, that's quite a temperature change. If you don't get out immediately, you're never going to get out. The beauty of the Royal Air Force training came to my rescue and I instinctively reached for the harness and slid the hood back. I rolled the aircraft on to its back, kicked back the control column so the aircraft pointed its nose upwards, but as I was upside down, I popped out like a cork out of a toy gun.

I stupidly wasn't wearing any gloves, so my hands got a terrible burning, and face as well. My mouth and nose were saved by my gas mask. I found myself tumbling head over heels through space. I remember seeing my right arm and extending it, making myself pull the metal ring of the ripcord on my parachute – and that was agony. It was like an electric shock through my burnt hand. Again, you don't have a choice, because, if you don't, the parachute won't open.

Fortunately, my parachute wasn't on fire. One then took stock of the situation, and I noticed a funny thing had happened. My left shoe and my trousers had been blown off completely by the explosion. I was almost naked from the waist downwards – my legs were slightly burnt. Then I could hear the fight all around me, and it took me about ten minutes to float down into the water.

I had various problems to deal with. First of all, I had to get rid of my parachute, but you had to turn this metal disk on your stomach. You turn it through ninety degrees and then give it a hard thump – but it was difficult because I was badly burnt. Then the parachute was on top of me, so I was really inside a tent with the cords trapping me like an octopus's tentacles. I knew I had to get it away quickly, otherwise I would sink. Again, desperation comes into the issue, so you do turn it, and you do thump it.

The next thing was to blow up my life jacket. I got hold of the rubber tube over my left shoulder, but when I blew into it, all I got was a lot of bubbles. It had been burnt right through. My face was swelling up at this point, and my eyesight was bad because my swollen eyelids were closing up. The distant view of England, which I could see a few miles away was a bit blurred, but I started vaguely in the right direction.

Then a happy thought came to my mind, and I remembered that in my jacket pocket I had a brandy flask that my dear mother had given me – which I had filled with brandy just as an emergency measure. I thought that this probably qualified as an emergency, so I rolled on my back. This was a painful process, but I got it out and held it between my wrists and undid the screw cap with my teeth. I thought, 'Well, life is going to feel a bit better.' But as I lifted it up to take a swig, a dirty big wave came along and the whole lot went to the bottom of the Channel. I was a bit annoyed about that, but there was nothing else for it, so I continued swimming.

I heard, rather than saw the boat. There were two men in it, and they kept asking me questions. By this time I had been swimming for half an hour, and I was fed up with the whole affair, so when they asked me if I was a Jerry, I'm afraid I let loose with every rude four-letter word that I could think of, and that immediately assured them that I was an RAF officer. They picked me out of the water, and took me to the big ship, where the captain dressed my burns and gave me a cup of tea. Then the Margate lifeboat came out and took me in to transfer me to Margate hospital.

For the first time for an hour or more, I was able to laugh, because waiting on the quayside was the Mayor, dressed in his top hat and tails, saying, 'Welcome to Margate.' When you'd been in an air fight an hour before, and then there's a chap in top hat and tails, it is two different worlds. As it happened, it was the beginning of grouse shooting that day, August 12th. There was a certain irony in that.

ORDINARY SEAMAN DOUGLAS DAVIES

HMS *REPULSE*, SOUTH CHINA SEA, 1941

These aircraft came in at various heights. It was impossible really for the best of gunners to direct as to which aircraft should be shot down – the ones at sea level, the ones at 3,000 feet, 6,000, 10,000 or even 15,000 feet.

We were below in the boiler room when there was a terrific explosion. The place went dark. There was no shouting – no nothing. The men were undoubtedly dead, and yet I was still alive and able to find my way to the ladder, which led to the top deck. I got out through the air intake on top deck, but now I could just about see with one eye – the other had been burned.

I felt all alone. I saw men being mown down by aircraft coming in at sea level, as I just lay on the deck.

But in time, I was taken down below, quite a distance down in the ship, where I was given an injection of morphia. But the morphine didn't do its work as it should have. I was still dazed. So I remained, with the countless other members of the ship's company that had been injured in the A magazine. Then there were seven or eight explosions – then I heard on the tannoy, 'Prepare to abandon ship, and may God be with you.' Why the morphia hadn't worked, I'll never know, but it actually saved my life by not working. I managed to climb towards a deck where there was a porthole.

The ship was now heeling over. Countless lads were doing what I was trying to do – escape from the ship by going through a porthole. As I hit the water, everything went black. Some time later, a lifeboat came, and the lads just heaved me aboard. I was taken to an escorting destroyer – the *Express*.

I was pulled up by rope to the quarterdeck. It seems that my clothing had been burnt off completely. On looking down I could just see the tops of my shoes. The soles had been burnt off, and I think that was about the only thing that had remained – otherwise I was completely naked – severely burnt. I had also been hit by five bullets. I was given another injection of morphia – which worked – and was sent to Singapore General Hospital. I was in a very bad condition – I was unconscious for three days with double pneumonia.

I had lost all my fingernails, I'd lost all my toenails. I had my ears burnt off, my back had been burnt – my legs, my feet had been severely burnt. I still don't know how I survived.

SERGEANT ROBIN MURRAY

214 SQUADRON, RAF, 1942

It was a cold day on the 12th February – overcast, 10/10ths cloud – and from 9,000 feet down to about 900 feet was solid cloud, snow cloud. We took off in our Wellington, and flew out on course – but we didn't see a thing because of the cloud. Then we iced up very badly. The port engine packed up, and after about twenty minutes, part of the propeller broke away – came through the side of the aircraft and damaged the hydraulics. We eventually came down in the sea at about a quarter to five in the evening.

When we hit, the Perspex area behind the front turret broke and the wave took me right back up against the main spar. I came to underwater, pulled myself along on the geodetics and came up by the pilot's controls. There were four of them already in the dinghy, which was still attached to the wing. I was the last one in. We'd lost Flight Lieutenant Hughes and George Taylor. We paddled around with our hands looking for them, and Andy Everett swam round to the turret which was under water, because the plane had broken its back just behind the main spar – but it was no good. I had swallowed a lot of salt water and was very sick. We were all sopping wet. We made ourselves as comfortable as we could. There were five of us in the dinghy – McFadden, Stephens, Wood, Everett and myself.

For the first few hours there was nothing around – just

the sea. It was quite choppy, and that was uncomfortable. Unfortunately, whoever had put the rations in the dinghy had forgotten the tin opener, so we couldn't open the tins. Then the knife fell overboard, so we didn't have that either. So all we had was Horlicks Malted Milk tablets. It was cold – the coldest winter for nearly a century.

We were hoping that someone would come out and pick us up, because the wireless operator had sent out a Mayday signal – but what none of us realised was that the navigator must have got his co-ordinates wrong. We had done a 180 degree turn, and we were heading out to sea again, so we landed off the Frisian Islands instead of, as we thought, twenty miles off Orford Ness.

I had read about how you mustn't go into a deep sleep when you're cold, because you get hypothermia and that's it – you die. So I suggested that we always had two people awake so that we didn't all go right off into a deep sleep – and that's what we tried to do.

Everyone survived the first night. We thought that any moment somebody was going to pick us up. We saw quite a few aircraft flying very high – unrecognisable, of course. There were flares on the dinghy, but we didn't see any aircraft that was low enough to have seen us. Once we thought we saw a ship – that was on the second day. We set off a flare, but nothing happened, and we tried to send off another. But it wouldn't work – it was damp. None of the flares worked at all after that. We saw quite a few aircraft that evening, just before dusk, flying very high. We came to the conclusion they were probably German.

We hadn't got a paddle on board – we were just sitting there. It was very strange, because people just went into a coma. They just sort of lost themselves. Stephens went first, on the second day at four o'clock.

That second night was very cold. We just talked about various things. There was no despondency – we never thought we weren't going to be picked up.

At dawn of that morning, Wing Commander McFadden died. There were no visible signs of injury. McFadden was firmly under the impression in his last hours that he was in his car, driving from the hangars back to the mess. He was the only one who got delirious in that way. People sort of went into a coma. They would be talking quite normally and they would gradually drowse off. You'd shake them to try to keep them awake, but they'd gone. You could feel that they were going. But it was peaceful – there was no suffering at all. They weren't in pain – they just quietly died.

Pilot Officer Wood died about three hours after Wing Commander McFadden. He was very quiet. Finally, Sergeant Everett died at dawn. I was disappointed that he had gone so quickly. He went while he was talking – just drifted off. I kept them all on the dinghy, and was able to keep my legs out of the water by resting them on them. It sounds terrible, but by this time they were beyond help.

The final morning was the worst time, because we drifted in towards land. The water was as calm as a millpond, and the cliffs were about 150 yards away, with a gun emplacement on the top. It was about eleven o'clock, I suppose, by the time I drifted into the shore. I got a tin lid and caught the sun, and somebody came out of the gun emplacement.

Then the tide started to go out. I was starting to drift out to sea. That was a bad moment. Then a German Marine Police boat with a Red Cross came out and they hauled me aboard. I was able to stand up, and they got me on to the deck. They tied the dinghy on the back with the bodies of my crew and came slowly back.

They took me into Flushing dock. I'll never forget that

moment – the deck was above the quay, and they put a ramp down, and as I walked down the ramp to the ambulance, there were five or six German sailors there, and they all came to attention and saluted me.

FLIGHT LIEUTENANT HAROLD HOBDAY

617 SQUADRON, RAF, 1943

We were going to try and hit the aqueduct which carried the Dortmund-Ems Canal over a valley, to release all the water. We had a different bomb – we didn't have a bouncing bomb – we had a very large bomb on board.

We took off, but fog in the area meant we couldn't see the target, so we had to return and land with a bomb on board. I think it bent the hook it was on when we landed, because we weren't supposed to land with this bomb on board – but we had to because there were no other supplies of the bomb.

The following night they decided to send us again. Mosquitos were sent in advance to reconnoitre and beat up the defences. But we couldn't find the aqueduct because the weather wasn't good enough. The moon wasn't bright enough either, and so we were stooging around, trying to locate it. We did a wide circle a couple of times, with our pilot trying to see if he could see the target, when suddenly the bomb aimer in front of our aircraft said, 'Pull up, Les!' and Les and I pulled up, because we were aiming straight for some trees on a hill. We brushed the trees and two of the engines were damaged – and the tail.

We managed to ditch our bomb and climb up, but because of the damaged tail, the aircraft kept wanting to go around in circles. Eventually it got worse and worse, and the pilot couldn't hold it, so he told us to bail out.

The crew in the front bailed out, but the people in the back, who were shovelling ammunition out to lighten the load, didn't hear the 'bail out' order. They sensed Les was coming down, and called over the blower, 'Are you ditching, Les?' and Les said, 'Jump out quickly.'

He tried to land the aircraft in a field, but it hit a tree and he was killed – but the other two got out. Naturally we didn't find each other. I landed in a tree, clambered down and started walking.

I found someone who could speak English. I was given some clothes and told to shave off my moustache, as Dutchmen don't have them. The underground movement looked after me in a wood for a month, then eventually they fixed up that I should go up to Rotterdam, stay with somebody there, and get used to mixing with Germans.

Then I was met by a fellow who took me down to Paris on the train, which was very overcrowded. This was done on purpose, of course. We had to go through the customs where the Germans were on the Holland/Belgium border, and also on the Franco/Belgian border, which was a little hair-raising, because there were two Gestapo people at each place. I had to hand my papers in. I'd got forged papers in which I was supposed to be a deaf and dumb Dutchman working on an airfield in the South of France. Sounds a little bit of a tall story. They were just about to ask me a question, the Germans, and then said, 'Well, go through,' and I didn't have any trouble.

WILLIAM 'BILL' JORDAN

CAMERAMAN, ARMY FILM AND PHOTOGRAPHIC UNIT, ITALY, 1944

I always feel that sound could have captured far more than the visual medium. You'd hear a shell burst, but by the time you'd swung your camera round, all you got was just a cloud of dust drifting away. You were incapable of capturing the physical situation you found yourself in.

We got to the outskirts of Cassino – crawled, literally on our tummies into a couple of shell-holes, I suppose just half a mile short of the foot of castle hill. There were one or two Indian soldiers passing through and there was sniper fire everywhere. Literally just to put your head up above ground was fatal. They'd got it so pinpointed that one couldn't move during daylight. We did a bit of filming – general stuff of Cassino itself – and then decided that we still weren't getting enough, so we came back and found a first-aid post. I spoke to the sergeant there and he said, 'Well, there might be a bit of material for you here. We go out every now and again with a stretcher party and pick up the wounded. We go between the lines and pick up our own and sometimes German wounded.' I said, 'Well, that's excellent. I'll come along with you.' He offered me a Red Cross armband, but I said, 'I don't think I need that,' and off we went.

I tagged along with the stretcher party and we got within five or six hundred yards from the foot of castle hill again. Walking along, suddenly I thought to myself, 'Terrific shot – first-aid party going along with the ruins of the monastery in the background and castle hill, as they're picking up the wounded.' I went down on one knee – I think I'd got a

25-mm lens on, which is a fairly wide angle – I wanted to catch the whole situation with the whole section of medics. Let them get no more than fifty yards in front of me to get the shot . . . and boom. I knew no more. I got a mortar bomb right by the side of me. I woke up four days later in hospital with so many holes in me they thought I was a pincushion.

Sergeant Bill McConville, who came to see me in hospital about four days later, told me that at one time, when they put me on a stretcher, they said I was dead, because I was bleeding from the mouth and nose, had blood in my eyes – and I don't remember a single thing. They cut me from the base of the stomach, right up to the chest. This was all done under canvas, just outside Cassino. I don't know whether they used a penknife or a boy scout's knife, or what, but it's the most amazing scar you could ever see. The surgeon got half way up the stomach and decided he'd gone the wrong way, so he came back again and made another cut. Some stitches are something like six inches long, some are a couple of inches long – but thank God I'm still here.

Flight Sergeant David Russell

RAF, Far Eastern prisoner of war, 1945

We were taken prisoner by the Japanese in 1942 and sent to an established prison camp in Java where there were 600 Dutch. The Dutch women were still free, but because the men had joined the home guard, they were all in the camp.

After we'd been there about two weeks three Dutchmen were caught climbing back over the wire at night, having visited their wives. A few days later we were all taken on to this football field where they had dug three graves. A Japanese sergeant-major got us all on parade, arranged on three sides of a square, staggered, so that nobody could miss what was going to happen. Eventually these poor creatures were led out, hands tied behind their backs, bleeding profusely from cuts and bruises all over them, staggering as the Japanese prodded them. One was placed opposite each grave. Two ranks of Japanese soldiers, none over seventeen years of age, seemed to be the firing squad. A black Dutch chap standing beside me translated the sentence read out in Malayan by a Japanese officer. He said, 'They are going to kill them, but they are not going to shoot them. They are to die by thrusting.'

While all this was going on, the Japanese officer lit a cigarette in a tortoiseshell holder, put his hands in his riding breeches' pockets and stood beside the three victims, really enjoying the scene. Then he signalled and three young Japanese left the ranks. One stood opposite each prisoner with a fixed bayonet. The officer looked to see if we were all watching, threw away his cigarette, took out another and put it in his holder. The three Dutch guys refused to be bandaged. The Japs thumped them with their rifle butts and they had to submit to the bandage. They were standing each in front of his grave.

The Japanese officer made his men practise bayonet drill on these men – forward, retreat, forward, retreat, forward and then a lunge. Eventually they lunged for the stomach and the three men fell on the ground kicking. They kept thrusting at them and threw the men still kicking into the graves. By then my mouth was just dry.

After that we were marched into Bandoeng, a very big camp which was highly organised. I became the camp librarian under the aegis of Colonel van der Post, who was quite a character. He got all the talent together and started a school – a gunner called Rees, who was a lecturer in French, started giving French lessons; another guy was teaching Italian, and another Russian. My navigator friend, Ken Wibley, started Russian in prison camp and later became Senior Lecturer in Russian at Bangor University. Van der Post spoke Japanese, but he was getting information from all sources by pretending he didn't understand a word of it. He was a great morale-builder – he would come round the sergeants' lines and say 'Morniiing!', singing it out as if life was just perfect. He was charming and very inspirational. He'd been fighting guerrilla warfare against the Italians. He was well built and strong, because he had been out in the jungle so long. He loved cowboy stories – open-air spaces got him away from the close environment of a prison camp.

I had quite a reasonable life for four or five months and then they decided to take us to Japan. We had five days on a ship to Singapore and another twenty-eight days on a ship battened down. We lost quite a number of people on that trip. There were burials every day at sea with canvas bags overboard. It was a terrible journey. We couldn't lie down. We slept sitting up, back to back. There were rats everywhere, running over your face at night. Feeding was very difficult. They would bring a big wooden barrel full of mushy rice to the top of the gangway. The mess tins had our names on them and were passed hand over hand. When we landed I was eventually moved to a place called Ikuno, where I became a copper miner. Most of my friends were there.

The Japanese soldiers wouldn't come down the mine – it was only us and the civilian miners. Our job was to get great big heavy buggies and fill them with copper ore. My abiding memory is of starvation. The food was just minimum. We were trying to do a ten-hour shift in the mines on a few grains of rice a day. It was unpolished rice, full of weevils just scraped off the floor of some store. We stole like mad. I became a very accomplished thief. In summertime the Japanese gave us little cotton shorts, which was all we wore, and you could see everybody's ribs. We were burnt black from working outside. On one day a week we worked in the gardens outside the camp, but weren't allowed to touch the produce. They grew magnificent crops of oranges, plums, breadfruit, eggfruit and rice. Sometimes they let us take the white radish tops which we put into the soup. There was no soil. They grew everything on sand covered with manure, which we supplied. They had these huge concrete pits behind each billet, for latrines. They gave you a long pole with a big tin on the end of it and you filled the wooden barrels with loose shit – everyone had diarrhoea and dysentery, and you had this pole which you placed in hoops attached to the top of the barrel and you carried the honeypots out to the plants and you fertilised them.

It sounds odd but our morale was high. We lived on hope. We were getting information, and that was important for morale. We had a fellow called Arthur Brady who taught himself Japanese. We stole newspapers and he was able to translate a lot of it. We knew when Germany packed up because first of all the Japanese put us all on parade at 3 a.m. and beat the hell out of us. We knew something big had happened. We were delighted. Arthur got hold of a paper, and was able to translate the word Eisenhower. We thought he was a bloody German. We'd never heard of him.

We had no library when we went to the mines. We'd each taken one book. Some fellows took the Bible. I took The Essays of Elia. Those were the only books we had. It was an odd funny thing in the mining camp, books became in such short supply that you took pages 1–50 of, say, The Murder of Roger Ackroyd and you gave it to somebody else.

So you'd get guys coming round the billets saying, 'Anybody got pages 145–190 of such and such a book?' We read books by instalments. I managed to keep mine. No one wanted to read it.

After the end of the war in Europe we thought maybe the Japanese would go easy. But they didn't. They were getting all sorts of propaganda. The women were out practising bayonet drill, the kids were out practising throwing hand-grenades – pieces of rock – on the sand outside the camp, and the newspapers were full of how to defend the country against the American invader. The Jap guards were saying, 'The Americans come, you die!' They cut down on the food because they were beginning to starve themselves. And they kept reminding us of what they were going to do to us. It was terrifying.

But there was one big act of kindness that happened to me after the German capitulation. I was working down the mine and Taff and I had just been given a beating for not working hard enough. We discovered that, in addition to the pit props, if you got a great big piece of copper ore into the buggy, that filled up quite a big space. I lifted this huge piece, and as I got to the edge of the buggy my stomach muscles just collapsed and the thing dropped over the edge and cut the end of my finger off. I was bleeding like a stuck pig and Taff was flapping around saying, 'You're going to die!'

He went and fetched the Japanese foreman. The Japanese didn't think you were sick until there was blood all over the place. So he saw the blood and got on the blower to the surface and down came the Japanese sergeant we called the King of Jazz, because he used pomade on his hair. He saw the blood and marched me back to camp two solid bloody miles with me leaving a river of blood behind me. We had two doctors in that camp. Harold Knox wanted to know why I hadn't brought the end of my finger, because he could have sewn it back on. He could only put a tourniquet round my arm, because he had no anaesthetic. The little bone was sticking up and had to come off. It wasn't pleasant because the nail-bed was still intact and he had to get the nail to go over the end of the bone. He did it. But he had to cut the end of the bone with a pair of scissors, and I nearly went through the roof. After that a Japanese did my work for me for a solid month, wouldn't let me lift a thing. People won't believe that of the Japanese.

Kanyu Riverside Camp: Dysentry Ward
STANLEY G GIMSON

CORPORAL DEREK GLAISTER

7TH PARACHUTE BATTALION, GERMANY, 1945

When we got to the Rhine, myself and ten others came down near a farmhouse which had an 88 mm gun just outside it. Just before my feet touched the ground a bullet smashed through my left elbow, so I lay on my stomach and pretended to be dead. I saw nine of the others come down – some into trees. The Germans shot them as they hung there helpless – it was a sickening sight. I was in big trouble. I am left-handed and my left arm was useless. But when five Germans came towards me I got my Sten gun in my right hand and as they got close I fired and I think killed them all. Then I made for the farmhouse, hoping to get some help – but as I peered round a corner I saw German rifles poking out of every window. I tried to give myself some cover by throwing a smoke bomb, but just as I was making for the nearest ditch, a German SS officer came up and shot me in the back from ten yards with a Luger pistol. I spun round and fell down, and this officer grabbed my left arm and shoved it through the straps of my webbing, then he took hold of my water bottle, flung it in the ditch and looted whatever he could. I was worried that he'd finish me off with my knife but I had the presence of mind to lie on it and when he'd gone I got hold of it and threw it in the ditch. I lay there feeling pretty rough – my left arm was like a great black pudding by then, all swollen up – and watched those poor fellows swinging in the trees. Then one of our gliders came over, but the 88 mm cracked it open like an egg and the jeep, gun, blokes all fell out. Point-blank range – they couldn't miss at fifty feet.

Towards the evening I was still lying there, in one hell of a bloody mess. I was finding it difficult to breathe because the second bullet had touched my lungs. Then a couple of captured airborne soldiers came by – a glider pilot and Lance Corporal Butler from my own battalion – and they asked their German escort if they could pick me up. So they gave me a shot of morphine, which helped, and put me in this wheelbarrow. They carted me along in this farm wheelbarrow along a bumpy old road, until the Germans took them away for interrogation and I was wheeled on to a big mansion near Hamelken. At dusk a German lorry came along and two Jerries picked me up like a sack of spuds and dumped me in the back of the truck on top of some dead blokes sewn up in sacks. They must have thought I was dead. That was the first time I fainted – my wounds had opened up and were bleeding again.

I came to in a German toilet with my head near the pan. That was where all my troubles started. Two orderlies took me into an operating theatre and pulled my clothes off, which was very painful. They'd just been operating on some chap and they slithered me straight on to the aluminium table which was still covered in his blood. Then they put an ether mask over my face and out I went. I woke up five days later, my arm in a Nazi salute in plaster and paper bandages all around my back. No medicines or antibiotics. My back had opened up again as the stitches had come apart, so I was carried off to be restitched. When we got to the top of some massive stairs I was tipped off – deliberately I'm sure. I landed at the bottom on my head, breaking my nose and smashing the plaster. There was a hell of a row about it and those orderlies didn't appear again. They stitched me all up again and put another plaster on, still in a Nazi salute. Then they had a go at my nose with no anaesthetic. They probed about pulling bits of bone out but they went too close to my eye and damaged it so I've got permanent pain and double vision from that.

I lay in that hospital until the British arrived. They flew me over to the RAF Hospital at Wroughton and sent for my wife and parents as they didn't expect me to live. My father was also in hospital at the time, having his leg amputated as a result of World War I. When my mother and wife came into the ward they walked right past my bed – they didn't recognise me. I had pneumonia by then, so they put in a tube to drain off the fluid and sent me by ambulance to an orthopaedic unit. The tube came out in the ambulance, so they just pushed it in again, nearly choking me when it reached my lungs. When at last they got around to getting the German plaster off, one of the nurses fainted; the stench was bad enough, but the plaster was full of maggots, put in by the German doctor to eat the dead flesh. No wonder it itched. A surgeon took one look at my arm and said, 'Off', just like that. But there was a lady doctor, Miss Wagstaff, who said she'd like to have a go at saving it, since I was left-handed. The surgeon said it would take years and still might not work, but they tried. It took three years in hospital and fifty-five operations to get me where I am now, which is 80 per cent disabled.

Corporal Jack Sharpe

1st Battalion, Leicestershire Regiment,
Far East prisoner of war, 1945

In solitary confinement, every hour during the night the sentry would bang on the door and I would have to call 'yes' in Japanese, so long periods of sleep were impossible. Then for something to do they would just beat me up. I had a bucket for a toilet, three bowls of rice a day and a mug of dirty water. There was nothing for me to do but dream of home and my mother and hang on to the insult from the court martial. After fourteen months I was let out. The Japs cut my hair and beard and put me in another cell.

During the day we prisoners cut grass and worked on rope-making, but all the time the guards would just beat us. So many were dying. If they weren't dying they were executed. We had no doctor. The Japs began to worry about the reputation of the place and started moving some prisoners to Changi Jail, which had some medical facilities. They wanted to move me but I refused. I was so determined to walk out of Outram Road Jail a free man. My friends pleaded with me to go but I wouldn't. In the end I was the longest survivor in that jail. During that time I got scurvy, which made my eyes like balls of fire, all matter coming out. My mouth was all swollen and red raw. I could barely swallow. Then I got scabies, which killed so many. I was covered in scabs from head to foot. There was no treatment. Mother Nature or death took over. I kept saying, 'Keep going, keep going,' and months later the scabs disappeared. So many around me were starving to death or simply giving up.

The only time I faltered was when my best friend died. I couldn't see the sense in going on. But I had to. In May 1945 we heard about the end of the war in Europe so I was determined to stay alive. Then in August the American bombers arrived and blasted Singapore. Two days after the raid the Japs surrendered.

When the camp was relieved the lads picked me up like a conquering hero. As I was being carried out I saw the sign over the gate and I asked the lads to put me down. I was determined to walk for freedom. I managed a few steps, got outside and then the lads had to pick me up again. I had weighed eleven stone when I was captured – I was now only four.

I'd contracted dysentery and was unconscious for forty-eight hours in Changi. When I came round I saw the padre so I thought I was in heaven. Later, a really thoughtful NCO came into the ward and called me outside to sit on the verandah. He gave me thirty-eight letters, all from my mother. She had never believed I was dead and had written to me every month for more than three years. Reading them I just wept and wept. I thought of my dear mother and all the pain she had been through. That was the first time I'd allowed myself to cry. After a few weeks' rest I was flown to Bangalore to recover.

One day in Bangalore, I was sitting on my bed and feeling a bit low – and heard footsteps. I looked up and there was my older brother, Jess. I'd made him promise to stay home and look after our mother, but he had joined up. Now he had got special extended leave to come to find me. He stayed with me and taught me to walk again as he had done when I was a child. All the same, it was a year before I was fit enough to go back to England. There at long last I saw my mother.

12

THE KINDNESS OF STRANGERS

Often when warring for he wist not what,
An enemy-solider, passing by one weak,
Has tendered water, wiped the burning cheek,
And cooled the lips so black and clammed and hot;

Then gone his way, and maybe quite forgot
The deed of grace amid the roar and reek;
Yet larger vision than loud arms bespeak
He there has reached, although he has known it not.

For natural mindsight, triumphing in the act
Over the throes of artificial rage,
Has thuswise muffled victory's peal of pride,
Rended to ribands policy's specious page
That deals but with evasion, code and pact,
And war's apology wholly stultified.

'OFTEN WHEN WARRING'
THOMAS HARDY

Sergeant Richard Tobin

Hood Battalion, Royal Naval Division, 1914

On a brisk October morning we arrived in the threatened port of Antwerp. The people lined the street, they cheered, they waved, there were flowers and wine. The war was young and so were we. We felt gallant, they felt relieved. Out to the trenches we went. We settled, opened reserve ammunition, fixed our bayonets and said, 'Now let 'em come!'

Night came but not the enemy. We posted sentries and settled down, but not for long. Heavy rifle fire broke out on the left, then on the right. We manned the firing step and peered over. Searchlights from the fort swept the front. We could see nothing. We held our fire and felt neglected.

Morning came but still no enemy. Suddenly high in the sky was a train-like rumble and whistle followed by an explosion. Smoke and flame shot up in the city. An old hand said, 'Them's howitzer shells. The bastards must be a dozen miles away.'

At intervals throughout the day these rumbling shells rolled over, flames shooting up after each explosion. Then the oil tanks by the dockside were alight. The smoke gathered over the port to join the autumn mists and the glow from the fires. It looked like hell. We could only wait. We felt useless.

On the 8th of October an order came, 'Prepare to move.' Just at the back of our trench was a deserted farm. Odd men had gone scrounging in the farm and as we were about to move, an officer shouted to me, 'Sergeant, see the farm's clear.' Coming back through an outhouse, I saw some pails of milk and I did a most unsoldierly action. I emptied my half-full water-bottle and filled it full of milk. We soon got orders to move to the right and onto the road and we thought, 'Ah, they won't come to us. We're going out to them.'

On reaching the road, instead of turning left to the enemy, we turned right to the city and we received the most deadening, soul-racking order a soldier can receive. Retreat. We picked our way through the burning buildings, past the flaming oil tanks to the flaming pontoon bridge the engineers had built for us to cross and then destroy. On each side of the bridge stood hordes of refugees of every kind – children, women, nuns, priests. This was the bridge of sighs. They had been stopped so we could cross. The flare from the burning lit their faces, expressionless and hopeless, and we felt ashamed. An officer called to me, 'Sergeant! Shout "Break Step!"' It should have been 'Break Hearts!'

We were soon across and in open country. After a few miles we arrived at a Belgian village, marched into a cobbled square, and the orders were, 'Rest where you stand. Be ready for any alarm.'

'Sad' is not a soldier's word – browned off, fed up, yes, but the only time a soldier is really and deeply sad is when his line of duty takes him among refugees, those weary, shuffling, hopeless columns, chiefly women, children and the aged, carrying or pushing-pulling pram, wheelbarrow, farm cart, piled high with their world and often perched on top – granny. If his unit is rushing forward, pressing these weary souls aside so that the troops could get ahead and engage the enemy – he is sad, but feels he's giving them hope, but if his army is in retreat and they are in the press at the side of the road, the troops and guns rush past to take up another fighting position, he is sad but ashamed because he knows they think he is running away.

Just by was the church. Straw had been placed all round

it and there were dark forms lying on it. My pal and I moved to the straw and were about to settle when we noticed two young women. With a mumbled apology, we were moving away when a voice said in good English, 'Don't go, please.' We squatted down, and I saw that one of the young women was nursing a whimpering baby. For something to say, I said, 'Is your baby all right?' With a sad smile she said, 'It's not my baby. I don't even know its mother. We are tired and hungry.' My pal and I emptied from our haversacks two tins of sardines and army biscuits. She sighed and said, 'The baby needs milk.' 'Milk!' I swung my water-bottle round. I think even the baby was surprised. Quite soon, we fell in and marched away. The British government had lost a water-bottle, but a baby found a meal.

Sergeant Stefan Westmann

29th Division, German Army, 1914

All of a sudden the enemy fire ceased. Complete silence came over the battlefield. Then one of the chaps in my shell-hole said, 'I wonder what they are up to,' and another answered, 'Perhaps they are getting tea.' A third one said, 'Don't be a fool, do you see what I see?' And we looked over the brim of our shell-hole and there between the brick heaps, out had come a British soldier with a Red Cross flag that he waved at us. And he was followed by stretcher-bearers who came slowly towards us and collected our wounded. We got up, still completely dumb from fear of death, and helped them to bring our wounded into our trenches.

LIEUTENANT MONTAGUE CLEEVE

ROYAL GARRISON ARTILLERY, SOMME, 1916

I came across a sergeant lying dead on the ground with his hand on an open bible. It was a Douai Bible and from that I knew he was a Catholic. The shrapnel was pouring over our heads, but I closed his eyes, then closed the book and put it in my pocket before crawling back to the front line. Later on I took his address from it and sent it home to his widow.

SUB LIEUTENANT WILLIAM BENHAM

HAWKE BATTALION, ROYAL NAVAL DIVISION, 1917

When I got to France there was snow all over the Western Front. There had been a very severe frost and there were lots of frozen corpses that couldn't be moved or buried. Before I got there the Germans had made an early dawn attack across the snow, wearing white sheets and using whitened rifles. They'd managed to drive back the last battalion with great casualties because they hadn't been seen, and we still had several bodies lying there frozen, unable to be moved because of the frost.

When at last the frost broke, we were able to get the bodies down, and one of them was Sub Lieutenant Alan Campbell, the son of Mrs Patrick Campbell, the actress. We managed to get these bodies to a burial ground five or six miles behind the front line, and I had the unenviable job of being in charge of the burial party. We carried the men over the trenches until we got to where the transport could come, then the bodies were put in GS wagons and taken down for burial. Afterwards, I turned to walk the five miles back to the line. It was a pouring wet afternoon, with squally sleet going down our necks and the roads full of puddles and shell-holes.

My orderly, a dour Scot, was with me and presently we heard the sound of a car coming along. My orderly commented, 'Some ruddy staff wallah, Sir.' I said, 'Yes, I expect so,' but instead of swishing past us in a shower of mud and water, the car stopped and a cheerful young voice said, 'Would you chaps like a lift?' I was being offered a lift by the Prince of Wales, who was on one of his tours of the front line. My orderly sat beside his driver while he and I sat in the back with his equerry. We had a long talk and I found him more than interesting. After three or four miles his way was different from mine, so he put us down and we trudged on back to the trenches.

Mrs Scott-Hartley

Voluntary Aid Detachment, 1917

I was working as a VAD in a hospital in Bulstrode Street, in West London. It was a big house taken over by the authorities, and all the cases were shell-shocked, which meant they couldn't keep their hands or their heads still. I had to hold them gently behind their heads and feed them, and I also used to write their love letters. Many couldn't say what they wanted to say, or they were probably too shy to tell me, but I used to write them for them, and let them read them back. I used to say, 'My dearest darling,' you know, and 'Forever yours'.

Dunkirk: Embarkation of Wounded, May 1940
EDWARD BAWDEN

CORPORAL FRANK HURRELL

3RD FIELD ARMY WORKSHOP, ROYAL ARMY ORDINANCE CORPS, DUNKIRK EVACUATION, 1940

When we got into Dover we were put into old customs sheds. In there were these ladies from the women's services – the Red Shield Club – all the various ladies' associations. I had no tunic – I'd lost it – and one of the elderly ladies took off her fur coat and put it round me whilst I sat down, and gave me a cup of tea. Then she produced a stamped envelope – stamped and sealed – and she said, 'Right. Address it to go to your wife or whoever. Put the message on the back. Use it like a postcard – it will get there quicker.'

CAPTAIN ANTHONY RHODES

———

253 FIELD COMPANY, ROYAL ENGINEERS, DUNKIRK, 1940

About an hour after the setting of the sun came the familiar drone, as the Luftwaffe came along and dropped flares, so they could see us. The sky was alight as they dropped their bombs.

Where the boats came in, there was a little nucleus at the head of the water, and then a great queue, running up from the dunes behind, perhaps a quarter of a mile long. The idea was just like a London bus queue. Nobody told us to do that – it seemed the decent thing to do. There must have been about ten or twelve of these queues running up. When we were halfway up in our queue, the bombing started, and one man ran to the head of the queue when he saw a boat coming. A naval officer turned on him and said, 'Look, go back to the place you've come from – or I'll shoot you.' He said it very loudly for everybody to hear, and the man went back with his tail between his legs.

We'd been on the fishing boat, I suppose, an hour at the most. We were trying to lie down – we hadn't had any sleep for several days – when there was a cry came up. All the men who'd been rescued and were on the fishing boat were to be transferred to a destroyer.

When we got on board, an officer came round and said, 'We shall shortly be sailing for Blighty – England, Home and Beauty.' I went right down into the hold, where I was put into a hammock, because I was dead – we all were.

At Dover when we arrived, there were a whole series of trains. All the units had been dispersed and one hadn't got any of one's own men – one was isolated, and we were simply told, 'Each of you get on the train and get up to London. You'll find the RTO at Waterloo, and he'll tell you you'll have a couple of days to go home, and where you're to assemble to join your new units.' So we went up in the trains – they were full of civilians who got in and were going to their office in London. Sitting next to you, there might be a man who was going up to his bank. One very nice man, a civilian, pressed into my hand two half crowns – which was rather nice.

REVEREND DOUGLAS THOMPSON

CHAPLAIN, ESSEX REGIMENT, WESTERN DESERT, 1942

We got stuck. We were ordered to stay just five miles west-wards of the Alamein line, to hold the Germans back while the Alamein line was completed and Montgomery's plans came into effect for the push forward that he made later. The South Africans were in entrenchments, deep fortifica-tions on our right. The New Zealanders were out on the desert on our left, and we were in the middle of this line. It had to hold for perhaps forty-eight hours while things happened behind us.

I was up with the Regimental Aid Post, just behind the front line of troops – the first dugouts – and between there and the second line. That's the station for a chaplain in an infantry division, and I was there with the doctor. We made for the hole which was to be the Regimental Aid Post. I was there, going from there up to the front line, back and forwards, and fetching chaps out who were wounded, with a couple of drivers. I was in that position when the line fell. We kept out the German motorised infantry, but then they pushed down the tanks on us. Then Rommel's own corps came down in its tanks, and it was a case of the sand and the rifle against the tank – which was no bargain at all, so they mopped us up. As they came through, there was one tank commander standing in the top of his tank in the turret with a heavy rifle, potting off British chaps in holes. He came as far as the Regimental Aid Post. I was outside it with a couple of drivers who'd been hurt. He just took one pot at me and I got it in the liver. Then a young German sergeant, who was a very decent lad, came up, and he talked to my driver, who asked him for a stretcher for me. The young German gave him one and got four of our chaps to pick me up. I was taken in and they laid the stretcher down just beside Rommel's command car.

I was moved by ambulance. My driver put a young artilleryman, who'd been shot through both legs, in beside me, so the two of us were humped off across the desert. This German driver had made friends with my driver, and he took us from one hospital to another. He couldn't get us in. On one occasion we got to an Italian hospital and the chaplain came out and gave him a drink. He wouldn't give me a drink because this German doctor had said I had three days to live, but if I didn't eat and drink, I'd stay alive for at least three more days. He just gave me a kiss and a sweet to suck. We got back and we landed up at a place just a mile or two out of Sidi Barrani, in an Italian hospital which was full of German troops which our RAF had caught coming ashore. They were in a shocking mess. I was laid with them in the hospital.

The chap next door to me had got third-degree burns. When the Italian orderlies removed his clothes, they took most of his skin off with them. He was in a shocking state. Sometimes he was calling for a maid, or a servant, in a Channel Islands café, for beer, and then he would change his tune. He would begin to cry for his mum. He was just raving. I put out one hand and took hold of his hand and held it. I think he must have thought it was his mother's hand, because it quietened him down, and he died in peace before the morning came.

Ursula Betts

British anthropologist working with refugees from Burma (known as 'the White Queen of the Nagas'), 1943

I and four Nagas went down and ran a canteen – supposedly for Europeans – and we did keep European food for the Europeans coming down on the refugee trains. But of course we got swamped every day by the two thousand-odd Indian refugees who were streaming out. And the temperature was in the nineties – up in the hundreds during the day. It was very hot, and we got through sixty gallons of tea in the day.

We went down to the railway station, and the water for the tea had to be carried in four-gallon kerosene tins with a wooden bar across. You carried one in each hand, and the five us carried sixty gallons that way. We stacked the cans – at first we just had open fireplaces on the platform with iron bars across to sit the tins on, but as we got a bit more organised, the railway built us a little shed with proper brick compartments. We went down to the railway coal bunkers and came staggering back with loads and loads of coal – it was very sooty coal. I used to go down a blonde and come back a Carmen brunette – hair absolutely black with smoke and soot. About five, the train would pull in, and we'd be swamped by these mobs and mobs and mobs of clamouring Indian refugees. And poor devils, it was very hot. They were packed into the trains. Half of them were sick with dysentery and cholera. If anybody died on the train they used to try and get the body out for proper burial or cremation.

Then, of course, the trains were being shunted into sidings for hours at a time. They were supposed to go right through. There was a complete breakdown of communication in all possible directions. You fended for yourself, but they were supposed to get through in eight hours. It was believed in Shillong the trains were getting through in eight hours. If they got through in twenty-four, everybody was lucky. And, of course, the body would start to go off, and they just chucked the corpses out on the line.

The wounded were marvellous. They'd be leaning out of the windows and see me doubling down the platform with my cans. Having had their tea, the train would pull out with everybody hanging out of the windows and waving and shouting, 'See you on the road to Mandalay!' Quite often they were badly wounded men who had smelly wounds, whose clothes were in a mess. One of my tasks was to do a patrol down the train – look in every carriage to see if there was anybody who wasn't getting anything.

I found one chap who'd obviously been next to a friend who'd been hit, because there was blood all over his uniform, and I said, 'Look here, go up and get some tea. Can you walk?' 'Oh yes, I can walk – but there's ladies there, and I didn't like to go.' I said, 'All right, here you are.' And passed him in his tea and bun. He was very grateful.

Sergeant George Teal

Coldstream Guards, Guards Armoured Division, Germany, 1945

We avoided Hamburg and stopped outside a town called Rotenburg, where we could see the Jerries walking about looking at us at the end of the road. Eventually, we moved in. My officer told me to take a row of houses, so I went in one house and said, 'Get all the civvies out. We're taking over this row of houses,' but inside the house was a man and a woman with a blind little girl. I think she'd been born blind and that melted my heart, so I said to the woman, 'Your husband better get out but you can stay in the cellar and keep out of sight of the officers.' She was terrified – she thought we were going to do her.

Eventually she calmed down and a couple of days later there was a knock on the door and a young lad in German uniform was stood there, about fifteen or sixteen years old, and he was her son. He'd been taken prisoner in Denmark by the British who'd kicked him off his backside and said, 'Go home!' and he'd walked back from Denmark. His mother was delighted, but when he came in and took his jacket and shirt off, he was alive with bloody lice – like all the German soldiers, because they didn't have DDT. So I said, 'Go outside!' and his mother said, 'No,' but I said, 'No, he has to. Lice cause typhus!' We stripped him bollock-naked, poor lad, burnt his uniform and dusted him with DDT from head to foot. He had little scratch marks over his entire body. Covered in them.

13

THE HUMAN COST

In Flanders fields the poppies blow
Between the crosses, row on row
That mark our place; and in the sky
The larks, still bravely singing, fly
Scarce heard amid the guns below.

We are the Dead. Short days ago
We lived, felt dawn, saw sunset glow.
Loved and were loved, and now we lie
In Flanders fields.

Take up our quarrel with the foe;
To you from failing hands we throw
The torch; be yours to hold it high.
If ye break faith with us who die
We shall not sleep, though poppies grow
In Flanders fields.

'IN FLANDERS FIELDS'
JOHN McCREA

Trooper Walter Becklade

5th Cavalry Brigade, 1915

I was wounded in the battle and taken to a casualty clearing station. I was beside a fellow who had got his arms bandaged up – I'd simply got my right arm bandaged. He was trying to light his pipe but couldn't get on very well so I offered to fill and light it for him. But when I'd lit it I suddenly realised he had nowhere to put it, as he'd had his lower jaw blown away. So I smoked the pipe and he smelt the tobacco, that was all the poor chap could have.

Private W. A. Quinton

2nd Battalion, Bedfordshire Regiment, gas attack, 1915

The men came tumbling from the front line. I've never seen men so terror-stricken, they were tearing at their throats and their eyes were glaring out. Blood was streaming from those who were wounded and they were tumbling over one another. Those who fell couldn't get up because of the panic of the men following them, and eventually they were piled up two or three high in this trench.

One chap had his hand blown off and his wrist was fumbling around, tearing at his throat. In fact it was the most gruesome sight I'd seen in the war. We manned the firing step, thinking the Germans would be on their way over by this time, but strangely enough they didn't attack us.

When we got relieved we made our way four or five miles

back from the line. Going along this country road we were just like a rabble – you know how men are when they're tired and exhausted. Then we passed by an orchard where there must have been two or three hundred men. They were reeling around tearing at their throats, their faces black, while an RAMC sergeant stood by and, well, I've never known a man look so despondent. He said, 'Look at the poor bastards, and we can't do a thing for them.'

PRIVATE HARRY PATCH

7TH BATTALION, DUKE OF CORNWALL'S LIGHT INFANTRY, 1917

I can still see the bewilderment and fear on the men's faces when we went over the top. C and D Company was support, A and B had had to go at the front line. All over the battle-field the wounded were lying down, English and German all asking for help. We weren't like the Good Samaritan in the Bible, we were the robbers who passed by and left them. You couldn't help them. I came across a Cornishman, ripped from shoulder to waist with shrapnel, his stomach on the ground beside him in a pool of blood. As I got to him he said, 'Shoot me,' he was beyond all human aid. Before we could even draw a revolver he had died. He just said, 'Mother.' I will never forget it.

The Receiving Room: The 42nd Stationary Hospital
SIR WILLIAM ORPEN

GUNNER WILLIAM TOWERS

ROYAL FIELD ARTILLERY, 1917

I was one of fifteen drivers taking thirty horses to try and get ammunition through to our battery's guns. Each driver had two horses, and you had a pack for each horse with eight shells in it. The Germans were watching for anybody who tried to come through and the first few times we were shelled and had to come back. Sergeant Emsley said, 'Towers, I want you to come up front about six yards behind me and when I give the signal, we gallop.'

So I was following the sergeant, but just after we set off

the Germans dropped a shell right by us and that was it. I remember going up in the air and landing on the floor. I wasn't in any pain but I could see that shrapnel had gone into my kneecap. It was a joy, actually, because I thought it wasn't too bad and therefore I'd soon be home and out of it all. Two men from RAMC came over and one of them got a bottle of iodine and tipped it into the hole in my knee. Oh! The pain was terrific. They ran some bandages round it and put me on a stretcher.

I couldn't see where we were going because all around was barren land, but all of a sudden they stopped and put the stretcher down. I said, 'What's up?' and they said, 'You're all right, don't worry,' and went to a trap-door. They lifted it up and they put the stretcher on a slide and lowered it down. There was a proper hospital underneath. It had been a German hospital. There was a full staff of hospital people there. They took me down to a theatre and a sister pressed a white mask over my face, the anaesthetic hit me and the next thing I knew, I was waking up on a train.

I was in a carriage on a stretcher fixed on the wall, and when I looked round Sergeant Emsley was next to me. He'd been wounded in the leg as well. They took us to a hospital at Étaples and then put me in a bed and fitted me with a Thomas splint, a round wooden ring with iron bars and a footrest. The pain from my knee was getting terrible, so when I saw an officer coming up with his arm around two sisters and laughing, I said, 'Excuse me, Sir, could you have a look at my knee? The pain is driving me crazy.'

He came over and he stank of whisky. When the nurses took the bandages off he said, 'Oh, there's fluid above the knee. We'll tap that tonight.' So they came for me to go to the theatre and I thought, 'Thank God for that.' But when I woke up in early hours of the morning I thought, 'Oh my

God. My leg's gone.' They'd guillotined it off without saying a word. There had been no hint at all that I was going to lose my leg. They hadn't even looked at it until I asked the doctor.

That day, I prayed to die. All I could think of were the men who stood begging on street corners with a crutch with a tin can. And I was a footballer and that was finished. It was terrible. Late in the afternoon, a nurse came up, took the blanket off and started tearing the gauze off that had dried on. As she was pulling it I think I called her every name I knew. I said, 'You're inhuman, woman!' but she didn't take any notice, she must have been deaf. She could have wet it, which would have made it come off easily, but she wouldn't. I was in agony.

After that, they put me on a boat and I was taken to Stockport General Hospital. A civilian doctor, Mr Fenwick, came to look at me and when he took the bandages off the smell was terrible. The flesh had receded, two inches of bone stuck out and it had gone black. He said, 'Send a telegram for his mother and father to come right away.' He thought I was going to die. He told a sister to get a bowl of sterilised water with peroxide in it and that my leg had to be syringed with this solution every four hours. And then it started to get better. The wound became beautiful clean red flesh. Mr Fenwick said, 'We're going to win, Willie.' My parents came, and my future wife, whom I'd met when I was home on leave. I think it was her that pulled me through. And Mr Fenwick was an angel. He arranged for a friend of his, a surgeon who specialised in amputations, to re-amputate the leg and make a proper stump. He did it and it was perfect. Everybody seeing it said, 'What a beautiful job.'

Private William Tilley

Clerk with Base Depot, Royal Army Service Corps, Dunkirk, 1940

It's something that you look back on with astonishment – that from the little trawler which picked us up, we were able to watch the final lurching and sinking of the Lancastria. She overturned completely in the end, so you could see the propellers, and even then, you could see men standing on her upturned bows, afraid to jump into the sea – and even try to propel themselves away. That was a pretty awful sight to behold, because you realised that when she went down, they would just be sucked down with her. That was awful.

Colin Ryder-Richardson

Welsh boy, evacuee on *City of Benares*, September, 1940

I think my father could see, with a huge German army standing off the French coast, there was what you called a sense of urgency about us leaving. So it was arranged for me to go to New York. We had left Liverpool on *City of Benares* four days earlier – then we were hit by torpedoes.

There was a loud bang, a very loud bang, and almost immediately a smell of, presumably, cordite – it was an unmistakable smell. There were a lot of shouts so I immediately knew what was happening and I had a slight problem because I was in my pyjamas and I hadn't got my lifejacket, but I immediately put it on as I got out of bed. I put on my slippers – and then I had a dressing gown and now I had a problem. Did I put the dressing gown under the lifejacket or on top of the lifejacket? It wouldn't go over the top of the lifejacket and things were beginning to happen rather fast. I thought I mustn't panic, on the other hand I must think these things through rationally.

To make things worse, there was a Force 10 gale. The ship's nurse held my hand and got me on to a lifeboat. It was freezing cold and the boat was waterlogged. I clung on to the nurse, then as the night went on, lots of people were dying. This man on the boat gently suggested to me that I should release the ship's nurse, as in his view she was dead, and I was so cold that really I couldn't move my arms and legs. I was holding on for my life, holding on to her, and I didn't really want to let go of her because I felt that I would then lose whatever resource that I had in my arms. Then it became apparent to me that she was dying, and possibly was dead, and I still couldn't let go of her. I just felt that at any minute we might be rescued and there might be the possibility of life within her and it seemed to be so. There was no need to let go of her – it would be cruel to let go of her. She was a person even though she was patently dead and her mouth was open.

They said, 'Come on, Colin, let go of her, let go of her,' and I just couldn't do it. Eventually the storm solved the problem and she was swept away. We were getting fewer and fewer in numbers. There was a young man, a student, an Englishman as far as I know, who said he wanted something to eat or drink and he started drinking the seawater and everybody was telling him, 'No,' in between the waves, because it was very difficult to talk. The waves were just flowing over you. He was insistent on it and the next minute he jumped from the relative safety of the lifeboat into the sea.

SERGEANT STEPHEN DAWSON

339 BATTERY, 104TH FIELD REGIMENT,
ROYAL ARTILLERY, 1941

We knew something was going on when we were ordered
to travel up to Tobruk in about January 1941, because of the
tension in the air – but we were just ordinary soldiers at that
time, and nobody told us anything. On the way there, the
convoy came to a brief halt. We'd found the body of a young
British officer. He'd been shot across the chest. He had blue
eyes and fair hair, with a revolver in his hand – just this one
solitary object lying in the middle of the vast desert. We
started to dig a grave and I made a little plywood cross but
suddenly we were told to go again, and we had to leave him
there – somebody's son.

CORPORAL VERNON SCANNELL

7TH BATTALION ARGYLL AND SUTHERLAND
HIGHLANDERS, WESTERN DESERT, 1942

One of the most memorable and still chilling and night-
marish things is hearing the voices of those who'd been badly
wounded, their voices raised in terror and pain. I can
remember one particular sergeant who'd always seemed to
me almost a kind of father figure. He wasn't that much older,
but at that time I was twenty and he'd probably be pushing
thirty, which seemed to me a lot older. He was rather a
tough, leathery kind of man. He was badly wounded and
hearing his voice sort of sobbing and calling for his mother

seemed to be so demeaning and humiliating and dreadful. I felt a kind of shock that I can't fully understand even now, because he'd been reduced to a baby.

Zero Hour: The Mareth Offensive
JACK CHADDOCK

STAFF SERGEANT GEOFFREY BARKWAY

GLIDER PILOT REGIMENT, D-DAY, 1944

I felt this bang in my wrist, and that was it. The next thing I remember was being in this house on the floor with my arm in a sling across my chest. My right arm was pretty mucky. Because I had lost a lot of blood, I was terribly thirsty all the time. The next thing I remember is lying on the beach, under this tarpaulin cover. Then we were put on a DUKW and taken out to a tank landing ship. The doctor had got a sort of emergency theatre. He redressed my arm, which by this time had begun to smell a bit because gangrene had set in. After a while, I felt wet and uncomfortable, so I called a nurse and she turned the bedclothes back and there was all blood everywhere. I had haemorrhaged, she left the clothes turned back and rushed off to get the sister. I looked down, and instead of my arm across my chest as I thought, there was nothing there. My arm had gone. Which was a bit shattering.

CAPTAIN FRANK KING

11TH PARACHUTE BATTALION, 1944

With five minutes to go before the jump, the crew chief should have been busy rechecking all our equipment. He was a nice young American encased in nylon body armour, but at that moment he made me angry because he was lounging in his seat, a picture of contented idleness. 'Bloody Air Force,' I thought, and shouted at him. There was no reaction. It was only then that I noticed a large and growing pool of blood beneath his seat. He was dead, shot through the floor of the plane.

PRIVATE FRITZ JELTSCH

5TH COMPANY, 214 REGIMENT, GERMAN ARMY

After Normandy, in early August 1944, our position came under fire. We were surrounded, they were shooting from every direction, and almost everyone in my unit died. It was awful.

I remember one of my mates was running just in front

of me, and we were attacked again. He was hit and he fell on me, so I got hold of him and dragged him to one side. An ambulance came along, and I was crying out to this first-aid man, 'Can I put him in?' and he said to me, 'It's too late. You can't do anything for him any more. Save yourself.' So I left him and ran into a field to join the other few survivors. I couldn't do anything about it, but it's laid on my conscience for years.

Ronald McGill

Post Office telegraph boy in London, 1944

I was a fourteen-year-old telegraph boy in London. I grew up very, very quickly because my job was basically delivering death telegrams. The girls in the instrument room used to say to us, 'This is a priority. It's death.' When we came down the road, we used to see the curtains go – they'd twitch – because we were feared. People knew our uniforms and they were scared of us. We were told to knock on either side of the house you were delivering to – it was better for a neighbour to break the news, I suppose. I remember one occasion, delivering a death telegram to a house near Hammersmith Bridge. I saw the curtain twitch as I knocked on either side and the lady in question came out. 'That's for me, isn't it?' she said. 'Yes,' I said and she just fainted. She fell on the ground. Her two little kiddies ran out and saw their mother lying there. What was I supposed to do? I was fourteen. I knew nothing. She hadn't even opened the telegram. I managed to get another neighbour to come along and we pulled her into the house. The lady woke up and she and the neighbour opened the telegram. It was her husband – he'd been killed. I just stood there. I didn't know what to do. When I got home that night, I told my mother and she cried as well.

HANS BEHRENS

9TH PANZER DIVISION, ARDENNES, 1944

I remember Christmas – we were at our most westerly point between Bastogne and St Hubert in the Ardennes. The turning point for me about the folly and the terror war instils, was that Bastogne was taken several times, to and fro, and one of those times we were coming down a hill and on the left side was a Sherman tank with its turret open. I don't know why, but I got out of my vehicle and looked down inside in this tank. What I saw there was a young man absolutely charred black and one clean hole in the side of the turret. At that moment I realised that this man could be me and that he had a mother and a father. It became hard to carry on.

KARIN BUSCH

GERMAN SCHOOLGIRL, DRESDEN, 1945

Before the 13th February 1945, there had not been any air activity over Dresden. We had warning exercises but that was all. It was considered a safe city and we believed that culture-loving people would never destroy a jewel like Dresden. We felt safe in that knowledge. A few anti-aircraft guns had been placed around Dresden but a few nights before the raid, they were removed. No shelters had been built in Dresden. The only defence measure was to provide buckets of sand.

My father and brother were both at home on leave and my mother had broken into her food rationing cards and bought a lot of food and then, the following evening, the bombing started. At about half-past nine I was sitting sewing a bag for a friend when I heard a roaring noise. I didn't know what it was – we had no warning at all. In case of an air raid, you were supposed to receive a pre-warning and then a full warning but now we heard the full warning and suddenly the town was lit up by flares in the shape of Christmas trees all over the sky. Then hell broke loose. It was terrible, absolutely terrible.

We ran into the cellar. My mother grabbed two Japanese lacquer boxes – one had food in it and the other had all our documents – and we ran down. My father and brother, who were both in uniform, began organising people and telling them what to do. It was very hot and we heard all this noise going on when suddenly a bomb fell into the cellar. It didn't go off, but total pandemonium broke out and we tried to climb out. I tried to help my mother out, I held her and tried to force her through but as I did, I lost my grip on her and she disappeared.

Outside, I was hit by an inferno of wind and firestorm. It was like looking into a huge burning oven. I saw my twin brother sitting down, holding his eyes. He couldn't see, so I held him and together we were swept along by the storm. Flames were licking all around us and somehow we found ourselves by the River Elbe. I could see phosphorus dancing on the water, so for people throwing themselves into the river to get away from the fire, there was no escape. There were bodies everywhere and the gasmasks that people were wearing were melting into their faces. The massive throng of people was moving aimlessly and we started looking for a cellar to hide in, but in every cellar we looked into, we saw people sitting dead because the fires had sucked the oxygen out and suffocated them. I have no idea how long the hell lasted – time had no meaning when all this was going on.

I looked around and I saw the whole city in ruins. Everything, all the beautiful churches, everything was destroyed. We stood on Marshallstraße with its huge houses – now a mass of rubble with a few chimney stacks standing out. When I called out to someone I thought I knew, one of these chimneystacks fell down just from the echo of my voice. My brother had lost his sight from the heat. One eye recovered later but the other did not.

We found our father and older brother by calling out their names and together we went back to the cellar where we had first taken shelter. Inside, I saw a pile of ashes in the shape of a person. You know when you put wood into a furnace and it burns and becomes red hot and it keeps its shape with an inner glow but when you touch it, it disintegrates? That's what this was – the shape of a person but nothing left of the body. I didn't know who it was but then I saw a pair of earrings in the ashes. I knew the earrings. It was my mother.

BOMBARDIER MARTIN ADDINGTON

ROYAL ARTILLERY, ATTACHED TO ROYAL MARINE COMMANDO, GERMANY, 1945

I can remember one town we went through. As soon as they saw our green berets, they shouted out, 'Churchill's butchers!'

and slammed the doors and windows and bars. They were scared of us. They thought we were like the SS, I think. They must have heard terrible rumours about the Commandos. We'd been through so much, we just took it. One particular incident I'll never forget. One of our mates got mail – which was very rare – he got mail from home to say that his whole family had been bombed and killed. Well, that sent him berserk. They shouldn't have given him the letter – but not knowing, they should have opened it first. The first thing he did was to burst into a house. We followed him. He burst in on this family, lined them all up in a bedroom and held them at gun-point. Then he went through their belongings shouting, 'You've got this! My wife never had this! What's this? My kids never had this!'

David Bradford

British volunteer medical student at Belsen, Germany, 1945

A lot of them were starving. They hadn't had solid food for a long time and the only thing you could give them was fluid to get them used to it. A lot of them had been in the camp for a number of years but I think the reason why Belsen was so bad was that as the British advanced from the West and the Russians advanced from the East, many inmates were being brought into this part of Germany and so the numbers were swollen by people from other camps. At Bergen, which was the military establishment in the next village to Belsen, there was a room which was full of watches which had been taken from the inmates. There was another room full of human hair because they were nearly all shaved

– their hair was cut off before they were incinerated. There was another room full of other trinkets. It was beyond imagination. In our little hutted hospital, we had a family come in – two brothers and a sister all under twenty. The girl had been looking after her two brothers but then one of the brothers died and she clung on to him. She clung on and she wouldn't let go and eventually several of us had to drag her off his body so that we could take his corpse outside.

GEOFFREY SHERRING

MERCHANT NAVY RADIO OPERATOR, FAR EAST PRISONER OF WAR IN NAGASAKI, 1945

The day the bomb was dropped was beautiful to start with, with very little cloud. It was for this reason that the secondary target, which was Nagasaki, was selected by the bombers after they'd got over their primary target. They'd gone to the primary target and found it covered with cloud, and had therefore gone hurrying south to Nagasaki to give us the benefit of the bomb. We had a practically clear sky and a nice southerly breeze, but our foremen at the works had been terrified by the news that had been spreading throughout Japan about atomic bombing.

We didn't know this, of course. We knew that they were very, very air-raid-conscious. We went down to the foundry where we had an air-raid warning, and were immediately taken back to the camp because we had, by this time, begun digging trenches in our encampment as air-raid shelters. We went down into the shelters and when the 'raiders passed' signal was given, we all fell in and marched down to the foundry again – where, to our surprise, we found nobody.

There were no foremen or work people there to take over from us. What had happened, of course, was that they'd all left their place of work and gone away, having heard about the atomic bombing of Hiroshima. So we were all marched back to camp again.

I was working with an Australian whose name was Bernard O'Keefe. I said to him, 'There's nobody about – let's nip in there and have a smoke.' This we did, and it must have been a couple of minutes to eleven. I had a burning glass, and we each had a cigarette end somewhere about us, so we set alight our cigarettes with the sunlight, and retreated back into the trench, which was roofed, to smoke in peace. The atomic bomb went off whilst we were in there. Bernie said to me, 'I can hear a car on the road.' I said, 'Don't be ridiculous – there's no petrol in Japan, let alone cars – it must be an aeroplane.' He said, 'I'm going out to have a look.'

He began crawling away from me towards the hole in the roof of the trench that he could get out of. As he did so, and I was looking after him, I saw the flash from the bomb – which was exactly like the sort of bluish light that you get from an electrical welding operation. It was very blue, and it came in exactly the opposite direction from the sun's rays – it completely eclipsed them. It was this thin, blue blazing light, shining down a square hole in front of Bernie, who hadn't, fortunately, reached the hole – or he would have been burned too. Then we heard the vibration and shaking, which wasn't a bang by any means. It was a continuous shaking of the whole air and earth about it. It was separated by several seconds from the flash, because we were not directly underneath the bomb – we were about 1,100 yards away.

Then this thundering, rolling, shaking came along, and

everywhere went completely dark. What had happened was the shock wave had rolled over us, lifting as it went all the earth and dust around us and blowing the building flat at the same time. So when we came out, in a matter of seconds, we came out into a choking brown fog. This fog lasted for quite a while before the south-westerly breeze blew it back up the city. As it did so, we had a shower of most peculiar rain. It was in very, very large droplets, about as big as grapes, and it was almost entirely mud – just thick blobs of mud falling from the sky.

It didn't take us long to realise that there was something seriously amiss, because the camp had collapsed and there wasn't a building standing anywhere near us. We could see further than we'd ever seen before across the city, which was all in a heap. Most of the buildings had been made of wood and some of them nearer to the site of the bomb had already been set on fire and it was spreading. I ran to a storehouse nearby and the Japanese in charge of this must have been standing in the doorway, because his skin was completely burnt off him, and he had fallen on the ground. He was a distressing sight, with a lot of his insides hanging out. I was trying to make him comfortable but all the skin came off his arms on to my hands, just like thin wet rubber. He, of course, was in great pain, and shouting for a stretcher – which I couldn't provide for him so I left him.

On a horse and cart we made our way out of the town, up into the hills. By early to mid-afternoon, we had made ourselves as comfortable as we could on a terrace over-looking the city, and thought we should stay there for a while. But the houses, each of which was on its own terrace, had begun to burn from the bottom upwards. We exhorted the Japanese who lived in the house on the end of the terrace we were sitting on to move their stuff before their house was burnt down. Nothing would induce them to go. Absolutely nothing.

I said, 'Come on lads – we've got to do something.' So we all dashed into this house and collected everything we could take out – for instance drawers with all their contents – and passed them from hand to hand out on to the field. The Japanese were pitifully grateful about this, but they would never go in to help themselves. I got the feeling they felt this was almost a supernatural occurrence, and that they couldn't do anything about it.

We were feeling very tired from our exertions and hoping nothing more would happen, when a Japanese soldier came along. He had his rifle and still had his bayonet fixed. He told us that the bulk of our prisoners were on the opposite side of the city – over on the other side, occupying a similar hillside position to ourselves. He pointed out that they had no stores, food or blankets – nothing. I was very impressed by the way he went about his duties in the middle of all this terrible chaos, so I got three Dutch East India men and we put buckets on thick bamboo poles, and we loaded these up with tinned food of various kinds and we folded blankets on to the poles, and carrying these burdens, we set off into the burning city.

It was very impressive to move down these roads, and in many cases we had to wait until the flames had blown aside until we could run like mad to get past the fire. We went straight into the middle of the city where we saw a tram that was still on its rails, but with absolutely no woodwork left – just the metal chassis of the tram sitting on the rails. I remember at one point lighting a cigarette from a nearby wooden pole. Most of Japan's services – telephone, electricity and everything like that, was carried overhead, so there were huge numbers of poles and quite a lot of these had begun to burn at the top, and were burning steadily downwards. The one that I lit my cigarette from was just about head-height, and I remember going to it the following morning and finding it was in a five-foot cavity in the ground. It had burned its way steadily down all through the night and there was a little heap of ashes in the bottom of this five-foot cylindrical hole.

The dead were lying everywhere. This problem of corpses became very severe, so we gathered all the timber we could find, that had been used in the construction of houses, and put it in long rows down the middle of the concrete road, and then we stacked the corpses neatly on top of this pile of timber. We were left with rows of corpses a hundred yards long. The police chalked the identity of the corpse on the pavement beside the body. Then, as we left in the afternoon, we set fire to the timber, and the following morning the whole thing had burned out. The calcified skeletons were lying in a row on the road with their names beside them. They were then able to be picked up with chopsticks and put into their little wooden boxes with their name on. The box was about as big as a seven-pound tea chest.

It was interesting to remember that within three or four hours of the bomb going off, we – that is to say my Dutch comrades and myself – had worked out what it was, how it was, and where it was. On a wooden building which was a very small one, and didn't completely collapse, a new nail had been driven into the woodwork. The building itself was in the full light that fell from the bomb, and therefore it was burned like toast to a crisp – but the shadow of the nail fell down the building in such a way as to make it look like a white knitting needle with a big head. If you laid a straight edge from that big head to the nail's head, you could look up it and see where the light came from, that had fallen on this nail, so it was quite possible, with two or three markers like that, to come to the conclusion the bomb had gone off above the baseball stadium about 1,500 feet high.

We also knew by the size of it, that one single bomb, delivered by one single aeroplane, could only contain that kind of energy if the atom had been split – so we instantly assumed this was done by the splitting of the atom. We were right.

There were shadows of all kinds. Wherever anything had been sheltered and the light from the bomb had not actually been allowed to fall upon it, the surfaces were quite different from the places that had been irradiated. The heat must have been intense. Everything that was made of ordinary wood crisped and roasted before it actually caught fire. For instance, our camp fence turned a dark brown. The rice crop had been green in the fields – but by the end of the afternoon it had turned brown and ripened prematurely. All the trees went autumn-coloured, and the leaves fell off them – those that didn't actually catch fire.

All these effects on the natural order of things about us were fascinating to see. For example, kites were always hovering over Nagasaki – big brown birds of the buzzard type – very big birds. A number of them must have been hovering when the bomb fell, because I came across two or three of them, walking about in the city with no feathers on. Their feathers had been burnt off them in mid-air, and they'd collapsed to the ground. They were wandering around on foot. Horrifying sight. It impressed me more than the sight of the Japanese and their sufferings, because, after all, the Japanese had scarcely endeared themselves to me. I felt they deserved it.

Corporal Patricia Coulson

WAAF, RAF administration, 1946

After the men came back from the Far East, they were given their Post Office books. We received a letter from a mother. Briefly, it read, 'My son who is living with me, has been given his Post Office book. Could you please give me authority to draw out the money to look after him? He has returned minus his arms and legs.' He was twenty-three years old. This sums it all up. However much I may not remember of the past as I grow older, these things I saw and heard during this period of my life will always be with me.

14

BATTLE'S END . . . AND EVER AFTER

Pile the bodies high at Austerlitz and Waterloo.
Shovel them under and let me work—
I am the grass; I cover all.

And pile them high at Gettysburg
And pile them high at Ypres and Verdun.
Shovel them under and let me work.
Two years, ten years, and passengers ask the conductor:
What place is this?
Where are we now?

I am the grass.
Let me work.

'GRASS'
CARL SANDBURG

HERBERT SULZBACH

9TH DIVISION, GERMAN ARMY, 1918

On July the 15th our offensive started towards Rheims. Preparations were enormous. The bomb barrage and the gun barrage started at 1 o'clock at night and went on for four hours. The infantry moved on after the barrage ended, but we soon realised that the infantry could not move on very far. The first French prisoners came in and told us that they knew of our offensive. Our mood was not too good after we heard this, and especially at night when we were told that our division was to be withdrawn back into camps. During this night we found that many regiments were already in camps moved from the front towards the so-called back line. We were full of doubt. Suddenly came the order that our division had to move towards Fismes, about forty kilometres away. This order was rather more depressing, because it seemed that our offensive had failed entirely.

I never forgot this night. After terrific heat, thunderstorms, downpours, it was regiment after regiment moving towards another place. We were drenched wet and fell asleep on our horses. We arrived at Fismes a few days later and then came the Order of the Day, of July the 18th, telling us that enormous attacks out of the Bois de Villers-Cotterêts had started. It seemed too that the Americans had arrived, because the orders said that the forces were so great that they couldn't have been French and British alone. After the 18th of July we moved into the front line and were attacked by a barrage which was absolutely unbelievable. It was the worse barrage and the worst gunfire I ever heard, and I had been through the Somme and everywhere else since then.

The night came and the infantry moved a little backwards, we moved forwards, but we moved more backwards than forwards. It went for days like this, until the retreat came at the end of July. It was hardly possible to get through the gunfire of the Allies. Their aeroplanes were flying very low and seeing everything that we were doing and bombing us in daylight. So it went on until we moved to a new line far further back. We realised that something had gone wrong, our losses were enormous and the gas attacks fearsome. The gas stuck into the high grass so that even our horses had gas masks. We realised it was the beginning of the end.

In October I had leave to go home to Frankfurt, my home town, to my parents. I was very much looking forward to this leave after the terrific battles we had been through. I went through the streets of Frankfurt. I was not saluted. I was a commissioned offficer, yet no one saluted. Everything was rationed and there was hardly anything to buy. Dance halls were closed, the streets were dull and the mood of the people was really bad. We hadn't realised at the Front how bad it was at home. People were fed up with war. They wanted the war to be ended as soon as possible, victory or no victory. After a fortnight I went back to the front line, to my comrades, to my guns, and I felt at home amongst the mud, the dirt and the lice.

In spite of our retreats for weeks and months, we still received mail. The letters I received were not depressing, but some of my comrades received letters which were most upsetting. Their families wrote, 'We have nothing to eat, we are fed up with war, come back as soon as possible.' You can imagine how it affected the morale of these poor chaps.

On November the 1st we were at Étreux not far from St Quentin, where we had started our big offensive on March the 21st. Then we were so full of hope and broke through the British 5th Army. Now it seems a million guns of the American, French and British were bombing us. The war was entirely lost. As adjutant I had to give the order of the day. On the 11th of November it was: 'From noon onwards our guns will be silent.' Four years before, full of optimism, now a beaten army.

MARINE HUBERT TROTMAN

ROYAL MARINE LIGHT INFANTRY, 1918

We were still fighting hard and losing men. We knew nothing of the proposed Armistice, we didn't know until a quarter to ten on that day. As we advanced on the village of Guiry a runner came up and told us that the Armistice would be signed at 11 o'clock that day, the 11th of November. That was the first we knew of it. We were lined up on a railway bank nearby, the same railway bank that the Manchesters had lined up on in 1914. They had fought at the battle of Mons in August that year. Some of us went down to a wood in a little valley and found the skeletons of some of the Manchesters still lying there. Lying there with their boots on, very still, no helmets, no rusty rifles or equipment, just their boots.

The Manchesters, Arras. 'Just out of the trenches near Arras.
Been through the battles of Ypres and Somme untouched.
Going home to Sheffield to be married.'
SIR WILLIAM ORPEN

CORPORAL REGINALD LEONARD HAINE

1ST BATTALION, HONOURABLE ARTILLERY COMPANY, 1918

It wasn't like London, where they all got drunk of course. No, it wasn't like that, it was all very quiet. You were so dazed you just didn't realise that you could stand up straight and not be shot.

TROOPER ALEXANDER JAMIESON

11TH BATTALION, ROYAL SCOTS FUSILIERS, 1918

As we advanced we saw the terrible state of the Ypres salient.
There were wrecked tanks from 1917 all over the place. I was
used to dead horses and mules but not in the numbers that
we saw up there. Of course it was just shell-holes everywhere. By the end of the first day we were clear of Ypres
and on a ridge where we could look ahead and see trees and
a landscape that had not been affected by war. It was just
unbelievable. We knew then that things were going well.

We came back out of the line at a place called Vichte
and had gone to bed in a hay loft. Our sergeant came in
shouting that the war was over. Everybody got up and went
down into this wee village. The estaminet owner opened his
pub and issued free drinks and then went back to bed. We
were paraded at the usual time. We were made to do slope
arms by numbers till 11 o'clock. Then we were disbanded.
That was the Armistice.

MAJOR KEITH OFFICER

AUSTRALIAN CORPS, 1918

At 11 o'clock on the 11th of November I was sitting in a
room, in the Brewer's House at Le Cateau which had been
Sir John French's headquarters at the time of the battle of
Mons. I was sitting at a table with a major in the Scots
Greys who had a large, old-fashioned hunting watch which
he put on the table and watched the minutes going round.

When 11 o'clock came, he shut his watch up and said, 'I wonder what we are all going to do next!' That was very much the feeling of everyone. What was one going to do next? To some of us it was the end of four years, to others three years, to some less. For many of us it was practically the only life we had known. We had started so young.

Sergeant-Major Richard Tobin

Hood Battalion, Royal Naval Division, 1918

In the summer of 1918 came the breakthrough. We had left the trenches behind, those mud-sodden trenches that we had hated for so many years. We were out in the open country. We almost felt victory in the air. Admittedly the Germans were standing and fighting here and there, but they were going back and we were following them. The breakthrough had come. It was open warfare. We were in green fields once again. However, open warfare brought its difficulties. This was the test of the trained soldier and junior officer leadership. The battalion commander had to watch his flanks, wondering when to stop, when to dig in, when to go on. We also had our ration problems. But it looked like the end and the peace we had longed for.

The Armistice came, the day we had dreamed of. The guns stopped, the fighting stopped. Four years of noise and bangs ended in silence. The killings had stopped.

We were stunned. I had been out since 1914. I should have been happy. I was sad. I thought of the slaughter, the hardships, the waste and the friends I had lost.

Major Peter Carrington

2ND ARMOURED BATTALION, GRENADIER GUARDS, 1945

The Germans were very, very good soldiers to the last. After the Rhine crossing, we had 15th Panzer Grenadier Division in front of us, fighting a rearguard action all the way to the very end of the war, in circumstances in Germany when they must have known that they were going to lose the war and had very little hope. Yet they fought absolutely magnificently with great courage and skill. Looking back, I did at this time commit a war crime. We commandeered a house, and left tanks and jeeps by the house. I woke up in the morning to see the son of the house putting sticks of explosive under my jeep. I considered that an unfriendly act so I came down and said to the people in the house, 'You have half an hour to take everything out of your house, and then I'll burn it down.' After half an hour, I asked my CSM to put jerry cans of petrol all round the house and I threw in a match. The match went out and we let the son of the house go. The fact is that I did not feel sorry for the Germans. They had proved enormously inconvenient and this was the sixth year of the war. I don't think we behaved badly. We behaved rather well. We helped ourselves to one or two things which we shouldn't have. I found a marvellous Mercedes, which in the jargon of those days, I 'liberated'. The Divisional Commander saw me with it and said, 'Where did you get that?' When I told him I had liberated it, he said, 'That's the most disgraceful thing I've ever heard. Send it immediately to Div HQ.' The next day I saw him riding in it.

ROLF WEINBERG

OFFICER, FRENCH ARMY, 1945

I remember the day of victory. We were lodged in the Hotel l'Opéra in Paris. On that day the order came that at three o'clock in the afternoon de Gaulle would speak to us, and he came out of the Opéra together with Lily Pons, the well-known soprano, and there was an enormous multitude of people. He said Hitler was dead and that the war in Europe had ended. France was free again. It was such a moment that I fainted out of emotion. I was picked up and carried to my hotel room and a wonderful nurse was holding my hand and she said, 'You should be enjoying yourself with the others. Don't lie here. Come down and we'll have some champagne.' I said, 'You're right in a way. But for me this is not the time for a fiesta because I'm thinking of all my comrades and all of those who have been killed by this damn Nazi regime. I'm just glad that I had the chance to help to wipe the regime out.'

SERGEANT ALAN BREWSTER

58TH LIGHT ANTI-AIRCRAFT REGIMENT, ROYAL ARTILLERY, GERMANY, 1945

We came up to these marvellous wrought-iron gates, which the Germans opened for us to let us in. I think they'd been disarmed by now, they didn't have any rifles, and we drove in and these inmates, all in their striped uniforms, looked up at us. They were lying around on the ground. They had terrible sunken eyes and they put their hands out to try and touch us as we went past. It was a complete shock to us. We didn't have the faintest idea.

I walked to the main building and I heard this thudding noise. I recognised it from my days in a band. It was someone putting a bass drum on the ground. I wondered where the devil it was coming from. I kept on walking and I came across all these men in their striped uniforms, lined up in front of the main building with musical instruments and they started playing 'God Save the King'. I stood stiffly to attention. Some of the inmates who were lying dying on the ground struggled to their feet, they were helping each other up and they stood to attention too. And then a couple of the inmates who were in better health ran amongst the others, taking off their caps. It was an amazing sight. At the end of the anthem, they slowly sank down to the ground again.

SERGEANT GEORGE TEAL

COLDSTREAM GUARDS, GUARDS ARMOURED DIVISION, GERMANY, 1945

As soon as the armistice was signed, thousands of German soldiers appeared, lining the roads. Our officer said, 'Keep your guns loaded and your fingers on the trigger. First sign of trouble, we'll mow the bastards down.' We were itchy-fingered because there was so many of them. At Cuxhaven Airfield, we had to take the surrender of the German 6th Parachute Regiment and they came marching in, wearing brand-new uniforms with flags flying, swords out. Someone wanted to present arms to them but our CO, Colonel Gooch, wouldn't allow it. They halted and their commanding officer came forward and handed over his sword and put his hand out. Colonel Gooch said, 'This has not been a football match,' and refused to shake hands.

Listening to the BBC in St Peter Port, Guernsey, after the liberation in May 1945
HAROLD WILLIAM HAILSTONE

DAVID BRADFORD

MEDICAL STUDENT VOLUNTEER IN BELSEN, 1945

When VE Day arrived in Belsen, a lot of the inmates didn't seem to take it in at all. I think they probably couldn't see any future. What was VE Day to them? If they managed to live – well, that would be alright – but even then, what did they have to look forward to? The prospect of returning to their ruined home towns in Poland and Czechoslovakia to find their families and friends all dead.

PETER BENNETT

CHILD IN GODALMING, 1945

On VE Day, we broke into school and stole a shirt off one of the footballers and put it on the flagpole in the local recreation ground as a form of celebration. We had VE Day parties on the village green – bonfires and later on, the following year, we got a letter from King George VI – thanking the boys and girls for coping so well during the war and reminding us what our older brothers and sisters had done for us – which was a nice thought.

I remember having oranges during VE parties – but I was sick after eating the orange peel, having no idea that wasn't what you did.

Ellen Harris

Reuters reporter in Parliament, 1945

I shall never forget it. I couldn't move – I couldn't do anything, whatever had happened. Although we'd known this was coming, the House of Commons itself just went into one great roar of cheers, papers went up in the air, I just sat and the tears were rolling down – it was relief after all this long time. And this kept up, the roaring and cheering and shouting, for some time. And then the Speaker dissolved the House.

I came home quite early in the day and I said to my husband, 'What are we going to do?' He said, 'What do you mean, what are we going to do?' 'Well, this is a most momentous day, we can't stay home.' 'Can't we?' he said, rather surprised. 'We must go up the West End somewhere.' 'Where? It'll be so crowded.' 'Never mind, let's be in the crowd.' So we went to Whitehall, Charing Cross. We got through gradually. I was underneath the Ministry of Health balcony – thousands upon thousands of people packed tight. They shouted and shouted for Churchill. Nobody was quite certain where he was but he came out on that balcony and he threw his arms out. He said, 'God bless you all,' and said a few words. He praised them for their fortitude – they had won the war, he said. He thanked them all – it was short and sweet but lovely for the Londoners. And he finished up once more, 'God bless you all!' The cheers – it was a wonder the clouds didn't come down. It was a really most momentous occasion.

HERBERT HOLEWA

GERMAN PARATROOPER, PRISONER OF WAR, 1945

I spent the end of the war in a British prisoner of war camp. At the beginning of August 1945, our camp speaker went from hut to hut, telling us that the war was over and that Germany was decimated. He told us to pop a letter into the War Office, which would allow me to work. On the 11th August, we were put on a train and brought down to Market Rasen and were put into Working Camp 256. For the first couple of weeks, we didn't do any work but after that we started to go out in work parties to do jobs for farmers. On our third day there, we saw a forest fire on the opposite side of the road. We jumped over the three barbed wire fences to try to put it out, but after a while the fire service came and told us that they would take care of it. So they marched us back into the camp and they counted us and they counted us and they counted us again. No one had run away. The next day, they took up the three barbed wire fences and replaced them with a single wire. We were told that if we wanted to go out of the camp, we could use the gate. That was their way of thanking us and showing us that they trusted us.

After that, I remained in Britain. On the 3rd June 1946, I was billeted next door to the Brown Cow pub in Nettleham. I worked for a contractor and I built a garage. In 1947, I worked on a farm near Lincoln and in April 1949, I moved near to Doncaster. The following year, I met the woman I was to marry, a beautiful English nurse, and I have lived in this country ever since.

SERGEANT TERRY BROOKS

ROYAL MARINES, FAR EAST PRISONER OF WAR, 1945

Then came the day when I was standing at the door of the hut and the Japanese were marching along, changing their reliefs. There was something funny about them, I couldn't quite place it. So I decided not to come to attention – but they didn't notice. I thought, 'You bastards, it's over.' The next minute the British officers came and said, 'It is over.' We all sang 'God Save the King', and 'Abide with Me'. Then we heard explosions all over the place. The Japanese soldiers and Korean privates and corporals were committing hara-kiri by blowing themselves to pieces. All the Japs we hated were dead.

HMS Argonaut, the first British ship to enter Shanghai after the
Japanese Surrender, September 1945
JAMES MORRIS

MASAO HIRAKUBO

JAPANESE OFFICER, 3RD BATTALION, 31ST MOUNTAIN GUN REGIMENT, BURMA, 1945

We were taught to kill ourselves by hand-grenade rather than to surrender. Actually, I heard the noise of hand-grenades going off all over the jungle. If I had been cornered and I could see no way to escape, then I would have killed myself. One of my divisional classmates killed himself in the jungle at Kohima because he felt sick and he couldn't allow his orderly to support him. He couldn't allow the position to continue where his orderly was helping him every day. But on the evening of the 15th August, I heard from Divisional Headquarters the Emperor's broadcast of surrender. I had a feeling of having lost everything. I thought the war could go on. We felt that even though we were preparing for the next battle, Japan itself had decided to finish. We found ourselves crying.

Within a week, many things happened in Japanese units in Burma. As far as my group was concerned, I made a speech to the soldiers on how we should behave. I said that we had lost the war and that meant that our generation had lost the war. We had spoilt the whole country of Japan that had been constructed by the previous generations. So we could not pass it on to the next generation unless we could recover it, at least to some degree. So we should go back to Japan and work more, even harder, to compensate the people who died in the war, so we must work harder to make Japan recover. Until that time, I said that in relation to the British army, we must keep our pride and that no man could live without belonging to a nation. So we had to go back to Japan.

Not every unit did as we did, though. It depended on the commanders – some platoons escaped in the night with provisions and arms to the mountains, saying that they would continue to fight or that they would wait there for the next war to break out. We did not try to escape. The disarmament of our regiment was only done in the middle of October. I was in charge of handing weapons over to the British. In our camp, the British gave us rice, dried potato and corned beef, so we had to collect fruit and vegetables for ourselves. We were sent to the British camp to work, for repairing of roads, painting and so on, once a week. In the camp, I taught English and we played sports and games and each company competed in putting on theatre performances. Compared to the time of fighting, it was a very easy life. There was no mistreatment of Japanese prisoners. The only problem was that our gums were bloody because we were not getting enough vitamin C. We asked the British supply officer to provide more fruits and on the following day, we were given fruit and the problem seemed to stop. But even now, my gums are spoilt and I lost all my teeth years ago.

SERGEANT THOMAS WOODHOUSE

ROYAL CORPS OF SIGNALS, FAR EAST PRISONER OF WAR, 1945

After years as a prisoner of the Japanese, we embarked on the cruiser, the *Mobile*, after a hot bath on the quayside. There was all the food you wanted – in small doses, cigarettes, soap, changes of clothing, even a row of beads for Catholics. It was a lovely ship, together with big hefty American marines to help you up the gangplank if you wanted. He would carry your kit for you. It was a wonderful feeling. I had a big kitbag full of stuff but I didn't want him to carry it. 'No thanks, old son,' I said. 'I walked into this bloody country and I'll walk out of it, and lucky I've made it without falling on my chinstrap.' That first night, there was a film show on board and there was a band playing. I can remember the tune – 'Sentimental Journey'. I couldn't settle to sleep so I sat on the upper deck, smoking all night. By the next morning I'd started to readjust and I've never had any hang-ups since.

SERGEANT CLIFFORD BAILEY

RIFLE BRIGADE, RELEASED FAR EAST
PRISONER OF WAR, 1946

After I got back to England, I went home. I arrived at my house and I walked in, and it was quite an emotional experience, actually, because I'd been away since '41. My father had been reasonably fit when I left – now he was virtually bedridden with a chronic heart condition. He was being looked after by a cousin of mine who had made her home with us through the war, because my mother had died in 1940. She greeted me at the door – very emotional. She said, 'Oh, you know, be careful of your father – not too much shock.' She said, 'He's been very ill.' One of the rooms had been converted into a bedsitting room for him, because he couldn't go up the stairs. And I went in, and he greeted me calmly. He looked at me – he said, 'I knew you'd come back.' We talked well into the early hours of the morning, and eventually, about three o'clock in the morning I suppose, I went to bed.

That was quite an experience, because up to that time, I'd been with a crowd of people, so I'd never been completely on my own. To go into that bedroom and close the door . . . all the thoughts came flooding back then, you know, the preceding years. It was the first time you could stop and really come to terms with yourself and find out what it was all about.

PATRICIA CRAMPTON

BRITISH TRANSLATOR AT THE NUREMBERG TRIALS, 1945–49

I went to work as a translator at the Nuremberg Trials. While I was there, we were always free to go into the courtroom. On one occasion, we all went into court for the sentence of a man called Oswald Pohl, who had been in charge of the labour and concentration camps and who had been making fun of the judges throughout his trial in every possible way. On that last day, the judge was foolish enough to ask him to raise his hand to take the oath. How Pohl sneered because he was manacled, as the judge knew perfectly well. He just wasn't thinking. Pohl claimed to have been personally responsible for signing the documents that led to the deaths of six million people. After sentence was pronounced, he rose to his feet and said that he would do it again. And then he bowed to the judge. As if to say, 'You wait. You next . . .'

I was involved in the 'Doctors Trial'. That was about the experiments conducted by doctors using Jews and 'undesirables' as guinea pigs. I was translating the depositions of people who had come out alive. Some very well annotated records survived. One aspect that I never really got over was the fact that alongside the doctors were people who were carrying out this behaviour for no legitimate purpose. The insertion of mice into women's vaginas, the repeated breakings of children and adults' legs to assess the different healing capacities of different ages. There were people who were actually enjoying carrying out these experiments and there were no lengths to which they would not go. I remember, when I got back to England, my cousin asked me what I thought of the Germans now. I said, 'There but for the grace of God.' He said, 'You can't mean that!' but I'd seen that all sorts of people had been involved with these experiments. They weren't just Nazis, members of the party, there were all sorts of people, many saving their own skins by being involved. There but for the grace of God. Unfortunately, in England, people seemed to think that this was not a proper job for me to have done. I was lucky with my parents. They knew, like me, that it was hugely important. But no one else wanted to hear anything about it at all.

MAJOR CORRIE HALLIDAY

11TH HUSSARS, 1945

After the war there were times when I was so depressed that I came close to suicide. It wasn't so much that I was fed up with having survived the war or that I felt bad that some of my friends had been killed and I hadn't. It was the future. I'd had six years taken away from me. Whereas before the war there was a future – if I didn't like the bank I was working in at the time then I was free to change direction, but by the end of the war I'd got round to asking what good has the last six years done me? Why am I here? Where am I going from here?

I had no anchor in life and I was restless. I couldn't sit down and read a book – I'd done enough of that in a prison camp. So I decided that I'd do a labouring job that exhausted me completely so that I could put the mental strains and stresses in the background. And I moved out to New Zealand to become a sheep farmer. And it worked.

FLIGHT LIEUTENANT FRANK ZIEGLER

609 SQUADRON, RAF, 1945

The end of the war took away the purpose that for years had united young men of a dozen different countries in friendship and mutual loyalty. Flying together and fighting together, it had been a way of life and fulfilment that few would ever experience again, even if for so many others, it had been a way of death.

INDEX OF
CONTRIBUTORS

ACKNOWLEDGEMENTS

ILLUSTRATIONS

The following images are IWM copyright:

p65 IWM ART 518; p82 IWM ART 249; p129 IWM ART 520; p147 IWM ART 513; p169 IWM ART 3070; p213 IWM ART 3023; p252 IWM ART 3041; p320 IWM ART 2988.

The following images are Crown copyright:

p9 IWM ART 1605; p17 IWM ART 2323; p23 IWM ART LD 264; p32 IWM ART 1148; p37 IWM ART 1167; p44 IWM ART LD 305 ; p52 IWM ART LD 1698; ; p73 IWM ART LD 30; p87 IWM ART 1921; p91 IWM ART LD 251; p102 IWM ART LD 3157; p105 IWM ART LD 1095; p121 IWM ART 2271; p141 IWM ART 3011; p153 IWM ART LD 177; p161 IWM ART LD 3161; p175 IWM ART LD 5271; p179 IWM ART LD 1530; p192 IWM ART 1883; p224 IWM ART LD 1849; p235 IWM ART 1154; p244 IWM ART LD 4235; p268 IWM ART 16893; p282 IWM ART LD 6337; p293 IWM ART 2952; p299 IWM ART LD 3398; ; p326 IWM ART LD 5596; p330 IWM ART LD 5531.

POETRY

ABOUT THE IMPERIAL WAR MUSEUM

IMPERIAL WAR MUSEUM LONDON
Packed with fascinating exhibits and amazing facts, this museum tells the story of what life was like in the front line and on the home front during both World Wars. Visitors can experience the drama of an air raid, complete with sounds, smells and special effects, find out about evacuees and rationing, and discover the undercover world of wartime espionage.

CHURCHILL MUSEUM AND CABINET WAR ROOMS
Concealed beneath the streets of Westminster, the Cabinet War Rooms was Winston Churchill's secret underground headquarters during the Second World War. Visitors can see where Churchill worked, ate and slept, protected from the bombing raids above, and discover more about the life of this extraordinary man in the Churchill Museum.

HMS BELFAST
The museum's third London branch is a Second World War ship moored on the River Thames near the Tower of London. It gives a unique insight into naval history and the harsh, dangerous conditions which her crew endured. Visitors can explore nine decks to find out what life was like when living and working on board a warship.

IMPERIAL WAR MUSEUM DUXFORD
Based near Cambridge, this is one of the country's biggest air museums, sited on a former Battle of Britain station. It has a

unique collection including bi-planes, Spitfires, Concorde and Gulf War jets. During the summer, many of these legendary aircraft take to the sky for Duxford's world-class airshows.

IMPERIAL WAR MUSEUM NORTH

The Museum's newest branch in Manchester is housed in an unusual and dramatic building representing conflict on land, sea and air. This Museum offers exhibitions, family events and a dynamic audio-visual show called the Big Picture.

All sorts of interactive family activities take place throughout the year at every branch of the Imperial War Museum. These range from code-breaking activities to art and sculpture sessions and the chance to handle wartime artefacts as well as opportunities to meet veterans and find out first-hand what life was like during wartime.

For further information about the Imperial War Museum visit:www.iwm.org.uk

FINDING OUT MORE ABOUT THE FIRST
AND SECOND WORLD WARS

If you are interested in finding out more about the First or Second World Wars there is a huge amount of material available. Your local bookshop or library should have a range of books that will tell you about different aspects of the war. Many films, documentaries and television series have been made on this subject over the years including the well-known classic films are *All Quiet on the Western Front* (1930), *Dawn Patrol* (1938), *Lawrence of Arabia* (1962), *Gallipoli* (1981), *The Dambusters* (1954), *The Bridge on the River Kwai* (1957), *The Longest Day* (1962), *The Great Escape* (1963) and *A Bridge Too Far* (1977), but there are numerous others. *The World at War* is probably the best known factual series about the war and the companion book, *The World at War* by Richard Holmes, is published by Ebury Press.

Many towns and cities have local museums, some of which will have information about the effects of the war in your area. You may be able to find some interesting accounts and photographs of what life was like during the war, particularly during the Blitz. You may even have relatives who actually lived through the war and who are able to tell you their own stories.

There are many hundreds of eyewitness accounts from the both world wars. A wonderfully varied selection of these accounts can be found in the books and the CDs: *Forgotten Voices of the Great War* and *Forgotten Voices of the Second World War* both by Max Arthur, the sources for the stories contained in this edition.

The Internet contains a great deal of information about both world wars. Here are some good websites to browse:

www.firstworldwar.com
www.nationalarchives.gov.uk/pathways/firstworldwar
www.schoolshistory.org.uk
www.bbc.co.uk/schools/worldwarone
www.bbc.co.uk/history/war/wwone
www.spartacus.schoolnet.co.uk
www.channel4.com/history/microsites/F/firstworldwar
www.bbc.co.uk/history/war/wwtwo/
www.spartacus.schoolnet.co.uk/2WW.htm
www.historylearningsite.co.uk
http://www.worldwar-2.net/
www.channel4.com/history/microsites/H/history/browse/britain-ww2.html